**Michael Broadbent's Wine Vintages**

First published in Great Britain in 1992 by Mitchell Beazley
an imprint of Octopus Publishing Group Limited
2-4 Heron Quays, London E14 4JP

Revised editions 1995 and 1998

Reprinted 1999

A CIP catalogue record for this book is available from the British
Library

ISBN 1 84000 090 2

Commissioning Editor: Sue Jamieson
Executive Art Editor: Fiona Knowles
Editor: Hilary Lumsden
Designer: Geoff Fennell
Production Controller: Rachel Lynch

Typeset in Veljovic Book

Printed and bound by Toppan Printing Company in Hong Kong

# Contents

# Foreword to new edition

Time flies, as do vintages which in the original publication were recent and are now part of the recent past. The purpose of this pocketbook is to answer two basic questions: "what is a vintage?" and "why are vintages important?" and then to rate every significant vintage of all the world's principal wine districts and wine types, assessing quality, advising whether, and for how long, one should keep young wine, and summarising the maturity and current drinkability of the wines of former vintages.

The main text, arranged by district and type of wine, listing up to a century of vintage years, goes far beyond the familiar vintage charts both in range and scope, explaining briefly the conditions which produced the good, bad and indifferent vintages and wines. Yet the handy pocketbook format will, I trust, make it both a practical and convenient work of reference.

**Michael Broadbent**
Christie's, London, Spring 1998

## ACKNOWLEDGEMENTS

| | |
|---|---|
| Alberto Fornos | Lindemans Wines Ltd |
| Alex Hargrave | Luis Pato |
| Andrew Williams | Lynn Murray (BRL Hardy) |
| Australian Wine Bureau | Madeira Wine Co. Ltd |
| Bernard L Rhodes MD | Miguel Torres |
| Bureau Interprofessionnel des Vins du Centre | Mondavi Winery |
| | New York Grape Foundation |
| Columbia Winery | Penfolds Wines Ltd |
| Comité Interprofessionnel du Vin de Champagne | Peter Cobb |
| | Peter Devereux |
| Comité Interprofessionnel des Vins d'A.O.C., Côtes du Rhône et de la Vallée du Rhône | Peter A Sichel |
| | Port Wine Institute |
| | Rebecca Wasserman |
| | Richard Mayson |
| Decanter Magazine | Royal Tokaji Wine Co. |
| Edward Berry (Cape Mentelle) | Simi Winery |
| Eyrie Vineyard | Vicky Bishop (New Zealand Wine Guild) |
| Gabor Egressy | |
| German Wine Info. Service | Victoria Morrall |
| Italian Trade Centre | Wines from Spain |
| James Halliday | Wine Institute of New Zealand |
| James Symington | Wines of Portugal |
| John E. Fells & Sons Ltd | Wines of South Africa |
| John Platter | Yarra Yering Wines Ltd |

# Introduction

Wine, the oldest, most natural and healthiest of beverages, is the combined product of nature and man. It is part natural, part man-made. Vines are planted and tended. They produce an annual crop of grapes which, after harvesting, is fermented into wine. Nature produces, man guides.

Unlike most other agricultural products, soft fruits for example, wine is to a certain extent manufactured, its natural fermentation controlled. Its "shelf life" is as varied as its colour, smell and taste. Grapes for the making of good wine can only be grown in a temperate climate, the basic differences of type being due to the variety of vine cultivated, the soil, subsoil, aspect and drainage. Once the vineyard is planted these elements are to a certain extent "fixed". Thereafter the hand of man, his skill in tending the vines and of winemaking, introduces a controllable variable. The other variable, more or less beyond man's control, is the weather. The weather is the key to the vintage.

## WHAT IS A "VINTAGE"?

The word vintage has two meanings. "The vintage" is the time of grape harvesting, "vintaging", less often used, refers simply to the picking of grapes at harvest time, that short or extended period in the autumn which follows the growing and ripening season, when – all being well – the grapes are at their optimum state of maturity with the desired levels of grape sugar, acidity and other component parts.

The growing and ripening season is annual which means that there is a vintage every year: every wine, strictly speaking, is therefore a vintage wine. Whether it remains so depends on its quality, the best being nursed and nurtured to retain its individuality. In practice a high proportion of the world's annual production of wines loses its vintage identity shortly after it is made as it is blended either with other wine made in the same year or with vatted wines of previous vintages. Examples of the latter are sherry and "wood port".

In the broader context, however, the term "vintage" in relation to wine has an implied quality connotation, not necessarily good, but sometimes most specifically so, as in the case of vintage port and vintage Champagne.

## WHY ARE VINTAGES IMPORTANT?

The producer of fine wine, the importer, merchant, investor and consumer are acutely conscious of vintages. They have a direct bearing on the value of the wine, whether youthful and immature or old and mature. For the connoisseur vintages provide an endless fascination – nuances noted, understood and appreciated.

The value of a vintage wine is directly proportional to its perceived quality, though the price demanded at source, or paid on the open market, is greatly enhanced by its scarcity value – where production is small (for example Château Pétrus, a small vineyard compared to the first-growths of the Médoc; also the world demand for the minute supply of Romanée-Conti and Le Montrachet) or where availability of a great, mature and mostly consumed vintage is limited (for example Château Mouton-Rothschild 1945 or Château d'Yquem 1921).

That poorer vintages of the wine of great estates command lower prices than those of the best vintages is amply borne out by prices in the London salesrooms. For example the 1968 vintage of Château Lafite sells for roughly one-eighth the price of the 1959, the 1963 one-sixteenth that of the 1961.

Quite apart from price, there is the important matter of how good the wine is as a drink: its unready immaturity, its agreeable young fruit, the perfection of one carefully cellared and perfectly developed, its balance of component parts, its harmony, its imbalance, over-acidity, and so forth: all are functions of vintage. In short vintages vary, and a knowledge and understanding of this is an important part of wine appreciation.

## WHAT MAKES A GOOD OR A BAD VINTAGE?

Given the fixed elements of temperate climate, soils, vine stocks, and winemaking traditions and techniques, the joker in the pack is the weather. No matter where in the world vines are grown, all are subject to variations of weather conditions during the grape growing and ripening season which vary from minor and subtle to dramatic and highly significant. Growers can do little except take evasive action, by no means always effective.

The timing and permutations of cold, heat, dryness, rain, sunshine, lack of sun, and humidity have a direct bearing on the eventual quality of grapes and of the style and quality of the wine made. Rather like the human face, none is identical despite the commonality of eyes, nose, mouth, hair etc; the vine's growing season has bud-break, flowering, grape set, ripening – yet no one year is alike another.

Whether the vineyard is a small holding managed by a part-time farmer who has a job in town, a major full-time family operation, a managed estate, or vast rolling acres of vines owned by a multinational, the basic elements of vine husbandry are the same. The vine management season begins soon after the annual grape harvest.

**Late autumn/winter** After the harvest, long shoots are removed, and ploughing between rows is carried out to cover the base of the vinestocks as a protection against severe chill and frosts. Pruning can start from mid-December (for simplicity I am assuming that the vineyard is in the northern hemisphere). A cold winter is good for the vines. They are dormant, resting after the exertions of the previous season and harvest. The bigger and better the crop, the greater need for rest.

**New year and spring** Pruning continues until early March when the sap starts to rise. The winter covering of the vines is reversed, the soil being removed from their base. This period can be one of happy anticipation or worry. If too mild, the vegetation is advanced, and the likelihood of frost-damage far increased. Just one frost in April or early May can wreak havoc, critically reducing the potential crop (as was the case in 1991, the new shoots being literally nipped in the bud) or, if severe, can even destroy the vines.

Action can be taken as a precaution against frosts – "smudge pots", stoves in the vineyard, wind machines – but can be expensive and often ineffective. A severe frost will be crippling, but it can also have a beneficial outcome, for what is in effect a drastic pruning results in a small crop which, if the summer is hot and dry, can lead to concentrated, high quality grapes – as was the case in 1945 and 1961 in Bordeaux.

**Late spring, early summer** Let us assume that there has been no crippling frost. Weeds are cleared and vines are sprayed with fungicides to prevent two potentially leaf damaging diseases, oidium and mildew. The next period is also crucial: the flowering of the vine.

Ideal conditions are warm and dry so that the flowering takes place early and over a short period. The earlier the flowering the sooner the vintage. If the weather is cold and wet, flowering is delayed and prolonged, resulting in failure to pollinate (*coulure*): the embryo grapes do not develop, and eventually fall off. Another problem is partial pollination (*millerandage*) resulting in tiny seedless berries which, though usually very sweet, reduce the volume of grape juice. Shoots are thinned. More spraying is carried out if necessary.

As a rule of thumb the vines need 100 days of sun between flowering and picking. The later the flowering the later – and generally the more risky – the harvest.

**Mid- to late summer** Ideally, what is needed is a judicious mixture of warm sunshine and light rain, the one to bring on the ripening, the other to swell the berries.

August can be uneventful. There is more thinning and weeding as the grapes change colour (*véraison*). In particularly good years with potentially bountiful crops, some growers in the best vineyards "green prune", cutting off whole bunches to reduce quantities, nourishment from the soil is then concentrated in fewer grapes. This is an expensive process and only justified if the increase of quality is matched by a satisfactory price for the wine.

**Early autumn** If the spring and early summer – bud formation and flowering – are responsible for the potential size of the crop and earliest possible date of picking, the very late summer and early autumn ripening period is responsible for the creation of adequate sugar content and richness of component parts. The balance of acidity and sugar is important. The riper the grapes, the higher the sugar content and the stronger the alcohol after fermentation. But as grapes ripen beyond a certain stage the level of acidity is reduced.

Acidity is vital for the life, vigour, refreshing quality and longevity of the wine. I personally think of acidity – tartaric, the grape acid – as the nervous system of the wine. Conversely, unripe grapes have too little natural sugar and an insufficiency of potential alcohol, a situation which can be remedied, if officially sanctioned, by the addition of cane sugar to the grape juice or "must" prior to fermentation. In unripe grapes, acidity tends to be high and of the wrong sort: malic acid, which is tart, like cooking apples.

The harvest – "the vintage" – itself takes place when the grapes have achieved optimum ripeness and before the cold weather sets in. In Bordeaux mid-September is considered early, the end of September usually satisfactory, early October not abnormal, but later is risky. After exceptionally hot summers the picking of white grapes for dry wine can start in August, though this very rarely happens for reds. The grapes for naturally sweet wines made in classic districts like Sauternes and in Germany will generally be picked later than those for the dry whites and reds to obtain the extra ripeness.

Destalking and fermentation – in short winemaking – are man-controlled operations, and depend on the whim and expertise of the owner or oenologist, on local practices, and on the style and quality of wine aimed for. The differences are important but are either predictable, because the methods are well tried and known, or can be ascertained.

The only unpredictable variable is the weather. This, I stress again, is what makes vintages important.

## POSTSCRIPT

It is often said that good wines can be made in bad vintages just as bad wines can be made in good vintages. This is a half-truism. Mistakes, carelessness, sheer ineptness can spoil a potentially good wine. Conversely, a skilled and conscientious vine-grower and winemaker can mollify disasters, making the best wine that inclement weather will allow. But in the final analysis, good wine can only be made from good grapes, and good grapes can only be grown in suitable weather conditions.

## STAR RATING

| | |
|---|---|
| ☆☆☆☆☆ | Outstanding (vintage or wine) |
| ☆☆☆☆ | Very good |
| ☆☆☆ | Good |
| ☆☆ | Moderately good |
| ☆ | Not very good, but not bad |
| No stars/ ~ | Poor |

# French Classics

## Bordeaux

Bordeaux, one of the oldest, largest and most famous classic wine regions of the world, is situated in the southwest of France. The various districts which radiate from its hub, the surprisingly big and now sprawling city and port, produce a vast quantity of red wine ranging in quality from everyday to the finest, a substantial volume of dry white, some of the highest quality, and sweet white wine from the merely pleasant to the sublime.

Bordeaux has a maritime climate, temperate and perfect for vine growing. However, rather like an island, the weather throughout the growing season is subject to manifold changes, some minor and subtle, others major and crucial: conditions that effect the timing and success of the budding of the vine, its flowering, ripening and harvest. In short, each season has its variations, resulting in wines of different style, weight and quality. Here, as elsewhere, the vineyard manager must tend his vines, cope with the exigencies of weather and take evasive action against pests and diseases; the *maître de chai* and oenologist must make the best of the grapes harvested. The wines of Bordeaux are an infinite challenge for producer, broker, *négociant*, importer, merchant and, perhaps most important of all, the consumer.

## RED BORDEAUX

One of the most important and significant differences between red Bordeaux and red wine of many other classic districts is that it is made not from just one major vine variety, but several, each with different characteristics; the choice between them being dictated by the soil type which, again, varies throughout the region, and the style of wine aimed for. Moreover, each grape variety has, in effect, its own life style: Merlot, for example, is an early ripener, susceptible to rot, and the small-berried Cabernet Sauvignon is firmer and ripens later. The latter grape has the strongest association with Bordeaux, the proportion cultivated usually being by far the highest, certainly the most dominant, in the Médoc and Graves, yet rarely planted in the Pomerol and St-Emilion districts where Merlot is favoured. Cabernet Franc is a major partner to the Merlot in these hillier districts to the north and east of Bordeaux, but is just one of the supporting cast of grapes in the Médoc. Other varieties, notably Petit Verdot, are grown but only as a small proportion, two to five per cent, of the varietal or *cépage* mix, if at all.

The importance of these different grape varieties is that in juxtaposition they provide the correct balance of component parts to create red Bordeaux. To a lesser extent they are a sort of insurance: if the Merlot fails the Cabernet Sauvignon and Franc might well survive for the winemaker to use; if the Merlot is ripe but the weather deteriorates and the Cabernets fail to ripen, a Merlot dominated wine will be made.

It is these infinite variations, of *cépage* mix, of age and maturity, of soils and subsoils, of literally thousands of individual vineyards, of weather throughout the growing season, and of the subtle manifestations of change as the wine matures, first in cask then in bottle, that make red Bordeaux – claret – so endlessly fascinating. A kaleidoscope, warranting a life-time's study; an endless challenge, affording endless enjoyment.

A word of warning: it is not possible in a paragraph to sum up the characteristics of the wines of every district, let alone of individual châteaux. Though the overall weather pattern in a given year is common to all, microclimates do exist, and vine growers and winemakers are only human.

Lastly, a word about longevity. Only major châteaux, the classed growths and their equivalents, with vines on prime sites, are capable of producing true *vin de garde* wines which will not only keep but improve with bottle-age. Minor wines from less favoured vineyard sites and districts will, in a good vintage, keep but they will not necessarily improve: softening a little perhaps, but not developing the richness of bouquet, the extra dimensions of flavour and refinement of the great growths. Bourgeois claret is best drunk between three and eight years of age, depending on the vintage, whereas classed growths need, in a good vintage, from six to 15 years, great wines in great vintages keeping and improving for over 20 years.

## 1997 ☆☆ to ☆☆☆☆

Expensive and highly complicated. Producers had to react quickly to whatever mother nature decided to throw next. This makes it difficult to give a general comment about the vintage, it all depends on how each individual reacted.

Winter was short with snow in early January allowing the vines to rest. February then became unusually warm and the conditions stayed this way until June (recorded as the warmest spring in 50 years). Consequently bud-break was two weeks premature and long, causing uneven development. Flowering then followed, it was three weeks early and also very long. Unfortunately, due to May being cool and wet, *coulure* and *millerandage* resulted in poor berry set. At this point most producers green pruned to even out development. Rain again in late June and August made *véraison* slow and some rot was evident, requiring more pruning. It was also obvious just how much energy the vines were putting into foliage growth. Late August saw the first real sun and this fortunately continued throughout the harvest.

Harvesting commenced on September 8 and took longer than usual: 50 to 60 days altogether. The weather was warm, clear and sunny (similar to 1990), while cooler nights ensured potential quality. Differences in style occurred here as some opted to pick early, giving good acidity and aroma to a lighter weight wine. Others waited, leaving grapes on the vine up to 140 days, giving phenolic ripeness and a fuller, deeper wine. One generalisation could be made – Cabernet Sauvignon benefited from its later ripening, fortunate for the left-bank producers. The right bank made some good, supple Merlot but were caught by rain in early

September. Blends of the two varieties made very successful wines. This was definitely a year for the extra diligent producer.

*Hard at this early stage (spring 1998) to predict the future development when the quality varies so much. One thing is certain, the top and dependable châteaux properties will have done a good job. For mid-term drinking?*

## 1996☆☆☆to☆☆☆☆

A vintage definitely not to be ignored. Underestimated at first, due to the market's continuing obsession with the previous vintage, which happened similarly with the 1989 and 1990 vintages. After a very unsettled growing season the results are exceptional, possibly the best vintage of the 1990s, particularly in the Médoc. Frost prevailed in February and March with a slightly delayed budding starting in mid-April. Flowering was quick, even and completed by June 20. This was due to very hot temperatures in June, resulting in an explosion of growth and a general feel of well-being about the vineyards. As this weather continued, there were some problems of *millerandage*, particularly for Merlot.

August temperatures were very cool early in the month, but by the end, sunny days and cool evenings were welcomed and any rot danger did not materialise. Rain dampened high spirits pre-harvest and then again towards the end of September. This was to see the division of the right and left banks, in terms of vintage. As a result Pomerol and St-Emilion suffered reduced crops and dilution in the grapes, especially Merlot. However, in the Médoc rainfall was far less – about half that of the right bank, if at all in the very north of this region.

Later picking dates made it a year for Cabernet Sauvignon. The vintage started on September 12 and those grapes harvested between September 30 and October 12 were to give the finest wines. Strong, rich and concentrated wines resulted from skins toughened by changing conditions throughout autumn. In the Médoc, some compare the wines to those of 1986, but with more balanced tannic structure. A "classic" claret style produced wines for ageing. Unfortunately, the right-bank producers suffered large losses and not such high quality, largely due to the rain.

*This is definitely a Médoc vintage, particularly in the northern half, where even the petits châteaux of the Bas-Médoc made exceptional wines. Most right-bank wines are for present to mid-term drinking.*

## 1995☆☆☆☆

This vintage was hailed a success after the previous four rain-plagued years. The wines show excellent ripeness, the result of the high sugar to acid ratio found at the time of picking. Concentration, balance and aroma are all reflective of the wine style, with supple, balancing tannins to support mid-term ageing.

Winter was one of the mildest of the 1990s. Substantial rainfall also raised the water-table, equipping the vines for a long, hot summer. As a result the growing season was early and consistent. Bud-break was regular with rapid flowering before the end of May, and the vines were seen to be in fine health. The driest summer in 20 years made producers worry about drought as temperatures soared to 30°C (86°F) – with the average usually 22°C (72°F). Winter rain had provided well and *véraison* was ten days early.

The vintage started one week early on September 11, and potentially disastrous rain threatened soon after, persisting lightly and sporadically until September 20. Most producers picked after this time, when temperatures rose again and October saw an Indian summer. Cabernet Sauvignon was picked last with sugar levels almost unheard of for Bordeaux. Some Merlot was caught by the early rain, but Cabernet Franc achieved success, producing aromatic and supple styles.

The result: ripe wines backed by a firm structure, deemed tender and charming. With wines at the time likened to those of 1982, the yields this vintage were up by 14 per cent compared with that of 1994, yet keeping good concentration. Most areas did well with the Cabernets performing outstandingly.

*Definitely a vin de garde, though the minor reds will make pleasant early drinking. The best growths to 2010 and beyond.*

## 1994☆☆☆

A difficult year, but some potentially good wines were produced. The overall style is of ripeness, deep colour, high natural tannins and varying ageing potential. The worry is that the fruit will be eventually overwhelmed by the tannin, most notably when extensive maturation in oak has taken place.

The winter of 1993 was one of the warmest on record; rainy with mild temperatures and a lack of sunshine and budding took place at the end of March. Once into April, temperatures began to drop and heavy rain fell during the first ten days. By April 15 the entire region had been hit by frost. Generally the damage amounted to 50 per cent but was as much as 70 to 100 per cent in some plots. Warm weather picked up again – temperatures in the high 20s°C (70s°F) and continued well into May. Quick re-budding of the frost-affected vines was facilitated and although the weather became more unsettled with storms and even some hail, the vegetation was not harmed. June and, particularly, July were hot and these heat-wave conditions consolidated a rapid flowering and the grapes continued to ripen in perfect conditions. By the end of August the region was on course for a great vintage and the grapes were in a strong, healthy condition – physiologically more advanced than 1993 by about a month.

September 9 was set for the *ban de vendange*, the opening of the harvest, and many châteaux started picking the following day. From September 7 heavy rains hit the region. Picking resumed or started on September 19 and was completed by September 29. As usual, Merlot and Cabernet Franc were picked ahead of the later ripening Cabernet Sauvignon, the majority of which was harvested on September 24/25 before heavy showers fell during the following two days. Some properties chose to wait until fine weather returned on September 28 and brought in their final Cabernet Sauvignon by October 7.

The overall response to the vintage was favourable. Yields were small and the quality of Merlot and Cabernet Franc was good as maturity had been reached before the rains fell. Cabernet Sauvignon was variable, but with a greater level of ripeness than in 1993. The best wines were the result of careful selection.

*Minor wines for drinking now to 2000, top châteaux from the Médoc probably best mid-term, say 2000 to 2010 or beyond, the more successful right-bank wines now to 2010. Time will tell.*

## 1993☆☆to☆☆☆

This will never be perceived as a great vintage, but the wines do have good colour and where careful selection took place, they have substantial body and character. Unfortunately, the overriding climatic feature was rain that occurred on 160 days out of 365. The first three months of the growing season were unusually, almost worryingly dry and by contrast, the final four months were wet to the same dramatic extent. Unfortunately, the wettest month of all was September. Despite the wet conditions the vines were generally in favourable shape. Merlot-based wines are potentially the most successful as by mid-September these grapes were extremely close to perfect ripeness. The risk of dilution was greater for the slower ripening Cabernet Sauvignon. The harvest began and in most cases was completed in the rain.

Overall, the results were satisfactory and some properties produced impressive wines due to extremely careful selection and advanced technology in the winery. St-Emilion and Pomerol produced wines with good colour and fruit density. The Cabernets have a lighter, more elegant style and with marked differences between the Médoc communes.

*Frankly variable, the Médocs and Graves depending on the quality of wine making and selection, the most successful quite clearly is the right bank – Pomerol and St-Emilion. The latter for drinking from now to well beyond 2000, most Médocs are pleasant and refreshing now, not for long cellaring.*

## 1992☆

Traditionally, a sodden year such as this would have been a complete disaster. Technological advances and the rejection of as much as half the crop by those who could afford to, enhanced the potential of the vintage. The wines are extremely varied and too many are simply mean and dilute.

The problem with 1992 was that the growing and harvesting conditions were execrable. The summer was the wettest for over half a century and sunshine hours were the least since 1980. The spring was warm and humid and during June heavy rains delayed and extended flowering causing uneven ripening. Rot had set in by this point, only to progressively worsen as rains continued through the summer. August was particularly torrential and some localised hailstorms occurred, most notably in Cantenac on August 8. The better properties removed many bunches of grapes that realistically had no chance of ripening. The harvest for this unprecedentedly large crop was extremely wet and prolonged.

Fortunately, most of the Merlot crop was brought in during three dry days: September 29 to October 1 and did not suffer as much dilution as Cabernet Sauvignon which was harvested during the heaviest downpour (October 2 to 6). Pomerol was the most successful commune due to the high proportion of Merlot. Bordeaux's better wines from this poor year are generally soft and fruity with low acidity and moderate tannins and concentration.

*Frankly, disappointing wines, no fault of the growers and winemakers. Rather thin and uninteresting. Not long keeping.*

## 1991 ☆☆to☆☆☆

An uneven year. Small production due to severe spring frosts. A vintage that veered from disaster to the verge of great success but did not, in the end, make it. Certainly nothing like the overall quality of the preceding three vintages.

The winter of 1990 was very wet; December was cold but ended with a record 19.5˚C (67˚F) on December 29. January was very dry, with eight days of frost and two of snow; February was also very dry, with five days of snow, during which time the vines were dormant. March was dry and mild, encouraging growth; April, until April 17, was mild with average rainfall and a little hail, vegetation advancing satisfactorily. On the night of April 21/22 the temperature plummeted to as low as –8˚C (18˚F). Vines were frozen, new shoots destroyed overnight, and the potential crop decimated. Cold weather continued, warming up as May progressed, with average rainfall. June was unsettled; first ten days wet; last ten days dry. Consequently flowering, from around June 15 to early July, was late, prolonged and uneven. There were early signs of mildew and grape worm.

July was hot, with above average rainfall which caused more worries about rot. August was dry and hot, in fact the hottest August since 1926. Above-average temperatures continued into September, advancing ripening and encouraging some growers, particularly in the Médoc, to anticipate another high quality, small, concentrated crop like 1961. However, the riper the grapes the greater the rot problems. The *coup de grâce* was delivered towards the end of the month, with eight days of rain prior to harvesting. Those whose vines had survived the big frost had now to sort out the ripe from rotten grapes, this separation being crucial for quality.

Despite these vicissitudes some good wines were made, particularly in the more favoured areas of the Médoc. The surviving grapes were fully ripe, had excellent acidity and good soft tannins, the Merlot attaining the best sugar levels. Some proprietors anticipate quality superior to 1981, possibly on a par with 1962, even 1985. But throughout the region the crop was small, the worst off being St-Emilion, the production of some châteaux being down to ten per cent of normal.

*As always, the minor reds can and should be drunk young – between three and five years after the vintage. The better class wines are turning out surprisingly well, though best to consume in the short term.*

## 1990☆☆☆☆☆

A large and successful vintage. It is very rare, and indeed unprecedented, to have three successive vintages of the quality of 1988, 1989 and 1990.

January to March was unusually warm, resulting in an early budding, but progress slowed during a cold, frosty patch in late March and early April. Beneficial rain in April was followed by a very hot, dry, sunny May. A second spurt of growth resulted in unevenness in the vines in some parts of Bordeaux. In particular there were variations between Merlot and Cabernet Sauvignon.

Hot, sunny weather lasted until the end of August but, despite the heat and drought, ripening was excellent. Happily, gentle rainfall saved the day, swelling and ripening the grapes and giving colour to the skins. Picking only became general in mid-September. The best grapes came from estates where the bunches had been carefully thinned. The Merlot grapes were in excellent condition with some of the highest sugar levels ever recorded. The Cabernet Sauvignon grapes had a difficult, prolonged flowering and the berries tended to be small and thick, prompting fears that wines from the Médoc would be inferior to those from St-Emilion and Pomerol where Merlot dominates.

This was an abundant, exciting vintage, particularly for the Merlots which have enormous amounts of tannin. The best Cabernet Sauvignons were made by growers who held out before picking; giving enough acidity to balance the slightly lacking Merlot. Overall, well-constituted, fairly powerful wines. Best may well be the Crus Bourgeois rather than the second growths.

*Minor wines from lesser districts attractive whilst still young and fruity; good quality St-Emilion and Pomerol from now to 2010, and the classed growth Médocs well into the next century.*

## 1989☆☆☆☆☆

An extremely attractive vintage following an exceptionally hot summer – the hottest since 1949 – which produced wines of real promise, though not without a few problems along the way.

By May, growth was already three weeks ahead of normal. Early flowering in excellent conditions ensured a substantially sized crop. The hot weather continued through to September with uneven, but surprisingly good, levels of rainfall. Picking began on August 28 – the earliest harvest since 1893. Growers in the Merlot-dominated vineyards of the right bank found that the grapes, though technically ripe, did not have ripe tannins; where tannins were allowed to ripen, the acidity level dropped. Problems were further compounded throughout Bordeaux by the high sugar levels, which contributed to fermentation difficulties.

Despite the problems, these are rich, ripe wines with luscious fruit and good tannin levels. The 1989s bear comparison in many respects with the 1985s, perhaps richer overall.

*An extremely attractive vintage, full of fruit and charm. Virtually all precociously drinkable, but under that appealing "puppy fat" have component parts to ensure good development. For the top growths, a fairly long life, well into the 21st century.*

### 1988☆☆☆☆

Undoubtedly an excellent vintage – particularly from those estates where the growers nervously sat out the late-September storms and harvested in an exceptionally warm, sunny October.

A mild, wet winter and spring necessitated widespread spraying and resulted in an uneven flowering. This was followed by a hot, dry summer which lasted right through from July until September. This produced wines with great depth of colour and high levels of tannin, especially in the Merlot-dominated vineyards of the right bank. Where the grapes were picked late, the tannin was complemented by good levels of fruit.

A firm, well-structured vintage, suitable for laying down; not as immediately charming as 1989 but capable of longer life.

*Classed growth Médocs will mature well into the 21st century. The best Graves, Pomerols and St-Emilions from the late 1990s to around 2010.*

### 1987☆☆

This year suffers from comparison with the two good vintages it followed – and the three it preceded. However, these were, on balance, light, attractive wines, suitable for early drinking.

A long cold winter and spring followed by a cool, humid June, resulted in prolonged and uneven flowering. A relatively cool and dull July and August, thereafter, apart from some rain in early September, the weather was generally fine, hot sun being succeeded by an unsettled October, the grapes being harvested in dull and rainy conditions.

This year yielded an average sized crop of sound wines. A useful stop-gap vintage, providing pleasant drinking while more important vintages – 1986, 1988 and younger wines are maturing.

*Even top growths can/should be drunk soon. Others drink up.*

### 1986☆☆☆☆

The biggest crop since World War II: 15 per cent larger than that of the 1985 vintage. A cool, damp spring delayed bud-break, but the weather improved during May and June. After a successful flowering, the summer was hot and dry until the harvest, which began during the last week in September.

The size of the crop provoked some worries about its quality. These are, however, intense, powerful, tannic wines and those with sufficient extract and flesh will last well.

*Try to leave the first-growths until after 2000. Other classed growths will be ready sooner, say from now, and those of lesser quality are drinking quite well now.*

### 1985☆☆☆☆☆

Very appealing wines produced after a growing season veering from one extreme to the other. Winter was one of the coldest on record, causing considerable frost damage in some areas. A very early, successful flowering took place at the start of a long, extremely hot summer. This continued until the harvest, which took place in ideal conditions in late September/early October.

The 1985s combine high quantity with high quality. The wines are ripe, opulent and luscious with soft fruit. Some lesser areas showed a tendency to overproduce, resulting in slightly diluted wines. Overall, however, beautifully-balanced claret.

*Attractive to drink now, yet the best should be kept and will continue to evolve to 2010 and beyond. The lesser wines might as well be drunk while relatively young and fruity.*

## 1984☆

Difficult weather conditions, including the arrival of hurricane Hortense on October 5, resulted in variable wines. After a cold February and March, conditions improved with a warm April. The cold weather returned in May and an incomplete flowering took place during an excessively hot, dry June.

The summer was fair, followed by a humid September and wet October. Picking began in late September/early October and was interrupted by the hurricane. Merlot vines suffered from coulure, reducing crops drastically, the result was that few quality wines were made on the right bank. In the Médoc wines were virtually all Cabernet Sauvignon.

The 1984 vintage does not compare well with other excellent vintages of the same period: they are lean, hard, ungracious wines which also suffered from over-pricing. This made them, in some instances, more expensive than the superior 1983s and 1982s.

*My advice: drink soon. The best will not improve much, nor will the minor wines soften.*

## 1983☆☆☆☆

A large crop of good quality, which produced some very appealing wines, more typical of Bordeaux than the 1982s.

After a poor start to the year conditions improved in time for flowering and the summer was hot and dry. Graves experienced hail during early July and other areas suffered disease due to excessive humidity. The harvest, which began September 26, took place in ideal conditions. Margaux was the most favoured district. Wines from the right bank were generally less fine.

This vintage has a good balance of tannin, fruit and acidity and is ageing reasonably well. The 1983s lack the power and substance of the 1982s and are not as well-balanced as the 1985s.

*Virtually all are drinking well now though the better Médocs will continue to develop, some beyond 2000.*

## 1982☆☆☆☆☆

An exceptional vintage throughout Bordeaux – the 1982s were immediately perceived as a potential "vintage of the decade". Not, however, typical Bordeaux: described by some as more like California Cabernet than claret.

Flowering was early and even. The climate provided ideal growing conditions for the vines. Consistently hot, dry weather held throughout the summer, though some areas in the Médoc and Graves experienced a hot, stormy July. The harvest started on September 14 in perfect conditions. A substantial crop of exceptionally ripe grapes was gathered, causing some concern that the wines would not, as a result, have the necessary structure to mature into good claret. The results, however, are huge, opulent, luscious wines with high extract masking considerable tannin content, which will take some time to mature.

*The top wines of the Médoc might well go through an extended period of seemingly little development but should prove magnificently rich and long-term. Most Pomerols, St-Emilions and red Graves are drinking well now but will keep. Minor wines: drink up while the young fruit is still evident.*

## 1981 ☆☆to☆☆☆

A small crop of good quality wines. This vintage has been overshadowed by the more immediately impressive 1982s and by other successful vintages of the 1980s.

Flowering took place early in hot, dry weather which held throughout the summer. September saw some gentle rain which cleared up in time for the harvest, which began on October 1. Some skinny, light wines are not worth pursuing, but many others are well-constituted and will benefit from more bottle-age.

*More of a claret man's claret than the 1982 and, on the whole, drinking well. The top growths should improve, soften, though most are on the lean side. Some particularly good Pomerols. Minor wines: drink up.*

## 1980 ☆

With the odd exception, this is an average vintage which, like 1981, has suffered in comparison to the high quality of most of the other 1980s vintages. A cool spring resulted in a late and uneven flowering; June was consistently cold and wet, followed by a moderate summer. Grapes ripened very slowly, delaying the harvest. Picking started as late as October 20 in some areas.

These were "lunchtime" clarets, ideal for early drinking. While it is unlikely that any will age particularly well, this was a useful and surprisingly attractive vintage.

*Few to be seen but drink up.*

## 1979 ☆☆

The biggest harvest since 1934. Initially unwanted, upstaged by the 1978s, the 1979s began to be appreciated in the mid- to late 1980s. But now overtaken by the better wines of that decade.

A cold wet spring, which followed a hard winter, delayed bud-break until mid-April, but the summer was fine apart from a cold spell in August. The harvest took place in good conditions in mid-October: a very large crop of small, thick-skinned grapes, lacking full ripeness and resulting in deep-coloured, tannic wines.

The right-bank vineyards – St-Emilion and Pomerol – had a very successful year, with a fine, ripe crop adding a more luscious note to the vintage.

*Many right-bank wines are drinking quite well, but the more tannic Médocs are drying out, lacking sufficient fruit. Though some will keep, relatively few will improve further.*

## 1978☆☆☆

The year described by Harry Waugh, then director of Château Latour, as "the year of the miracle": appalling growing conditions saved by perfect early autumn weather. The spring was late, with bud-break and harvest delayed a little. But after the late grape set in mid-August conditions improved, ripening taking place in unbroken sunshine until the start of the harvest on October 9. At some properties picking continued into late October.

The vintage was well received for several reasons: it turned out far better than originally feared; the 1977s were poor; the market was right.

*This vintage has been overrated and is on the decline. Some drinking quite well. I doubt if many will improve. Drink soon.*

## 1977

A poor vintage, the worst of an uneven decade. An early bud-break was damaged by spring frosts, then rain throughout the summer was followed by the driest September since 1851, which saved the crop from complete disaster. The wines were generally unexciting; colour was sometimes good but most lacked length and depth. The best showed a specious chaptalised fruitiness which soon wore off.

*Drink up.*

## 1976☆☆to☆☆☆

Upon release a deservedly popular vintage. A year of exceptional heat in northwest Europe, Bordeaux included, with a summer-long drought that broke during the harvest. Bud-break occurred at the normal time, during late March. Flowering, grape set and vintage were all early as the heat carried out its work. The harvest started on September 15, the earliest of the decade.

The wines turned out to be easy and agreeable, but many, from high to low class, lack flesh; more lean and supple than pleasantly fresh. this provided a good crop of lighter claret at the middle level, while some of the first-growths have surprised with their concentration and elegance.

Never a classic claret vintage, though some tasters were misled by its youthful appeal, attractive colour and initial fruit.

*Some continue to charm and delight. Many are flavoursome but fading. One or two top growths have time in hand. Drink up.*

## 1975☆☆to☆☆☆

Unhesitatingly pronounced a *vin de garde* by the Bordelais following three mediocre, graceless vintages. But, the wines are variable, all tannic, some lacking extract.

A mild, wet winter, followed by a mild spring with occasional frosts, provided favourable conditions for flowering. The summer was hot and dry with some gentle, welcome rain before the harvest (beginning on September 26); which was generally dry except for a few hailstorms. Fruity wines with a dark colour resulting from a deep pigment in the grape skins, plus a high sugar content assured a satisfactory alcohol level.

However, despite good fruit and high extract, the tannins were excessive: many wines have a "rusty" orange tinge, misleadingly mature-looking but still with a swingeingly dry and tannic finish.

*One of the most difficult vintages to assess. Some are still rich and delicious and the best-endowed will doubtless keep. The best made are drinking well. Lesser châteaux drying out. On the whole not for further cellaring.*

## 1974

A very large, unwelcome vintage at a time of slump in Bordeaux. Good flowering; hot summer; then a wet and increasingly cold autumn. Picking began on October 3. Raw, ungracious wines.

*Few remain. Drink up.*

## 1973☆☆

An enormous vintage of light, at best modestly attractive wines, which coincided with the severe recession in the wine market.

Fine weather all summer except for a very wet July. Vintage started on October 1 under satisfactory conditions, yielding a huge crop. The majority of wines lacked colour and substance. Had the market been more propitious it might have paid the growers to prune harder and be more selective. Better wines would have resulted.

*Drink up, though some can surprise.*

## 1972

One of the latest vintages since records began. Overpricing of these poor wines triggered the collapse of the Bordeaux market. A fairly large crop of immature, uneven quality grapes. Dismal but not undrinkable wines were made.

*Drink up, better still avoid.*

## 1971☆☆☆to☆☆☆☆

A good vintage with some elegant wines, though yields were much lower than in previous years. A cold, wet spring and early summer followed by warm and sunny weather with light rain – an ideal combination. Picking started on October 4. The Pomerols were outstanding and some Médocs excellent.

*Many pleasant surprises though some of the top Médocs are a bit lean. Many red Graves, Pomerols and St-Emilions are delicious now but should continue to please towards end of century.*

## 1970☆☆☆☆

An imposing vintage, combining quantity with high quality, though, in my opinion, possibly not as uniformly excellent as 1966. Spring was late but the vines blossomed in good conditions. July's great heat and drought was followed by a rainy, cool August with hot intervals. September was stormy and cold, but soon gave way to a long run of hot sunshine throughout the vintage which started on October 4. These weather conditions permitted all the main grape varieties to ripen fully and simultaneously. Some disappointments, particularly in the Médoc, but still impressive.

*Many of the top Pomerols and St-Emilions are perfect now and will keep. However, quite a few of the well-constituted wines of the Médoc have survived a rather long drawn-out, unyielding period. On the whole far less exciting now than their original promise implied.*

## 1969☆

Unappealing, lean, acidic wines, but flavoursome when young.
  *No future. Drink up.*

## 1968

Arguably the worst vintage since 1951; thin and acidic wines.
  *Few remain. Avoid.*

## 1967☆

Quite attractive when young. Flowering late, July/August hot and dry followed by generally cold weather with the odd fine period. Chaptalisation enabled some attractive wines to be made. They peaked in the mid-1970s but most were cracking up by the 1980s.
  *Drink up.*

## 1966☆☆☆☆

An excellent long-haul vintage. Lean rather than plump, though with good firm flesh. Flowering was early after a mild winter and early spring. The cool and fairly dry summer was counterbalanced by a very hot, sunny September. The grapes were harvested in perfect conditions on October 6. This is a vintage of real quality and great style; Bordeaux at its most uncompromising yet elegant. The first-growths all warrant five stars.
  *Drink up the lesser wines. Enjoy the top growths now and in some instances into the 21st century.*

## 1965

One of the worst post-war vintages. The result of a wet summer which delayed ripening; yielding some thin, short, acidic wines.
  *A pity to tip the skinny but flavoursome first-growths down the sink; do not hesitate with the rest, or keep for salad dressings.*

## 1964☆☆☆to☆☆☆☆

On the whole a very good and abundant vintage, one of the biggest since the war. Now, like the wines of 1962, undeservedly overlooked. A mild, wet winter and rather warm spring provided very good flowering conditions. The hot, dry summer resulted in a sound, healthy, ripe crop by mid-September, though the second half of the harvest was seriously affected by two weeks of continual rain, particularly in parts of the Médoc.

Château Latour picked early and made a magnificently beefy wine; Châteaux Lafite and Mouton picked late and the wines have the thinness and piquancy of a lighter vintage. At best the wines of this vintage are agreeable, chunky, fruity and flavoursome. Worth looking out for.
  *Many still drinking well.*

## 1963

A poor, though not execrable vintage. Cold summer caused rot. Light, acidic wines.

*Some thin yet flavoursome first-growths but otherwise avoid the few that remain.*

## 1962☆☆☆☆

A vintage overshadowed by the incomparable 1961. Abundant crop, *une très bonne année.* Cold and rainy conditions to the end of May; flowering in mid-June in good weather; very hot summer tempered by welcome showers in September which swelled the berries; and a late harvest, beginning October 9.

Firm, well-coloured wines, with some of the leanness of the 1966s. Never fully appreciated. Pleasant Pauillacs: excellent flavour and balance; hard, dry tannic finish. Fine classic wines.

*Drink now, and with considerable pleasure.*

## 1961☆☆☆☆☆

One of the greatest post-war vintages to date and one of the best of the century. The top 1961s are the gold dust of the wine world. As with the 1945 vintage, wine quality was due more to luck than management. Vegetation was advanced despite March frosts; cold weather during flowering, rain washed away pollen with the direct result of reducing the crop size. Persistent rain in July, drought in August and a very sunny September, left small, concentrated and well-nourished grapes. The pre-harvest sun brought them to full maturity, thickening the skins to a good depth of colour. The harvest began at the end of September.

The hallmarks of the 1961s are intense depth of colour, concentrated bouquet, sweetness, high extract, flesh and tannin, acidity levels enabling long keeping, and great length.

*Some, Château Latour for example, are not ready, needing a further ten to 20 years. Most are delicious mouthfillers now. A privilege to drink a vintage of this rare stature. Storage and provenance, however, are crucial. Some corks are deteriorating. Bottles stored unmoved in a cold, slightly damp cellar are best.*

## 1960☆

Some light and flavoursome wines made. Perfect flowering weather around May 25 despite a cold January and late frosts. A good June but a cold summer followed. Châteaux Latour, Palmer and Léoville-Las-Cases among the best of the 1960s, though all but the former now past best.

*Few seen. Drink up.*

## 1959☆☆☆☆☆

The press deemed this at the time "the vintage of the century". Hugely popular with the English trade and certainly one of the most massively constituted wines of the post-war era.

February and March were the finest in living memory: frost at night, early morning mists and hot sun. A cold April followed and a fine summer thereafter, with much rain falling from

September 13, but clearing up in time for the harvest which began on the 23rd of the month. A crop of average quantity was bought in, the results of which were rated *très grands vins*. At best opulent and magnificent.

*Despite some talk of "lacking acidity" many 1959s are still marvellous to drink, the best having the inner richness for an almost indefinite life. For once the press were more or less right.*

## 1958 ☆☆

An attractive but largely ignored vintage, bypassed by the English trade which had bought 1957s and then invested heavily in 1959s. Spring was cold, but a good flowering took place in June. Towards the end of summer, the weather improved resulting in a late harvest. The wines from this vintage have a soft, flavoursome character.

*All well past their best but can still be pleasing. Drink up.*

## 1957 ☆

Uneven, aggressive vintage. Perverse weather conditions: hot March, April frosts, poor flowering, the coldest August recorded. Unripe grapes picked in an early October heatwave. Despite this, popular with the trade.

*Mainly raw, ungracious wines, most long past their best. Some surprises though. My advice, drink up.*

## 1956

One of the most dismal post-war vintages. Most severe winter since 1709. Summer cold and wet.

*Avoid.*

## 1955 ☆☆☆

A good but always somewhat under-appreciated vintage. Alternating weather patterns early in the year; a fine summer with a perfect July and welcome rains in September; fine conditions for harvest on September 22. Optimistic reports at the time but not as attractive as the heavily bought 1953s. The best, and best kept, however, are still lovely – undervalued, some warranting five stars.

*The top growths, particularly of the Médoc and Graves, still delightful. All others, drink soon.*

## 1954 ☆

Despite one of the worst summers on record, some quite nice wines made. Rarely seen.

*Drink up.*

## 1953 ☆☆☆☆

A fine vintage: the personification of claret at its most charming and elegant best. An early, dry spring with insignificant frost; flowering started well but cold and rain caused some *coulure*; fine summer with perfect August; excessive rain in mid-September delayed the harvest which eventually started on October 2 in perfect weather. An average and ample yield. A vintage that has never gone through a hard or dull period. Attractive in cask; an appealing youth; perfect maturity.

*The finest still perfection but best to drink soon before they fade as, like the 1929s, they eventually will.*

## 1952☆☆to☆☆☆☆

Considered a *bonne année* at the time, but many wines lack vinosity and charm. A warm spring and hot June (flowering under exceptionally good conditions); July and August were hot; September was cold; the picking began on September 17 in unfavourable weather. Below average quantity. Pomerol and St-Emilion excelled, Graves were good, Médocs were hard and though good, firm and long-lasting, lacked plump flesh.

*Difficult to generalise for even the top growths were variable. Never as easy and delightful as the 1953s though sturdy. My recommendation: drink up.*

## 1951

One of, perhaps the worst, vintages since the early 1930s – thin, acid, decayed.

*Avoid.*

## 1950☆☆

An abundant vintage – nearly double that of 1949 – of uneven quality which filled war-depleted cellars. Good flowering, but harvested in changeable weather. Middleweight, lacking the charm and balance of 1949, but sometimes surprisingly nice. Rarely seen. Some good Pomerols, but most successful in Margaux and Graves.

*Drink up.*

## 1949☆☆☆☆☆

A great vintage following extraordinary weather conditions. After the driest January and February on record, flowering during cold and rain resulted in the worst *coulure* ever remembered; increasingly hot weather followed, with an almost unprecedented heatwave: 63°C (145°F) recorded in Médoc on July 11; storms thereafter in early September, fine harvest weather on the 27th, with a little beneficial rain. A small quantity of supple, beautifully-balanced wines. More finesse and elegance, and firmer than the 1947s; less intense and concentrated than the 1945s. Claret at its middle-weight, fragrant, superfine best.

*Many still perfect to drink, certainly all the top St-Emilions, Pomerols, Graves and Médocs – notably Margaux and Pauillac.*

## 1948☆☆☆

A rough diamond, lacking polish and charm; sandwiched between two more attractive vintages and consequently neglected. This year was characterised by perverse weather conditions: an exceptionally good spring then a cold summer which suffered much *coulure*, the critical month of September, however, provided good picking weather. The crop was three-quarters the size of 1947. Quality was good, but 1947 and 1949 were, rightly, preferred.

*Drink now.*

## 1947 ☆☆☆☆☆

Another post-war milestone, the "Edwardian" summer produced wines of an entirely different character to the 1945s: big, warm, fleshy and generous. A late spring and fine, increasingly hot summer. Picking in almost tropical conditions began on September 19. A problematic fermentation caused by the heat resulted, for some winemakers, in "pricking" and acidity. But, there are some rich, ripe, exciting wines. Pomerols superb.

*Drink now, at their opulent best.*

## 1946 ☆☆

An odd rather than "off" vintage which suffered an invasion of locusts. Rarely seen. Some, tasted recently, are surprisingly good.

*Drink now – if you can find any.*

## 1945 ☆☆☆☆☆

A year which heralded a string of vintages to match, if not exceed, the quality of the 1920s. Welcome after the misery of the war; this, in my opinion, is one of the top three vintages of the century. The crop was severely reduced by late frosts, hail, disease and exceptional drought which lasted until early into the harvest.

The wines are generally deep and concentrated and, having drawn the nutrients from the soil which would normally have fed a larger crop, are still packed with flavour.

*Though some are drying out, top Pomerols and first-growth Médocs are virtually unmatched for depth of colour, richness and concentration. In my opinion a greater vintage than 1961.*

## 1944 ☆☆

A slightly larger than average crop. Rain towards the end of the harvest resulted in wines of irregular quality: lightish, short, and at best charming, spicy and flavoursome. But better than expected.

*Scarce. Drink now, before they fade away.*

## 1943 ☆☆☆ to ☆☆☆☆

The best of the wartime vintages. An average sized crop after good weather conditions. Overall there was richness and fruit, pleasant but lacking persistence.

*Drink now.*

## 1942 ☆☆

After a very cold winter, a small crop of light, pleasant and useful wines. Now variable, and risky.

## 1941 ☆☆

A small crop; vines suffered neglect and disease due to the war. More than merely interesting.

*Drink up.*

## 1940 ☆☆

Vines suffered wartime neglect. An average crop of uneven wines was produced. Some still very attractive.
*Drink up.*

## 1939 ☆

A cold and stormy summer resulted in a large but very late vintage of light, though fragrant wines.

## 1938 ☆

Bottled in the early days of the war. A below average vintage.

## 1937 ☆☆☆

An important, and originally highly regarded, vintage. A dry but cool summer produced wines high in tannin and acidity. Now austere, many distinctly raw and unpleasant. Margaux the best.

## 1936 ☆

Bottled in 1938. Rare, though some pleasant surprises.

## 1935 ☆

An abundant vintage of irregular quality. Rarely seen.

## 1934 ☆☆☆☆

The best vintage of the decade. The grapes were saved from a two-month drought by September rain, producing a good quality, abundant harvest. Rich, now somewhat overmature, but some exciting and attractive wines.

## 1933 ☆☆☆

Light, charming wines, upstaged by 1934. Some still delicious.

## 1932

The latest harvest on record (completed December 1). Avoid.

## 1931

Wines rarely seen but just drinkable.

## 1930

Bad weather, bad times, bad wines.

## 1929 ☆☆☆☆☆

Considered the best vintage since 1900. A good summer followed difficult flowering and an average sized crop was harvested.

The results were wines of charm and delicate balance. At this time Château Mouton-Rothschild was for many years the star-attraction in the salesrooms. The top wines can still be lovely despite being well past their best.

## 1928 ☆☆☆☆☆

A monumental year: an extremely hot summer with some much-needed rain produced a promising harvest. This is the longest-lived vintage of the decade. Initially overpoweringly hard and tannic, some of the top wines, Château Latour in particular, took 50 years to soften. The best, however, have mellowed and can still be superb.

## 1927

A poor year. Rarely seen.

## 1926☆☆☆☆

A very good year. A hard winter, cold spring and small flowering, followed by long, hot summer. The small size of the crop coincided with the 1920s boom period and resulted in prohibitively high prices.

*Top wines, if in perfect condition can still be incredibly rich.*

## 1925

A sunless year, producing weak and watery wine.

## 1924☆☆☆

Not unlike 1978, saved by three beautiful weeks in September following a cold spring and wet summer. Wines of considerable charm, rich but delicate, a few still drinking beautifully.

## 1923☆☆

Moderate vintage; some initial charm, few wines more than faintly interesting.

## 1922☆

Enormous crop of uneven quality. Few wines have survived.

## 1921☆☆☆☆

A year of exceptional heat and consequent problems of vinification. Good winemakers were rewarded with wines full of fruit, alcohol and tannin. The vintage that made Château Cheval Blanc's reputation. Some still impressively good, but risky.

## 1920☆☆☆☆☆

The first unqualified *grande année* since 1900. A mild winter; excellent spring; perfect flowering and an exceptionally cold summer. Oidium and black rot severely reduced the size of the crop to a third that of 1919. The best-kept have survived.

## 1910s

**1919**☆☆☆ began well with a good flowering, the grapes then suffered oidium and mildew during a damp July, and were scorched by ensuing heat. Château Lafite enjoyed abundance whilst others were reduced by the excessive August temperatures. Moderately good, flavoursome wines; though light and somewhat overtaken by acidity.

**1918**☆☆☆ a good summer with no extremes of temperature. A slightly larger crop than the previous year's: good colour and sound, reasonable body; can still be quite attractive.

**1917**☆☆ was a pleasant vintage, though the quantity suffered due to a shortage of labour; now scarce, variable, mainly risky.

**1916**☆☆ produced good if somewhat hard wines, lacking charm.

**1915** ~ the poor summer saw the vines suffering from mildew, pests, lack of treatment and shortage of labour. Never tasted.

**1914**☆☆ was generally disappointing after a bright start, but some excellent wines were made: the few that survive can still be quite good.

In **1913** ~ pests and miserable weather brought this year close to disaster. Now the wines are dried-out and tart.

**1912**☆☆ underwent unsettled weather; an abundance of light, fairly satisfactory wines; surprisingly some have survived.

**1911**☆☆☆ saw a small yield of good quality wines: now variable, some still impressive.

**1910** ~ a small yield of insubstantial wines: thin and faded.

## 1900s

**1909**☆ produced an average crop of light wines; distinctly *passé*.

**1908**☆☆ was an average year, but now risky; some wines still clinging precariously to life.

**1907**☆☆ an abundant crop of appealing wines was produced in but they lacked staying power: now well past best.

**1906**☆☆☆ an unusually good start to the year was followed by excessive heat and drought in August which reduced the yield and produced wines of robust, high quality: now faded yet still some remarkable survivors.

**1905**☆☆☆ produced a large crop of light, moderately elegant wines; now variable, faded but flavoursome.

**1904**☆☆☆☆ excellent growing and harvesting climatic conditions produced an abundant crop, some lovely wines. Amongst the great survivors.

**1903** ~ saw a freezing April and sunless summer: poor wines.

**1902**☆ a moderately large crop: light, ordinary wines.

**1901**☆ a big harvest of very uneven quality.

**1900**☆☆☆☆☆ the start of the 20th century, was heralded by one of the finest vintages ever: excellent weather throughout the year led to a superabundant harvest; the best, and best kept, wines still beautiful to drink.

## PRE-1900

**1899**☆☆☆☆☆ was to be the first of the great *fin de siècle* twins: outstanding and of exquisite flavour and delicacy, the best, and most prudently stored, still beautiful to drink.

**1898**☆☆to☆☆☆☆ produced uneven and tannic wines, which generally took time to soften; some have survived.

**1897**☆ was the smallest crop between 1863 and 1910 due to unusual salt winds from off the sea.

**1896**☆☆☆☆ favourable weather conditions in produced an abundant crop, and good wines: fine, delicate and distinguished; now faded.

**1895** at best☆☆☆☆ saw uneven weather conditions and picking in an exceptional heat which made winemaking very difficult:

those saved, including Château Lafite which sought scientific advice, turned out remarkably well.

**1894**☆ produced a small crop of thin, uneven wines; now faded.

**1893**☆☆☆☆ after 15 dismal years, the weather was exceptionally good, no frosts, diseases or pests. The harvest was the earliest on record (August 15), yielding the biggest crop in 18 years of good quality grapes. Some wines still superb, but risky.

**1892**☆to☆☆☆ saw a small crop of weather-ravaged grapes: irregular in quality; one or two survivors.

**1891**☆ green, mediocre wines; yields severely cut by cochylis.

**1890**☆☆ colour and body at the expense of quantity – average.

# WHITE BORDEAUX

A great deal of white wine is made in the vineyards of the Gironde. Most is dry and of an everyday standard, some is of superior quality; there are also fairly sweet wines of modest pretensions and, arguably, the greatest sweet white wines of the world.

Although the climate is common to all Bordeaux districts, the weather conditions in the late autumn, after the grapes for the dry wines have been picked, are crucial for the sweet wines, and can vary significantly; moreover the methods of making the classic sweet wines are so different that they warrant separate descriptions.

**Dry white Bordeaux** Though a quantity of fair to middle quality wine is made in the Entre-Deux-Mers, to the southeast of Bordeaux, the finest dry whites are made from grapes, almost exclusively Sémillon and Sauvignon Blanc, grown in the vineyards scattered throughout the extensive Graves district south of Bordeaux; the two finest, white Châteaux Haut-Brion and Laville-Haut-Brion, are actually situated in the suburbs due west of the city centre.

No white wines are made in Pomerol and none to speak of in St-Emilion and its hinterlands. In the Médoc, the classic claret district, only one dry white of note is made, Pavillon Blanc de Château Margaux, though Château Lynch-Bages has recently entered this field too. The white Château Lafite is also made occasionally, in tiny quantities for family consumption.

The white wines of the Graves share an identical climate and enjoy – or otherwise – similar variations of weather during the growing season as do the reds. For this reason, the notes on the white wine vintages will not restate in full those that appear in the preceding red Bordeaux section unless there has been some significant aberration. Differences that arise are due also to the grape varieties, their ripening dates and their specific characteristics; generally, but not always, the Sémillon and Sauvignon Blanc are picked before the red grapes, principally to capture the fresh acidity that is so essential a feature of all dry white wines.

Importantly, the majority of the dry white Bordeaux are meant to be drunk young and fresh, those made predominantly, sometimes exclusively, from the Sauvignon Blanc, within a year or so of the vintage. Only the relatively few whites made at classed-growth châteaux will benefit from bottle-age and others, made, classically, from the Sémillon and Sauvignon Blanc, should be consumed within three to five years. There are exceptions, depending on the vintage. The two great odd-men-out have already been mentioned. Both white Châteaux Haut-Brion and Laville-Haut-Brion benefit from bottle-age. In a top vintage these wines are too powerful to be drunk young and are both best somewhere between five and ten years after the vintage: both capable of lasting, and drinking well, for more than 20, even on occasions up to 50 years.

**Sauternes** A relatively small rural district of rolling hills and hamlets at the most southerly end of the Bordeaux wine region, with a fair concentration of vineyards, and "châteaux" ranging from modest farm house to medieval castle and grand mansion.

The four communes, or parishes, plus the neighbouring lower-lying Barsac, specialise in sweet white wine. They grow the same grapes as in the Graves: Sémillon and Sauvignon Blanc, with a *soupçon* (as little as one percent) of Muscadelle occasionally added at the discretion of the proprietor.

The essential difference between these and the dry whites is that the grapes are left longer on the vines and allowed to develop a beneficial mould, *Botrytis cinerea* or *"pourriture noble"* (noble rot), the effect of which is to reduce the water content, increase the concentration of flesh and augment the sugar. *Botrytis* also adds a distinctive and highly desirable scent and flavour.

But it is a risky business. The crucial autumn weather can change for the worse or, less disastrously, lack of early morning mists will prevent or slow the formation of *botrytis*. It is also expensive: labour costs are high as the vineyard must be combed several times to select only the grapes at an optimum state of development; and the juice, reduced and concentrated, produces very little wine per vine.

The vintage notes that follow concern principally the classic sweet wines of Sauternes and Barsac though the same conditions apply to the lesser but similar style sweet wines of Loupiac and Ste-Croix-du-Mont across the River Garonne to the east.

Top quality Sauternes, particularly from good vintages, not only keep well but need bottle-age to arrive at their peak of perfection. The quality, state of development and anticipated best drinking dates are summarised below.

## 1997

**Dry White**☆☆ **Sauternes**☆☆☆☆ A roller-coaster year for the vines, as in the rest of Bordeaux, made very variable results here also. One major problem was the incidence of both grey and sour rot. The latter occurred due to the changing conditions in June causing berries to split, attracting the attention of insects. This then caused vinegar to be produced in the grapes, affecting Sauvignon Blanc in particular.

The vintage started very early on August 18 in the region of Pessac-Léognan. The Sauvignon Blanc grapes showed high sugar content, but below average acidity due to low malic acid levels. The later ripening grapes surviving into September, especially Sémillon, achieved good levels of ripeness. Sauvignon Blanc was elegant and fragrant, but not as concentrated as 1996; consequently it was used less in the blends. Sémillon gave broader wines, with a good depth of fruit.

Frost affected Sauternes in April, as did the aforementioned rots. A rigorous *trie* system helped raise quality by weeding out the unsalvagable grapes. These were in small lots as pickers had to frequently move around the vineyard to find suitably ripened bunches. The *tries* taken mid-season around October 17 produced the finest results. Yields were especially low, but of great concentration and gave very classic styles.

*Dry whites for drinking as soon as they appear on the market, the exception being châteaux of the eminence of Haut-Brion. Sauternes are unlikely to be bottled before the year 2000. Their potential longevity will be determined between now and then.*

## 1996

**Dry White**☆☆☆☆ **Sauternes**☆☆☆☆☆ A very favourable crop and larger than usual. In fact, this vintage was possibly even more successful for the whites than for the reds. A long and slow ripening occurred as a result of fluctuating weather patterns during the growing season. This produced wines with wonderful aromas and fine structure.

The dry whites marked the onset of vintage, starting with Sauvignon Blanc on September 12. Luckily most had picked before the rains, but the harvest still proved difficult. The majority had to be hand harvested, with much sorting of grapes required. Sémillon had a less consistent vintage, with very powerful wines made in the north and softer styles in the south. The result, when blended with the austere and highly aromatic Sauvignon Blanc, are wines of great finesse and longevity.

After the best *botrytis* year of the 1990s, the sweet wines also showed great volume and richness. *Botrytis* was slow to start on the sugar-rich grapes. It first appeared towards the end of August on Sauvignon Blanc and necessitated some thinning as some grapes shrivelled to dryness before harvesting began. The first two *tries* were hard due to the September rain. However, the third *trie* on October 4 (Château d'Yquem's first) and fourth *trie*, after a final burst of *botrytis* on October 17, were collected in perfect conditions. The most concentrated and pure wines of the past six years for the majority of Bordeaux's sweet wine producers.

*The best white Graves from the Pessac-Léognan appellation will benefit from three to five years bottle-age, except those with a high percentage of Sauvignon Blanc, which are best drunk young and fresh. Sauternes are not yet bottled (Spring 1998) and in due course will benefit from a minimum of three years bottle-age. The top châteaux will develop well, say 2010 to 2020.*

## 1995

**Dry white**☆☆☆☆ **Sauternes**☆☆☆☆☆ The growing conditions throughout the year benefited both dry and sweet wines, with yields increased by 22 per cent over 1994. Vintage started early on August 28 and the dry wines were mostly harvested by September 4 before the onset of rain in the second week. Excellent wines were made with aromatic Sauvignon Blanc and full, ripe Sémillon. This resulted in robust, perfumed styles with great structure and more balanced acidity than the 1994s.

The sweet wines were blessed with an Indian summer, resulting from rain in early September followed by warm weather into October. Producers took small first *tries* before the rain started, between September 6 and 13. By September 20 the weather had dried up, three quarters of the crop remained on the vine and *botrytis* spread rapidly. The grapes ripened quickly and there was an urgency to start picking. Harvest finished in record time by the second week of October. The resulting wines were fat, yet soft and clean with heavy floral and aromas of *botrytis*. An extraordinary vintage – as concentrated as 1990 and comparable with some of the best in the last 50 years.

*Drink the dry white now, except for top châteaux like Haut-Brion blanc and Laville Haut-Brion. Sauternes, despite being temptingly attractive now, will benefit from ten years in bottle.*

## 1994

**Dry white**☆☆☆☆ **Sauternes**☆☆to☆☆☆ Despite April frosts, the conditions during the growing season in Bordeaux were highly favourable. Fortunately, rains that hit the region in mid-September failed to harm dry white wines as by that point most of the white grapes had been harvested. The must from fat, aromatic Sauvignon Blanc and Muscadelle grapes was of very high quality. Sémillon vines had much larger bunches and took distinctly longer to ripen. Good, yet soft wine was the result, perfect for blending with the more assertive Sauvignon Blanc.

The sweet wines from Sauternes and Barsac were affected more by these wet weather conditions. Their hazardous and prolonged harvest had to be postponed as the first selective picking was due to start just before the rains fell. However, the Sémillon grapes did have a good chance of developing noble rot if the weather cleared (which it ultimately did), but not without the risk of deteriorating in the meantime. The properties that harvested well into October (as late as October 17) had the best results. Selection was the key factor for the finer wines but the general quality of the musts was high – grapey and aromatic. As with the rest of the region the yields were severely reduced.

*Dry white: with the exception top dry whites – Châteaux Haut-Brion blanc, Laville Haut-Brion and Domaine de Chevalier, drink soon. Sauternes: pleasant, but not for long cellaring.*

## 1993

**Dry white**☆☆☆ **Sauternes** ~ In spite of the heavy rains that affected the region so dramatically, the production of dry white wines was comparatively successful. The harvest for these wines officially began on September 10 and arrival of the rains resulted in the grapes being brought in very swiftly. The harvest was 20 per cent smaller than 1992 and the resultant wines are generally well-made fresh, nicely balanced and will develop quickly.

However, mid-autumn wet weather was disastrous for grapes in the Sauternes and Barsac districts, one of the worst ever vintages for these great sweet wines. Beneficial *botrytis* scarcely appeared, black rot dominated. Passable wines were made by growers who delayed picking until the weather finally picked up.

*Dry whites: drink whilst young and fresh. Sauternes: sadly, a disaster. Some of the worst I have ever encountered, entirely due to the adverse weather conditions. Tread carefully!*

## 1992

**Dry white**☆☆☆ **Sauternes**☆ Despite the enormous amount of rainfall and lack of sunshine, the few successes of this disastrous vintage were white wines. For dry white wines Sauvignon Blanc and Sémillon were harvested in the first two weeks of September, before the deluge that hit the red wine harvest later in the month. The plentiful results were light, fresh and fruity with elegant balanced acidity and provided an important commercial success after 1991's reduced harvest. The concentration is not sufficient for longevity, but the wines are ideal for easy, early drinking.

A well nigh disastrous vintage in Sauternes. Very few sweet wines of any real quality due to lack of sunshine and the cold, damp conditions hampered development of *botrytis*. Many lack weight and richness, even taste a little green, but are nevertheless passable. The wine of Château d'Yquem was declassified.

*Dry white: drink up soon. Sauternes: overall poor.*

## 1991

**Dry white**☆☆ **Sauternes**☆ The Graves and Sauternes regions were even worse affected by the severe April frosts than the red wine districts to the north and east. It was a wet summer – August afflicted by particularly heavy rain: 304mm (12 inches) in one and a half hours. Well-drained vineyards were least affected.

September was better, with exceptional heat on September 21, yet within a week the temperature had dropped to 10˚C (50˚F). The dry white harvest began on September 15 and those who picked early did best, though the crop was a fraction of normal. It then rained for eight days prior to the vintage in Sauternes. Due to the onset of rot, both noble and ignoble, picking in Sauternes was the earliest in recent years, ending by October 17. The problem was sorting grey from noble rot. Yields severely reduced.

*Drink soon.*

## 1990

**Dry white**☆☆☆☆☆ **Sauternes**☆☆☆☆☆ An excellent year, possibly the best sweet whites of the 1988, 1989, 1990 trio. The dry whites were soft and agreeable. The winter was very mild and vines flowered very early, encouraging hopes for an early harvest.

Uneven temperatures prolonged flowering, however, and after May the summer was long and hot until the end of August.

Overall the dry whites have a better balance of acidity and alcohol than the 1989 vintage and are more exciting than those of the two preceding years.

A remarkable year for Sauternes and Barsac. At first the dry summer encouraged fears that there would be no *botrytis*, but the rainfall in August and September produced perfect conditions for the noble rot and *botrytis* appeared surprisingly early, developing exceptionally fast. Sugar levels were the highest since 1929 making vinification particularly difficult, the danger of volatile acidity being ever-present. Resulting wines, however, are superb.

*Dry white: drink now except for the top growths. Sauternes: now to well into the 21st century.*

## 1989

**Dry white**☆☆☆☆☆ **Sauternes**☆☆☆☆☆ The extreme heat this year resulted in very advanced growth. The vines flowered in May and picking in Graves began as early as the end of August. An abundant crop was harvested.

For dry wines, those winemakers who picked early, having anticipated low acidity and high sugar levels as a result of the heat, made impressive dry wines with a crisp finish. One of the most superlative ever years for the two first-growths, Châteaux Haut-Brion blanc and Laville-Haut-Brion. By September the heat had given way to mild, misty weather, ideal for the development of *botrytis*. These are amongst the best Sauternes of the decade, and possibly of many previous decades. Even richer than 1988.

*Minor dry whites drink now, great Graves to 2010. Lesser sweet whites drink now, classed growth Sauternes well beyond 2000.*

## 1988

**Dry white**☆☆☆ **Sauternes**☆☆☆☆☆ A hot, dry summer was followed by a wet, humid and ultimately stormy September, then an Indian summer. The hot summer benefited the dry whites and those who picked before the storms produced some good wines. The early autumn climate encouraged the spread of noble rot and provided ideal harvesting conditions for the sweet wines. Clearly an outstanding vintage for Barsac and Sauternes.

*Dry white: drinking well now, the top Graves will continue to beyond 2000 as will Sauternes.*

## 1987

**Dry white**☆☆ **Sauternes**☆ A year of uneven quality. A cool spring resulted in an uneven flowering. The summer, though, was generally warm and dry, providing good conditions for the production of light, fresh, fruity dry white wines suitable for early drinking. Much Sauternes production was marred by heavy storms in early October. On those estates where harvest took place before the storms, grapes affected by *botrytis* produced some good quality wines. But overall, not a good sweet wine vintage.

*Drink up.*

## 1986

**Dry white**☆☆☆☆ **Sauternes**☆☆☆☆ An attractive and abundant year for dry white Bordeaux and another classic year for Sauternes. A good spring and a very successful flowering were followed by a perfect summer. Heavy rains from mid-September, then humid, misty weather, unsuitable for high quality dry whites, better for the development of *botrytis*. The grapes were too diluted to make quality dry white wine at Château Haut-Brion.

The Sauternes harvest took place in drier weather and a substantial quantity of grapes was brought in before the rains returned on October 19. Best sweet whites need bottle-age.

*Dry white: drink now. Sauternes: now to 2010.*

## 1985

**Dry white**☆☆☆to☆☆☆☆ **Sauternes**☆☆☆ After a very harsh winter the weather improved and was fine and dry throughout the spring, summer and autumn; September was one of the driest on record. The climate, providing such excellent conditions for the red wines, was not so kind to the whites. Many of the lesser dry whites lacked acidity and were rather clumsy, but the wines of the top châteaux are benefiting greatly from bottle-age.

In Sauternes the drought resulted in highly concentrated sugar levels but insufficient moisture to encourage the development of noble rot. However, the harvest took place in ideal conditions from October 1 and those who prolonged picking managed to make some good sweet wines.

*Top dry whites drinking now to 2000; the rest should have been drunk. Sauternes: pleasant now.*

## 1984

**Dry white** ~ **Sauternes**☆☆ Erratic weather patterns early in the year resulted in uneven flowering. Summer was fine, but heavy rainfall interrupted the harvest. Some light dry whites for early drinking, though most were acidic and lacked grace. The effects of hurricane Hortense in early October were, to some extent, dissipated by two weeks of windy weather which dried out the vines. Sauternes started their harvest on October 15 and managed to produce some surprisingly attractive *botrytis*-affected wines.

*Dry white: drink up. Sauternes: now to 2000.*

## 1983

**Dry white**☆☆☆☆ **Sauternes**☆☆☆☆☆ The dry whites are lovely, stylish wines with good levels of acidity. Excellent and abundant for Sauternes: beautifully balanced wines with tremendous concentration of fruit. Certainly the best between 1975 and 1988. After a wet spring, conditions were hot and dry in June and July. Rain in August and early September caused anxiety among some growers, but following misty mornings and fine, warm days were perfect for the development of good levels of *botrytis* in Sauternes. The harvesting there began on September 29.

*The top dry whites will develop and improve further. Sauternes: now to well into the 21st century.*

## 1982

**Dry white**☆☆☆ **Sauternes**☆☆☆ A year which produced white wines of good quality, but not of the stature of the outstanding red Bordeaux.

The vines flowered and grapes ripened fully under perfect conditions, perhaps too perfect for the dry whites which, though pleasant, lacked acidity. Moreover, *botrytis* forming in Sauternes was completely washed away by three weeks of torrential rain towards the end of September. The wines were sweet but, like the 1970 Sauternes, lack "golden" *botrytis*.

*Dry white: except for Châteaux Laville and Haut-Brion blanc, drink up. Sauternes: from now to the end of the century.*

## 1981

**Dry white**☆☆to☆☆☆ **Sauternes**☆☆☆ Ideal weather conditions made this a good year in Sauternes. A hot, dry summer produced healthy, ripe grapes; autumn rainfall then encouraged *botrytis* development and harvesting took place between October 5 and November 13 during an Indian summer. Many attractive, elegant Sauternes: better than the 1982s but by no means great.

*Dry white: should have been drunk. Sauternes: beyond 2000.*

## 1980

**Dry white**☆ **Sauternes**☆☆ An average vintage. Cold, dismal weather early in the year resulted in a poor flowering. Conditions improved with a hot, dry August, but the weather broke, September being cold and wet. The dry whites were insubstantial but the Sauternes were saved by sunny weather at the end of October/early November, some quite pleasant wines.

*Drink up.*

## 1979

**Dry white**☆☆☆ **Sauternes**☆☆☆ A wet winter led to a cold spring and summer, a fine June provided good flowering conditions. A slightly larger than average crop was harvested, showers prevailing throughout. For Sauternes a late harvest with *botrytis*. Not an exciting year; bottle-age will improve the sweet wines.

*Drink up.*

## 1978

**Dry White**☆☆☆☆ **Sauternes**☆☆ The long, sunny autumn which followed the cold spring and wet summer ripened the grapes and resulted in good quality wine full of alcohol and extract. Firm, long-lasting dry whites. However, due to the absence of *botrytis*, the sweet wines lack real character.

*Minor dry whites should have been drunk by now, top wines still improving. Sauternes: drink up – top wines fully mature..*

## 1977

**Dry white**~ **Sauternes**~ The result of a cold summer and the driest September on record. A small crop of poor wines.

*Avoid.*

## 1976

**Dry white**☆☆☆☆ **Sauternes**☆☆☆☆ The year of excessive heat and drought; ripe grapes were harvested in late September. The dry wines, with the exception of those from Graves, were low in acidity, needing to be drunk quickly; the sweet wines show great style and opulence but will probably be overtaken by the 1975s.

*Dry white: drink up. Sauternes: now to 2000.*

## 1975

**Dry white**☆☆☆☆ **Sauternes**☆☆☆☆☆ Spring frosts then a very hot, dry summer with some welcome rain in September and good harvest conditions for dry and sweet wines. The top Graves châteaux made excellent wines. Perfect wines from Sauternes, well-constituted and firm.

*The top dry whites still drinking well. The best Sauternes should keep indefinitely though all are drinking well.*

## 1974

**Dry white**~ **Sauternes**☆ Miserable harvest weather resulted in mediocre Graves and poor sweet wines, Barsacs best.

*Drink up, if at all.*

## 1973

**Dry white**☆☆ **Sauternes**☆☆ In common with reds: inoffensive, unimpressive light wines. Better Sauternes quite good.

*Drink up.*

## 1972

**Dry white**~ **Sauternes**☆ A dreary vintage: many Sauternes were declassified, though some not bad at all.

*Dry white: avoid. Sauternes: drink up.*

## 1971

**Dry white**☆☆☆☆☆ **Sauternes**☆☆☆☆☆ The best vintage of the decade. After a late spring and slow flowering, hopes were lifted by a pleasant, sunny summer and well-nigh ideal ripening conditions. There was *botrytis* on the grapes in Sauternes for the harvest which commenced early October.

*Dry white: top wines at peak. Sauternes: perfection now but with an almost indefinite life.*

## 1970

**Dry white**☆☆☆ **Sauternes**☆☆☆ These wines enjoy a good but, in my opinion, not entirely deserved reputation. Ripe grapes producing wines more generous in alcohol than acidity. In Sauternes an Indian summer further ripened the grapes but inhibited the development of *botrytis*. Lacking colour and zest.

*Dry white: drink up. Sauternes: drink soon.*

## 1969

**Dry white**☆☆ **Sauternes**☆to☆☆☆ A poor year; the damage was done during the wet spring, with poor flowering conditions. The white grapes in Graves were somewhat unripe and acidic but in Sauternes growers were saved by an Indian summer. On the whole, rather skinny, short-lived dry wines with high fixed acidity, and variable quality Sauternes.

*Dry white: acidity does provide the zest that the 1970s lacked and, though minor wines are skinny and tart, the best are sustained by its life-enhancing properties. Sauternes: drink up.*

## 1968

**Dry white ~ Sauternes ~** A miserable spring and summer: cold, wet and sunless. Sauternes wholly declassified.

*Avoid.*

## 1967

**Dry white☆to☆☆☆ Sauternes☆☆☆☆☆** After a late flowering, a hot dry summer and wet September, the grapes for the dry whites were somewhat unripe and acidic. However, in Sauternes the harvest began on September 27 in sunny conditions, resulting in well-structured wines of breeding, good proportion and quality of flesh that gives richness and shape. A classic Sauternes vintage.

*Dry white: with one or two exceptions (Château La Louvière still excellent) drink up. Sauternes: perfection now but all will keep. Top two of the vintage, Châteaux d'Yquem and Suduiraut, will keep indefinitely.*

## 1966

**Dry white☆☆☆ Sauternes☆☆☆** A cool, dry summer with no real heat until September. Both dry and sweet have a lean, firm, sinewy character and fairly high acidity, the good Graves still drinking well but Sauternes, though fragrant, lack flesh.

*Drink up.*

## 1965

**Dry white ~ Sauternes ~** Appalling weather conditions; a tiny crop of rotten grapes. Thin over-acidic wines. The third poor Sauternes vintage in a row.

*Avoid.*

## 1964

**Dry white ~ Sauternes ~** A promising year, hot summer, ripe grapes. Early picking saved the dry whites but many lacked acidity and balance. Torrential rain ruined the Sauternes harvest.

*Drink up.*

## 1963

**Dry white ~ Sauternes ~** An abysmal vintage. The first of three disastrous years in Sauternes: little wine made.

*Avoid.*

## 1962

**Dry white☆☆☆☆ Sauternes☆☆☆☆** A fine summer with some rain and no disasters. Good and firm dry whites. A classic vintage for Sauternes. The harvest began on October 1. An abundant crop. Well-balanced, long-lasting, elegant wines.

*Dry white: the best still very good if you like Graves with bottle-age. Sauternes now beautifully mature, better than 1961s.*

## 1961

**Dry white**☆☆☆☆ **Sauternes**☆☆☆ A small crop of stylish wines, but not of a comparable quality to the majestic reds. After poor flowering conditions reduced the potential size of the crop, an August drought and sunny September further pruned the yield. The Graves, picked early, have good acidity. In Sauternes the wines do not have the lusciousness of a great vintage, but nevertheless have good shape and flavour.

*Sauternes: drink soon.*

## 1960

**Dry white**☆ **Sauternes**☆ A good spring, but cold, wet summer. Graves better than Sauternes.

*Avoid.*

## 1959

**Dry white**☆☆☆☆ **Sauternes**☆☆☆☆☆ Good but somewhat solid Graves, which lacked a little acidity. However, in Sauternes a monumental, heavyweight classic vintage. A long hot summer with some rain just before the harvest, which started in good conditions on September 21. The grapes had a high sugar content, producing rich, powerful, massively constituted wines.

*Sauternes: perfection now but will continue for many years.*

## 1958

**Dry white**☆ **Sauternes**☆☆ Good summer, late harvest. But of little interest now.

*Drink up.*

## 1957

**Dry white**☆☆ **Sauternes**☆☆☆ A good spring, followed by perverse weather patterns – the coldest summer and hottest October on record – with variable results. The Graves very dry and acidic. Sauternes somewhat better: clean-cut wines with refreshing acidity, but lacking flesh.

*Dry white: avoid. Sauternes: drink up.*

## 1956

**Dry white** ~ **Sauternes** ~ Bad weather conditions at critical times, except for a brief improvement in time for picking; a poor, ill-balanced year.

*Avoid.*

## 1955

**Dry white**☆☆☆☆ **Sauternes**☆☆☆☆☆ A classic combination of influences produced a great and abundant vintage for white Bordeaux. A fine July, hot and dry August made well-balanced dry whites, the best of the decade. Some beneficial September rain led to an early harvest in Sauternes on September 21, and to a dry October. Well-nigh perfect for Sauternes.

*Dry whites: well past their best; drink up. Sauternes: at their best, perfection; drink soon before they dry out.*

## 1954

**Dry white**☆ **Sauternes** ~ A dismal, damp and cold summer. Watery, ill-knit wines. Graves passable, Sauternes a wash-out.

*Avoid.*

## 1953

**Dry white**☆☆☆ **Sauternes**☆☆☆☆ An outstanding August and wet September. Picking in Sauternes from September 28 in perfect weather. The dry wines pleasant, ripe, perhaps lacking acidity. Sauternes almost perfect, making up in finesse what they lack in weight.

*Sauternes: drinking beautifully; most at peak, best will keep.*

## 1952

**Dry white**☆☆☆ **Sauternes**☆☆☆ Good, firm, well-balanced dry whites. Classic Graves. Barsac more successful than Sauternes: particularly attractive, rich, crisp wines. Hail completely destroyed the crop at Château d'Yquem.

*Drink up.*

## 1951

**Dry white** ~ **Sauternes** ~ An atrocious vintage, rightly avoided by the trade.

*Happily few, if any, to be found.*

## 1950

**Dry white**☆☆ **Sauternes**☆☆☆ A better year for whites than reds. In Sauternes the harvest started in damp weather but developed into an Indian summer which ripened the grapes. Some very good sweet wines.

*Sauternes: some extremely good wines showing few signs of fatigue; nevertheless, drink soon.*

## 1949

**Dry white**☆☆☆☆ **Sauternes**☆☆☆☆☆ A classic vintage with breeding and style, less abundant than 1947 and less concentrated than 1945. In Sauternes harvest began on September 27 and continued into the driest October on record. Good *botrytis*.

*Dry white: the top Graves still remaining good though deepening in colour, with ripe honeyed bouquet. Sauternes: if well kept, superb.*

## 1948

**Dry white**☆☆☆ **Sauternes**☆☆ A good though never popular year, rarely seen now. Sauternes not bad but on the lean side.

*Drink up.*

## 1947

**Dry white**☆☆☆☆ **Sauternes**☆☆☆☆☆ Despite the hot summer a good Graves vintage. A great year too for Sauternes, the harvest beginning early on September 15 in intense heat.

*Dry white: a few top wines, notably Château Laville-Haut-Brion, drinking well though untypically rich and honeyed. Sauternes: superb; rich wines at peak.*

## 1946

**Dry white**☆ **Sauternes**☆ A poor summer with wines to match. Sauternes saved by an extremely hot October. Rarely seen.

*Hardly an option: neither dry nor sweet exist now.*

## 1945

**Dry white**☆☆☆☆☆ **Sauternes**☆☆☆☆☆ The potential crop severely reduced by spring frosts. Hail, then a drought summer. An early harvest, beginning on September 10, produced small, ripe, concentrated grapes. A first-class classic vintage.

*Dry white: firm, dry, well-constituted; very scarce, can still be excellent. Sauternes: rare, firm and refined; perfection still.*

## 1944

**Dry white**☆☆ **Sauternes**☆☆☆☆ Despite high hopes, a light and uneven vintage. Some very good Sauternes.

*Dry white: no longer exist. Sauternes: surprisingly good though rarely seen; drink up.*

## 1943

**Dry white**☆☆☆☆ **Sauternes**☆☆☆☆ A rich, vigorous, well-bred year. Sauternes now drying out a little.

*Sauternes: the best still drinking well.*

## 1942

**Dry white**☆☆☆ **Sauternes** ☆☆☆☆ Very rich, long-lasting wines with finesse and bouquet. Château d'Yquem was a great surprise.

*Many dry whites still good. Sauternes still delightful.*

## 1941

**Dry white**☆☆ **Sauternes**~ Poor vintage: lean acidic wines.

*Drink up.*

## 1940

**Dry white**☆☆☆ **Sauternes**☆ Rarely seen, indifferent vintage.

## 1939

**Dry white**☆☆☆ **Sauternes**☆☆☆ Quite a good year generally.

*Drink up.*

## 1938

**Dry white**☆☆ **Sauternes**☆☆ A mediocre year which suffered wartime neglect.

*Rarely seen.*

## 1937

**Dry white**☆☆☆☆☆ **Sauternes**☆☆☆☆☆ The high acidity, which sadly spoiled the reds, produced long-lasting, crisp, dry whites. A classic year for Sauternes.

*Dry whites now over the top. Best Sauternes are still superb.*

## 1936

**Dry white**☆☆ **Sauternes**☆☆ A mediocre, uneven year.

*Rarely seen. Drink up.*

## 1935

**Dry white**☆☆☆ **Sauternes**☆☆ A reasonably good vintage. Wines were bottled just before the war and have rarely been seen since.

*Chateau-Laville-Haut Brion and some Sauternes still good.*

## 1934

**Dry white**☆☆☆☆ **Sauternes**☆☆☆☆ The second-best wine of the decade after 1937. The dry wines now well past best though interesting. The sweet wines delicious.

## 1933

**Dry white**☆☆☆ **Sauternes**☆ Not a great year for Sauternes.

*Good Graves can surprise.*

## 1932

**Dry white** ~ **Sauternes** ~ A disastrous year.

## 1931

**Dry white** ~ **Sauternes** ~ A poor year and worse market. But Château d'Yquem quite good.

## 1930

**Dry white** ~ **Sauternes** ~ A disastrous year.

## 1929

**Dry white**☆☆☆☆ **Sauternes**☆☆☆☆☆ A consistently good, luscious year; the best Sauternes since 1921. A particularly great vintage for Château Climens. Superb wines.

*Some dry whites good if well kept; Sauternes still riding high.*

## 1928

**Dry white**☆☆☆☆☆ **Sauternes**☆☆☆☆ Firm, distinguished wines which held well. Arguably, the best vintage of the century for the dry whites. Sauternes totally different in style. Crisper, paler and less luscious than the 1929s but with better acidity.

*Some top Graves good despite bottle-age; Sauternes superb.*

## 1927

**Dry white** ~ **Sauternes**☆☆☆ The terrible reds and dry whites of this year tarnished the reputation of the Sauternes, which had benefited from the late autumn sun. Rarely seen.

*The Sauternes can still be very good.*

## 1926
**Dry white**☆☆☆☆ **Sauternes**☆☆☆☆ A very good vintage.
*Now drying out.*

## 1920 TO 1925 SAUTERNES
**1925**☆☆ was a mediocre year: now variable. **1924**☆☆☆ a ripe attractive vintage, which can still be very good. **1923**☆☆☆ was a moderate, pleasant year, now drying out; and **1922**☆ saw a fairly early harvest of abundant grapes and wines which were light, but lacking quality (drink up).

**1921**☆☆☆☆☆ experienced an exceptionally hot summer and produced outstanding whites in all the European wine districts; arguably the greatest ever year for Château d'Yquem: deep-coloured, massively constituted wine, if well kept still superb. **1920**☆☆☆ was also a good vintage, though overshadowed by the 1921s: variable, some still drinking well.

## 1910s SAUTERNES
**1919**☆☆ variable; drink up. **1918**☆☆ a fairly good year, the wines were firmer than those of the previous vintage. **1917**☆☆☆ softer and riper than 1916, but not for long-keeping. **1916**☆☆☆ this was a good but tough vintage, now rarely seen. **1915**☆☆ a moderate year, little seen. **1914**☆☆☆ surprisingly good still, though some drying out. **1913**☆☆ drying out. **1911**☆☆☆ at best fading but sound. **1910** ~ no reputation and rarely seen.

## 1900s SAUTERNES
**1909**☆☆☆☆ a wonderful vintage; still drinking well if in top condition. **1906**☆☆☆☆ a classic Sauternes vintage; can still be superb. **1904**☆☆☆☆ a great vintage; powerful wines which can still be delicious. **1901–1903** ~ not very good and rarely seen. **1900**☆☆☆ a classic vintage; still rich, powerful wines.

## PRE-1900 SAUTERNES
**1899**☆☆☆☆ not quite as sturdy as the 1900, now variable. **1896**☆☆☆☆ an excellent vintage; at its best, as Château d'Yquem can be, superb. **1895–1894** ~ undistinguished. **1893**☆☆☆ an extremely hot summer; heavyweight wines, can still be very good.

# Burgundy
Burgundy's heart, the Côte d'Or, occupies the lower slopes of an escarpment facing southeast across the broad valley of the Saône. A relatively small strip of vineyards, its soil, vinestocks and climate differ completely from those of its major "competitor" Bordeaux. Of the quality factors and influences here, what the Burgundians call "climat" is crucial, embracing soil, subsoil, aspect, drainage and microclimate. Because of multi-ownerships of vineyards the individual winemaker's approach and ability is also of fundamental importance. But above all, as elsewhere, the weather is the great dictator.

The Burgundy region is particularly susceptible to spring frosts and severe summer hailstorms which, though localised, can cause severe damage to the grapes and taint the wine – at worst, stripping the vines of their leaves, grapes and branches. Otherwise the usual weather variations occur throughout the growing season, producing distinctive patterns of character and quality in the wines.

## Red Burgundy

The Côte de Nuits, at the top end of the Côte d'Or, is the most northerly of the great French classic red wine districts, producing at its best, well-coloured, well-structured wines capable of long life. Those of the Côte de Beaune are perhaps looser knit, broader – some, like the Volnays, with a certain delicacy. Continuing further to the south the red wines of Mâconnais are modest and for quick drinking, whilst those of Beaujolais have a character and life all of their own: mainly due to the Gamay grape, partly to the different soils of this hillier area, the most southerly of which being not far distant from Lyon and the start of the Rhône Valley vineyards. Although most Beaujolais is produced to be quaffed young, within a year, even within months of the vintage, in years like 1995 and 1989 those made in the old-fashioned way have remarkable depth and staying power.

The classic red burgundy, however, is made exclusively from the Pinot Noir grape and achieves its apotheosis in the famous village districts of the Côte d'Or.

## White Burgundy

Arguably the most successful, the most admired dry whites of the world. Demand exceeding supply, prices tend to be high. Nevertheless, made from the Chardonnay, the best white burgundies provide the yardstick against which the wines made from this now ubiquitous grape are matched.

Again, the heart of white burgundy is the Côte d'Or, this time the Côte de Beaune, its Meursault, the Pulignys and the great Montrachet vineyard producing archetypal wines. After that is Chablis, well to the north, halfway to Paris, with its classic, steely, bone dry whites – though in recent years more fruity and more oaky wines are emerging. To the south, the white Mâconnais and Chalonnais which are light, dry and usually good value: Montagny, Rully, and Pouilly, of which Fuissé is the best known.

All but the top Côte de Beaune whites should be consumed within one to four years after the vintage. Good Meursault and Puligny-Montrachet from, say, three to six years, the bigger whites like Corton-Charlemagne and Bâtard-Montrachet from five to 12 years, and the scarce and concentrated Le Montrachet, of a good vintage, up to 20 years.

## 1997

The third success in a row for this region, even in the face of a particularly variable year. The most important factor was lots of sunshine at the important times. Warm and dry conditions just before bud-break brought early development. Fears of a late frost were forgotten as the weather stayed fine for flowering also. Unfortunately, late June and July became unusually cold and wet which caused some flowering irregularities. By August it was hot, with some humidity and virtually no rainfall. This continued into September when a little rain occurred but obligingly stopped before the majority started to harvest.

Beaujolais commenced picking on August 31 – the earliest start many could remember. By September 13 the entire Côte d'Or had started to pick and Chablis followed on September 25. Unusually, the Pinot Noir had ripened before Chardonnay, but suffered a drop in yields due to poor fruit set. Total yields were down by 13 per cent against 1996.

**Red**☆☆☆☆ Grapes reached exceedingly high maturity levels – so much so that chaptalisation was redundant and some producers had to ask permission to exceed the usual alcohol levels. Results were variable and quality focused on tannic structure, as natural acidity was below average. Very satisfactory wines in general.

**White**☆☆☆☆☆ Stunning results here. The white wines also showed incredible degrees of ripeness, with balanced, but lower than average acidity levels. The wines of this vintage will be the ideal compliment to the 1996s – perfect to drink while waiting for the latter to mature.

*After justified criticism of overall quality in the 1970s, growers in Burgundy swallowed hard and took note. It has paid off, for connoisseurs are homing in on the superb wines made, albeit at a high price, by the top growers. Both white and red wines have a good future, the latter probably at best between 2005 and 2010.*

## 1996

A vintage of good quantity – yields were between five and ten per cent above that of 1995, and of even better quality. Very dry, rot-free conditions and a long, cool ripening season produced both Chardonnay and Pinot Noir with maturity levels which were higher than that of 1990. This meant that chaptalisation was not required in most areas.

Winter was cool until early April and a wet May prevented frost problems. June arrived with a burst of warm weather, which brought a quick and even flowering one week earlier than usual. This continued with a long, cool summer. Sunny days ripened the grapes and a cooling north wind helped maintain acidity levels. Some experienced a little rain in August, but elsewhere drought conditions loomed.

Uniform health reigned in the vineyards, while quantities looked large. Harvesting began in the latter part of September, in bright and cool conditions, continuing smoothly into October.

**Red**☆☆☆to☆☆☆☆ For those who pruned prior to flowering or in late summer – generous, charming and seductive wines were produced; possessing great balance of ripe fruit, good acidity and silky tannins. In some areas, the wines suffered from dilution due to the summer rain.

**White**☆☆☆☆☆ These wines definitely made a mark this vintage. The grapes were picked while astoundingly ripe, with balanced acidity levels. In Chablis the results were phenomenal, some stating that it could be the vintage of the century. Perfumed, racy, and less fat than the 1995s but holding immaculate constitution and great ageing capability.

*Wonderful white burgundies best between 2000 and 2010. Reds variable, best benefiting from three to five years bottle-age.*

## 1995

A temperamental growing season resulted in another smaller vintage, but one of high quality. A very mild winter preceded a cool March and a subsequent late bud-break around the middle of April. Then, unusually low temperatures brought frost and as producers took measures against this the result was a slow and irregular flowering. Some damage occurred and *millerandage* caused a drop in yields, but then a consequent increase in concentration and overall quality.

A hot summer followed, resulting in a fast maturation and the first grapes being harvested for *crémant* on September 9. Rain in the first half of September brought fear of *botrytis*. However, a fresh and early close to the vintage, around September 28 in Chablis, proved satisfactory.

**Red**☆☆☆☆ The Côte de Nuits wines benefited from their later picking, avoiding the rain. Small, thick-skinned berries from low yields; long malolactic fermentation and firm tannins gave supple, round wines with good ageing possibilities.

**White**☆☆☆☆ Yields were down nearly 30 per cent, but a touch of *botrytis*, gave further concentration and some super examples. Increased sugar levels and good acidity created rich, fresh wines with well-balanced fruit – very similar traits to the wines of 1985.

*The top white wines can still be hard though most are delicious now. Firm reds probably best between 2005 and 2015.*

## 1994

A relatively small vintage, the result of fifteen days of frost following a mild winter. Growers to the north, in Chablis, had to contend with snow in addition to severe frost. This retarded what had been rapid development of the vines. Considerably more damage was done in the Yonne than in the Côte d'Or.

Once into May the temperatures rose to more healthy levels. Flowering took place in early June in favourable climatic conditions and the beginning of the harvest was planned provisionally for September 20. The hot weather continued through the summer and by the end of August the potential quality of the crop was considered very high. Because of this the harvest began earlier than expected in mid-September but was almost immediately halted by the rains. Rot became a threat to both Pinot Noir and Chardonnay at this stage though it could be isolated. By the September 20 sunny weather returned and picking resumed. The harvest was completed in favourable conditions – considerable sunshine with gentle winds.

**Red**☆☆☆ Rigorous sorting and low yields resulted in wines with generous fresh fruit aromas. Some very fine examples. In Beaujolais well made, deeply coloured wines came from grapes picked early in the harvest, and early-drinking, supple wines from the later picked grapes.

**White**☆☆☆ Complex, heady, fragrant wines with personality for keeping. Chablis had more reduced quantities than elsewhere. Mâconnais made pleasant wines for early consumption.

*Unlike Bordeaux, Burgundy's reds range from passably good to excellent since 1990. Good red Burgundy for mid-term drinking, the 1994 whites for drinking now.*

## 1993

The year began well after a mainly dry winter. The final fortnight of March was hot and prompted early budding. Flowering was successful and even, taking place a few days earlier than usual at the beginning of June. Spring and summer were warm and wet until August – perfect conditions for the formation of mildew and, consequently, the vines needed twice as much attention as necessary. On June 19/20 a violent storm struck the central part of the Côte de Beaune and hail fell over St Aubin, Blagny, Meursault and the most eastern part of Puligny. This had a drastic effect on yields – more than halving them within some of the better Premier Cru sites in Meursault (most notably Perrières, Genevrières and Charmes).

Once into August the weather cleared and warm, dry conditions assisted the ripening, but as the heat increased towards the end of the month, its effects on both red and white grapes were quite different. The former benefited greatly from accelerated ripening and by the time the rain fell in mid-September had developed healthy thick skins. Chardonnay in the Grands and Premiers Crus ripened well and was in good health for picking before the rain. At other sites the vines became over-stressed due to lack of moisture, which blocked the sap and halted the ripening process. Rain at the beginning of September brought about recovery of these vines, enabling them to ripen further.

When the major rains started falling on September 22, the grapes were generally in good health. Pinot Noir was cleared first along with the Grands and Premiers Crus whites (due to their better exposure). The rest of the Côte de Beaune was then harvested in wet conditions – cool and showery rather than heavy, continuous rain and fortunately rot posed few problems. In Beaujolais, harvesting had finished before the rains fell.

**Red**☆☆☆☆ Quality is good to high – well ripened, intense and complex. Tannins are strong and well structured giving considerable ageing potential. High quality beaujolais with vibrant fruit and good levels of sugar and acidity.

**White**☆☆to☆☆☆ Quality is better than expected. The very best come from the hail-damaged vines in the Côte de Beaune where yields were so dramatically reduced. Unfortunately, many of the more generic whites suffer from over-production and higher than average acidity. In contrast, the results in Chablis are distinctly more uniform and favourable. The attractive, more reasonably priced dry whites of the Mâconnais and Chalonnais are as reliable as ever.

*Red Burgundy far superior to Bordeaux. Good mid-term drinking, say now to 2000. Lesser whites from the Côte de Beaune and the south – drink; better Chablis and best, storm-surviving classic white Burgundy drinking quite well now.*

## 1992

This vintage was a remarkable success given the almost disastrous results in other parts of France. The only significant rainfall during the harvest was a downpour on September 22 which had negligible effects on the overall results.

The winter and spring were exceptionally mild. Budding took place as normal, but the vines advanced swiftly towards an early flowering at the end of May and the beginning of June. In some areas, *coulure* and *millerandage* posed a threat because of the limited rainfall. This was no bad thing as it provided a natural check on what was clearly going to be an enormous harvest.

By early summer, growth was advancing at a precocious rate – around 15 to 20 days ahead of usual and necessary rain was provided by mid-June. At the end of July, some of the better growers performed a green-prune to keep further check on the size of the crop. Ripening took place under perfect conditions as the temperatures were high throughout August. By September, the vines were at the pinnacle of health.

The Mâconnais started picking on September 10 in glorious sunshine, conditions which persisted over the Burgundy region virtually throughout the entire harvest. The Côtes de Beaune and Nuits started their harvests on September 12 and 18 respectively. The rain in the third week of the month only affected the lesser sites of the Côte de Nuits and parts of the Côte Chalonnaise, as by that late stage, the rest of the Côte d'Or had finished harvesting.
**Red**☆☆☆to☆☆☆☆ Full and supple with good berry aromas, but many are lacking the necessary concentration for ageing. Generally, the better wines come from the Côte de Beaune. Beaujolais – very ripe and well balanced with fresh-fruit aromas.
**White**☆☆☆ Fat and well-rounded with complex ripe fruit. Acidity is a little low; wines are not generally suitable for ageing.

*The best reds will prove to be delightful drinking from now until the end of the century; the whites – best drunk soon.*

## 1991

Just about anything deleterious that can occur during the growing season did occur: April in the Côte d'Or was warm, with early bud-burst. May was colder with frost hindering development. In Chablis, the owners of the top vineyards managed to take effective action but the lesser vineyards were quite badly frost bitten, the yield being reduced to roughly a third of normal.

Cold weather continued in June, retarding flowering, and both *coulure* and *millerandage* further reduced the crop as did localised hailstorms. Thereafter the summer was hot and dry though

severe hail on August 22 cut a swathe through vineyards at the
northern end of the Côte de Nuits. Then in late September, 51mm
(two inches) of rain fell on the nicely matured grapes, just before
picking was due to commence. After this delay the harvest got
underway, but a week later there was more heavy rain causing
some dilution and rot problems. Those who managed to time
their picking right harvested healthy, ripe grapes which had the
added advantage of concentration due to the reduced crop size.

In the Côte Chalonnais the harvest was small and irregular.
Beaujolais appears to be the brightest spot: more southerly, less
susceptible to frosts, and in 1991 enjoyed one of the hottest
summers this century, even hotter than the great 1947.

**Red**☆☆ Overshadowed by the 1990s and variable in quality. A
classic Beaujolais year with deep coloured, rich, well-structured
wines. The best of which have benefited from bottle-age.

**White**☆ Also variable.

*Reds: drink soon. Whites: drink up.*

## 1990

Yet another successful year for Burgundy. Climatically similar to
the previous year, yet many feel that this will rank alongside the
very best vintages of the 1980s decade.

The winter was unusually warm in all regions of Burgundy;
February and March saw temperatures as high as 24°C (75.2°F)
in the Mâconnais, encouraging very early bud-break. However,
April and June cooled down with wet, cold nights everywhere
and frost in the Chablis area. Flowering was therefore later than
usual, finished by late June in Chablis, the potentially huge crop
being reduced by *coulure* and *millerandage*. The summer was hot
and near-drought conditions led to an irregular *véraison* and
shrivelling of grapes, particularly in the Mâconnais.

Picking was early, beginning on September 17 in the Côte
d'Or. Yields were up on 1989 and the grapes were generally small
and healthy with thick skins. September was cooler than normal,
making fermentation easier and allowing winemakers to extract
excess tannins.

**Red**☆☆☆☆ Côte d'Or reds are deep-coloured and concentrated
with fine tannins. The Pinot Noirs have many of the ripe,
raspberry fruit characteristics of the 1989s, but also have superior
extract and tannin. In Beaujolais wines were rich and ripe,
perhaps lacking fruit; not quite as good as 1989.

**White**☆☆☆☆ Growers throughout Burgundy were optimistic that
this was a promising year. A surprisingly large crop of rich,
elegant well-balanced wines for relatively early drinking.

*Beaujolais now, lesser Côte de Nuits and Côte de Beaune
ready; Grands Crus will develop further. Minor whites for
drinking soon, top white burgundies now to well beyond 2000.*

## 1989

The fifth consecutive successful year for growers in Burgundy as
the vineyards basked in the gloriously hot summer that all of
France experienced. A mild winter was followed by an early

spring in which growth was a fortnight ahead of normal. The long, hot summer resulted in an early harvest; exceptionally healthy, ripe grapes were picked from September 13 in ideal conditions.

**Red**☆☆☆☆ The harvest brought in a larger crop of red than white grapes. The Pinot Noir ripened well and produced high natural levels of alcohol. A very good year for Beaujolais.

**White**☆☆☆ The Chardonnay, like the Pinot Noir, ripened well, producing high natural levels of alcohol. This is undoubtedly a good year, although there were some contrasting views among growers about the real status of the vintage.

*Generic beaujolais should have been drunk, but single-vineyard Beaujolais excellent now and will keep. Lesser Côte d'Or reds and top growths lovely now. The best whites soon.*

## 1988

A very good year throughout Burgundy. For red wines this was the best vintage of the decade. The year had a poor start with a mild winter and long, wet spring. Despite this, however, bud-break was early and flowering and fruit set were problem free. Almost three months of dry and sunny weather followed, producing an excellent, slightly larger than average harvest which started on September 26 for the red grapes and on October 4 for the whites of the Côte de Beaune.

**Red**☆☆☆☆☆ These are deeply coloured, rich wines combining a good balance of fruit, acidity and tannin. Though attractive when young, they also have the capacity to age well. The Beaujolais also produced quality wines. Whites are keeping well.

**White**☆☆☆ Ripe, fresh, well-balanced wines. However, yields were high and some wines lack concentration as a result.

*Beaujolais, Mâconnais and minor reds from the Côte d'Or: drink now. Retain the top reds, particularly the leading estates, for drinking, say, now to 2020; the very best even beyond then. Minor whites drink up, better quality white burgundies soon.*

## 1987

This was quite a small vintage; its reputation improved as it matured, particularly the reds. A cool and unsettled summer resulted in a poor flowering and fruit set, prompting caution among winegrowers. A particularly beneficial period of unusually hot September weather followed, and picking began in October 5 in good conditions.

**Red**☆☆☆ The small yield of grapes had a high ratio of skin to juice, resulting in fairly concentrated, quite well-structured red wines for early to mid-term drinking.

**White**☆☆ This was a slightly less satisfactory year for the white wines. Firm and clean cut, but perhaps a little on the mean side.

*Lesser reds and whites: drink up. Best of both: drink soon.*

## 1986

A very large crop of good wines. A cold winter was followed by a mild spring; flowering took place successfully during a hot, sunny June. Excellent conditions continued through the summer with the exception of some late August and September storms, encouraging rot. The harvest began on September 29 in good weather; those who picked late made the best wines.

**Red**☆☆☆☆ The size of the crop prompted concern as to its quality. Fortunately, this was largely unfounded and where the grapes were not too swollen by the storms, quality was good. But, resulting wines lacked the charm of the 1985s being rather tough and tannic. Best appear to have come from the Côte de Nuits.

**White**☆☆☆☆☆ The whites were superb: dense and concentrated with excellent structure. Extremely good Pulignys; with increasing use of oak barriques becoming noticeable in Chablis.

*Most reds drinking well now. The Grands Cru wines should develop beyond 2000. Top quality whites still drinking well.*

## 1985

A phenomenally cold winter, during which the temperature fell as low as –25°C (–13°F) around the lower-lying vineyards of the Côte de Nuits in January, causing much damage. Nevertheless this was a consistently good year, partly because only the healthiest vines had survived the winter.

Spring was cool, resulting in a late and often difficult flowering. However, between then and the harvest the weather was fine and warm, becoming glorious in September and October. Picking began on September 26 and a larger than average crop of healthy grapes was brought in.

**Red**☆☆☆☆☆ Rich, ripe, clean and fruity wines. Probably the best balanced vintage since 1978.

**White**☆☆☆☆ Delightful wines. A late harvest of healthy grapes in the Côte de Beaune.

*Attractive reds, many drinking perfectly now though the best are currently reaching their plateau of maturity and will keep well beyond 2000. Drink the whites now except for the top growths which will be delicious until the late 1990s.*

## 1984

By no means a great year for Burgundy, largely due to the difficult weather conditions that prevailed throughout the growing season. Spring arrived late, delaying flowering until early July. A two-month drought thereafter was followed by one of the worst Septembers on record, with ceaseless rain continuing into early October. Unripe grapes were harvested, the only consolation was that the cool weather prevented the spread of rot.

**Red**☆ This vintage was low in natural alcohol and acidity which prompted widespread chaptalisation which produced unbalanced though not unpleasant wines.

**White**☆ These made light but elegant drinking.

*Reds: avoid. Whites: drink up.*

## 1983

An extremely uneven year, even by Burgundian standards, yet the reds can be outstanding. A successful flowering followed a poor, wet spring. The summer was generally hot with the occasional period of rain and even hail in some areas. The grapes ripened well but frequently suffered from rot. Picking began on September 29, yielding a fairly small crop, particularly around the Côte de Nuits where severe hailstorms did considerable damage.

**Red**☆☆to☆☆☆☆ May hailstorms in and around Chambolle-Musigny and Vosne-Romanée destroyed nearly one-third of the crop, though generally flowering was successful. A remarkable year; rot and hard tannins were the only problems and the wines that outlive the latter will be drinking well in the 21st century.

**White**☆☆☆☆ Very variable but exciting wines of character and quality. The best growths from the Côte de Beaune have kept well. Lesser wines should have been consumed.

*Reds of the best domaines have benefited from bottle-ageing and, all being well, should continue to develop beyond 2000. The minor whites should have been drunk but the best growths are still evolving.*

## 1982

A mild winter was followed by a warm, early spring and correspondingly early flowering. The summer was generally fine; September and October were both hot and sunny and the harvest started on September 20. Many growers found their cellars too small to house their bumper Pinot Noir crop and also encountered the inevitable problems of quality associated with large quantity.

**Red**☆☆to☆☆☆ The excessive production of the red wines resulted in a lack of concentration. They were, however, healthy wines with ripe fruit, suitable for early drinking.

**White**☆☆to☆☆☆☆ Both very good and very poor wines, most at their peak during the mid- to late 1980s. Top Crus worth keeping.

*Most reds should have been consumed. Some of the leading whites are still enjoyable.*

## 1981

Dismal weather during almost all the year produced a very small crop of mostly poor wines.

A cold winter ran into a warm spring, but frost attacked the vines once budding was underway and in Chablis this resulted in the loss of one-third of the crop. Miserable conditions did not relent until August during which there was some sunshine, but the harvest, which ran from September 24 until October 5, was continually interrupted by rain. Those who picked late, however, benefited from an improvement in the weather.

**Red**☆☆ With the odd surprise, this was a very poor year for red burgundy. The best wines were made from reduced crops of highly concentrated grapes.

**White**☆ Mediocre. Frosts reduced the Chablis crops considerably.

*Drink up.*

## 1980

A year of mixed results, but on the whole this was a good vintage. Bud-break was delayed by a cold winter and cool spring. A cold June led to extended and uneven flowering, though August and

September temperatures were above average. Some rain fell before the harvest which ran from October 10 onwards. Those growers who picked latest produced the best wines.

**Red**☆☆to☆☆☆ These were, as a result of the small crop deep, fairly concentrated wines, especially in the Côte de Nuits.

**White**☆ A disappointing and uneven crop, caused by the lack of sunshine, particularly in Chablis. This resulted in acidic, austere, unbalanced wines.

*Most reds and all the whites should have been consumed. However some of the best reds are still drinking quite well.*

## 1979

An abundant vintage of mainly good-quality wines. Vegetation was delayed by a cold winter and spring, then frosts during early May coincided with budding. The summer was fair with the exception of several hailstorms, one of which caused particular damage between Nuits-St-Georges and Chambolle-Musigny. However, the surviving grapes were healthy and a satisfactory harvest was brought in at the end of September.

**Red**☆☆☆ Overall, quite good wines.

**White**☆☆☆☆ Attractive wines with a more obvious, easy charm than the harder, firmer 1978s. Very good in the Côte de Beaune.

*The best reds still have a lot of life though most should be drunk soon. The top whites are still very good.*

## 1978

An excellent year. The small crop of good quality wines came onto the market at a time of high demand, encouraging growers to open prices 100 per cent above those of the atrocious 1977s.

Vegetation and flowering were delayed by an unusually cold spring and early summer; the weather turned on August 20 when the grapes were setting and an excellent autumn saved the vintage. The harvest produced richly coloured, alcoholic wines.

**Red**☆☆☆☆☆ Well-structured wines; their strength is from ripe grapes with a good balance of fruit, tannin, alcohol and acidity.

**White**☆☆☆☆☆ The best year since 1971. All areas, even the minor districts, produced wines of high quality. Very firm, well-built, alcoholic wines, with fruit, extract and acidity.

*A highly satisfactory vintage for reds, most of which are drinking well now, but the best will open up further and last until around 2010. Top quality whites can still be superb, with a maturity span beyond 2000.*

## 1977

Despite an ideal spring and perfect flowering, torrential rain throughout the summer, a two-week break in August, and then further severe storms later in the month, brought this vintage near to disaster. However, by September the weather turned fine and the harvest started on October 4.

**Red**~ An abundant crop. Sandwiched between two far superior years the 1977s attracted little attention, though considering the conditions some drinkable wines were made.

**White**☆ These were generally better than the reds. The small crop provoked much interest from the trade where stocks were low, consequently prices were higher than really deserved.

*Red: avoid. White: drink up.*

## 1976

This year had everything going for it: a mild, frostless winter followed by a summer of intense heat and drought. This relented slightly in time for an early September harvest.

**Red**☆☆☆☆ A very welcome vintage, coming at the end of the recession and following three poor quality years. Wines of colour, fruit, extract and alcohol, but with an excess of tannin which might never ameliorate. This was also a good year in Beaujolais – possibly comparable with the best 1947s, 1959s, and 1964s.

**White**☆☆☆☆ The excessive heat ripened the grapes very early and, in order to avoid loss of acidity and an excess of sugar, the harvest was bought forward (to September 15 in Chablis). Some grapes were gathered slightly underripe. The result was variable wines, some lacking life, others too hard.

*Most reds should be drunk soon. However, some are still very noticeably tannic, so, despite the risk of drying out, the best are worth keeping. The whites should mostly be drunk now though the firmest and best are continuing to develop.*

## 1975

A disastrous vintage, the worst since 1968, though marginally better for the whites. After a fine late spring and early summer the weather was generally unpleasant and grapes suffered widespread rot. A small quantity of thin, mouldy wines coincided with worldwide recession. A year Burgundians prefer to forget.

*Drink up.*

## 1974

A mild but occasionally frosty spring, difficult flowering and sunny summer were followed by the coldest September in years. Picking started September 21 in cold, wet and windy weather.

**Red**☆ Mainly dismal.

**Whites** Some passable wines made, though of little interest now.

*Drink up.*

## 1973

A successful flowering and dry start to the summer, driest since 1945, broke mid-July with heavy rain, particularly on the Côtes.

**Red** ~ Light, watery and unimportant wines. A late, wet and extended harvest ran from September 22 until October 18. This was a miserable year – the size of the crop ran over the permitted yield per acre and coincided with a drop in demand.

**White**☆to☆☆☆☆ Overall a good vintage for whites; comparable with, possibly better than, 1970, but the wines not as firm as the 1969s or 1971s. Wines of charm and fragrance but consequently at their best young. A tendency to be over acidic.

*Reds: drink up. Whites: some interesting survivors.*

## 1972

A severe winter was followed by warm weather at the end of March and the vines budded in April; summer was oddly cold but dry, and September mercifully sunny. A huge crop was picked late under good, if cold, conditions.

**Red**☆☆ Despite being unpopular with the English (due partly to being overshadowed by the three previous vintages, and partly to the association with the poor 1972 red Bordeaux) these were reasonably well-structured, pleasant and interesting wines, though with a touch of bitterness. They have little appeal now.

**White**☆☆ Mediocre, due to some of the grapes being harvested too early resulting in over-acid wines. Others were light, lacking finesse. But, there were many pleasant results, including some good Meursaults and Montrachets. Of little current interest.

*The reds are for drinking soon; only the very best are worth keeping longer. Drink up the whites.*

## 1971

An outstanding vintage throughout Burgundy: vigorous, well-constituted wines. Apart from a slightly problematic flowering, the summer was settled. August saw some hail and a poor final week but conditions picked up with a beautiful first half of September. A small but well-nourished crop of grapes was picked from September 16 onwards. In the Côte de Beaune, the area worst affected by the hail, the quantities amounted to a mere fraction of the 1970 harvest.

**Red**☆☆☆ An impressive vintage, regarded as untypical by Burgundians. The severe pruning caused by the harsh weather resulted in unusually substantial wines. Overall, big, rich and well-structured. Many were outstanding.

**White**☆☆☆☆ One of the loveliest white burgundy vintages of the period. Dry, firm, well-balanced and subtle; the Chablis, Meursaults and Montrachets were particularly successful.

*Reds still drinking well, best will keep beyond 2000. Whites now mainly consumed though finest and firmest still good.*

## 1970

April and May suffered bad weather but thereafter conditions were generally fine through to October. A large crop of ripe grapes was picked at the end of September.

**Red**☆☆ Sadly disappointing. Pale wines, probably due to over-production, many reaching maturity within five years.

**White**☆to☆☆☆ An uneven vintage which ranged from bad, somewhat dull, to good. The wines were often too soft, overripe and lacking in acidity. Most were speedily consumed.

*Reds: fully mature, drink up. Whites: drink up.*

## 1969

After a mild winter and cold, wet spring, the grapes budded late, but were then ripened by a fine, sunny summer. September was also wet, but fortunately sound, ripe grapes were gathered from October 5 onwards under exceptionally fine conditions.

**Red**☆☆☆☆☆ A superb vintage, and not unlike 1949 in its style. Unfortunately still somewhat underrated, 1969 being tainted by Bordeaux' poor reputation. The wines appeared to fall into two categories: light wines for quick drinking, and a higher class which had the body, tannin and acidity for long keeping – being the first year of such quality since 1966. A vintage that constantly surprises and delights.

**White**☆☆☆☆☆ A distinctly agreeable vintage. Firm, dry and well-balanced classic wines. The best of which took a full ten years to develop.

*The best reds excellent now and will keep, some comfortably into the 21st century. Whites: drink up all but the very best.*

## 1968

A very poor year. Such a catastrophic vintage that the Hospices de Beaune auction was cancelled. Some skilful winemakers who chaptalised their white wines did, however, manage to produce a few surprises.

*Mostly long consumed, few now seen. Avoid.*

## 1967

Favourable weather conditions, including a particularly sunny July and August, persuaded some vineyard owners to dispense with dusting the vines to protect them from disease. Ten days of rain in September produced some disastrous results. Many winemakers attempted to speed up fermentation. The wines produced were very uneven, some particularly high in alcohol.

**Red**☆☆ Variable, but the best, especially from the Grands Crus *climats* on the slopes, were delightful.

**White**☆☆☆ A better year for the whites: highly attractive dry, refreshing wines with good flavour. Mostly past their best but still some surprises around. Despite this the trade showed more interest in the 1966s.

*Drink up.*

## 1966

Crops were damaged by spring hail. The summer began poorly but conditions gradually improved. The harvest took place from September 28 in perfect conditions, the light September rain having gently swelled the grapes. At the outset growers were worried that the harvest would be small, but ultimately were pleasantly surprised by the good quantity and quality.

**Red**☆☆☆☆ Overall a firm, elegant vintage. The Côte de Nuits produced the best wines, and even the less good from elsewhere were attractive and lively.

**White**☆☆☆☆ Very high quality wines which combined austerity with fragrance, good firm flesh, plus sufficient fat and acidity to give them longevity. Not surprisingly, this was a very popular year which achieved consistently high prices.

*Reds: the best are perfect now, the greatest will continue to mature. Whites: most have been consumed though Grands Crus can still be superb, continuing to dazzle with style and richness.*

## 1965

A catastrophic year: rain waterlogged the soil and an appalling storm washed away some vineyards.

## 1964

A justifiably popular vintage with merchants. Record prices were achieved at the annual Hospices de Beaune auction. After the hardest, snowiest winter in 20 years, conditions finally picked up allowing a perfect June flowering and a hot, dry summer reduced the by now abundant crop. September alternated regularly between rain and sun, providing perfect pre-harvest conditions.

**Red**☆☆☆☆ Superb, meaty, open-knit wines.

**White**☆☆☆ The grapes were high in sugar and low in acidity. A popular vintage but lacking finesse, and quick maturing.

*Best reds can still be excellent. Whites should have been drunk.*

## 1963

A rather dreary summer and sunny autumn produced a very large crop of mediocre wines.

**Red**☆ A poor to fair vintage which was completely overshadowed by its two good flanking years.

**White**☆☆ A much better year for whites, though few were bought by the trade. Rather low in acidity; some good Montrachets.

*Few remain. Drink up.*

## 1962

A very good year. A cold April preceded a summer which gradually improved and culminated in a sunny August and welcome rain in September, delaying the start of picking until October 8. Exceptional harvesting weather produced a smallish crop of ripe, healthy grapes.

Hopes were that prices would come down to a more realistic level thanks to another satisfactory year. But this was not the case as sellers found themselves greatly outnumbered by buyers and prices strengthened. In retrospect, good value nevertheless.

**Red**☆☆☆☆ Fragrant, delicious, stylish wines. The best were slow starters but ultimately attractive, exciting and well-balanced.

**White**☆☆☆☆☆ The whites have a perfect balance of body, acidity, flesh and crispness.

*Reds are firmer than the 1964s, the best can still be superb and with years more life if well kept. Few whites remain but a Grand Cru, if perfectly cellared, can still be delicious.*

## 1961

A mild winter and warm spring pushed the growth of the vines months ahead of normal. However, due to uneven weather patterns in June, the flowering took nearly three times longer than average and this, coupled with a bad summer, meant that the vintage reverted to its usual timing. Conditions for harvest were good and picking began on September 25.

**Red**☆☆☆ A good, appealing, fragrant and popular vintage, though not comparable to 1961 red Bordeaux.

**White**☆☆☆ Undoubtedly a successful year, the wines were enormously popular – thanks partly to the success of the reds, the small size of the crop and the dismal previous vintage.

*Some of the reds still delicious but best drunk soon. The whites should have been consumed by now.*

## 1960

Unripe grapes, poor wines.

**Red** ~ Thin, almost all consumed early.

**White** ~ Equally thin, very acidic wines, refreshing in early 1960s.
*Drink up.*

## 1959

Excellent for the reds but not the whites. Good growing conditions with a hot, dry summer and sufficient rain to swell the berries.

**Red**☆☆☆☆☆ A magnificent vintage. From the first tastings these have always been highly flavoured, richly coloured wines with plenty of extract and tannin. The most dependable of the older vintages and the last of the great classic heavyweight reds.

**White**☆☆☆ Growers experienced difficulties with vinification and the wine tended to lack acidity. The more substantial wines such as Le Montrachet and Corton-Charlemagne can still be very good. In the northerly areas the hot weather was most beneficial and produced some interesting Chablis.

*The best reds are still superb. Few whites remain, drink up.*

## 1958

The market was already inundated with high-quality wines when this moderate vintage appeared; the English trade gave it a miss.

**Red**☆☆ Rarely seen. Now fully mature; drink up.

**White**☆ Not difficult to avoid: none to be had.

## 1957

Mild spring and early summer with extreme heat. Temperatures relented considerably with cool, grey July afternoons.

**Red**☆☆☆ A good, flavoursome vintage, the acid levels lending a zesty quality to the wines; better for Burgundy than Bordeaux.

**White**☆☆☆ Disastrous May frost in Chablis destroyed almost all the vines, including those of the top growths. Elsewhere wines were firm and fruity.

*Some reds have survived, can be flavoursome, but drink up.*

## 1956

A disastrous year, menaced by disease and pests. Rarely seen.
*Avoid.*

## 1955

After a slow, cold start to the year, the weather picked up and harvesting took place under the best conditions in 20 years.

**Red**☆☆☆ Sound and popular, though variable reds. The Côte de Nuits had depth and style but lacked length and finish; the Côte de Beaunes were light and at their best in the mid- to late 1960s.

**White**☆☆☆☆ A delightful vintage: elegant and beautifully balanced, sitting somewhere between the solidity of the 1952s and 1959s and the soft ripeness of the 1953s.

*Reds fully mature, drink now. Whites past best; drink up.*

## 1954

Pleasant spring, successful flowering, but wet summer. The harvest saved by a late, sunny autumn. Picking began October 7. An abundant crop of uneven quality grapes.

**Red**☆☆☆ Overshadowed by the 1952s and 1953s, this vintage was undeservedly neglected.

**White**☆ Unripe and a tendency to tartness. Few shipped.

*Drink up.*

## 1953

Apart from a mild April, the weather was generally wet and cold until August/September when the warm sun ripened the grapes. The harvest started on September 29 under excellent conditions.

**Red**☆☆☆☆ Ripe, supple, attractive wines.

**White**☆☆☆☆ As with the reds, these were highly popular, and with good reason. Soft, pleasant and very good value, though less firm than the 1952s.

*The best reds, though fading, can still be delicious. Drink up the few remaining whites.*

## 1952

A June drought and a hot July and August with some rain, then a cool September.

**Red**☆☆☆☆ A very reliable vintage, tough and concentrated as a result of the drought – a close second after 1959 as the most dependable of the decade.

**White**☆☆☆☆ As is so often the case with burgundy, the whites were better than the reds. The best reached perfection and all enjoyed great popularity, consequently few remain.

*The best reds are still firm and excellent; whites are well past their best, the few that remain can be more than interesting.*

## 1951

With 1956, one of the two worst years of the decade. Rarely seen but some surprises, for example La Tâche.

## 1950

A vintage menaced by hail throughout the summer, the latter half was wet.

**Red**☆ Feeble wines.

**White**☆☆☆ A far better vintage for the whites. Some excellent Montrachet, great variety in the quality of the Chablis. Among the less superior wines there was a tendency to fat and lack of length.

## 1949

A very wet start to the year, but worries were soon quelled by a dry summer with a little beneficial rain. Harvesting began

September 27. This vintage was highly popular amongst the buyers and was bought at exceptionally reasonable prices.

**Red**☆☆☆☆☆ First class results. Compared to the 1947s, the 1949s were better balanced and closer knit, consequently they held for longer – burgundy at its elegant best. Wines can still be excellent.

**White**☆☆☆☆ Superb, supple, well-balanced wines which lasted well. Now rarely seen and tiring.

## 1948

Cold, wet weather which gradually improved from mid-August.

**Red**☆☆to☆☆☆ A vintage unfairly sandwiched between two superior years. Some of very high quality, but some tired now.

**White**☆☆ Virtually bypassed by the English, despite being a moderately good year.

## 1947

Fantastic weather conditions throughout the year gave rise to much well-founded optimism. The usual difficulties associated with winemaking in great heat affected some areas, but those who overcame them made outstanding wines.

The 1947s came onto the market at a time when the old-established British wine merchants were anxious to replenish their war-depleted cellars. Wines were bought enthusiastically, and at very reasonable prices.

**Red**☆☆☆☆ Immediately attractive, ripe wines. More stable than their counterparts in Bordeaux.

**White**☆☆☆☆ A ripe, delightful, early-maturing vintage. Some excellent Chablis and Bâtard-Montrachets.

*Reds are still drinking well; English-bottled wines are worth looking out for. Of the whites, the top Côte de Beaune wines can still be delicious if of impeccable provenance.*

## 1946

Quite a good growing season. An abundant crop then reduced by hail, followed by a cold rainy period. Ignored by the trade.

**Red**☆

**White**☆☆

*Few ever seen. Drink up.*

## 1945

An impressive year. Nature's severe pruning of the crop was undoubtedly the key contributing factor. Severe frosts in spring were followed by a cyclone on June 21 which devastated the ten principal villages of the Côte de Beaune from Puligny to Corton. This reduced the crop to one-sixteenth of the estimated yield. The result was a small harvest of ripe, highly concentrated grapes.

**Red**☆☆☆☆☆ Dry, firm, substantial and deep-coloured. Well-constituted wines which lasted admirably. The best and best kept can still be magnificent.

**White**☆☆☆☆ A small crop of excellent wines with good finish. Few shipped to England. Rarely seen.

*The greatest reds still magnificent.*

## 1944

This might well have been a good year, had it not been for the dismal rain which fell continuously throughout the harvest.
**Red**☆ Light, washed-out wines.
**White** ~ A poor vintage. None tasted.

## 1943

The best war-time vintage: well-nigh perfect spring, summer and autumn. A shortage of labour, bottles and corks.
**Red**☆☆☆☆ Many of the wines had to be kept long in the cask, hastening decline and drying them out. Nevertheless, the wines had flavour, firmness and ripeness. Best are still drinking well.
**White**☆☆☆ The best vintage between 1937 and 1945 and those bottles that were well looked after make fascinating drinking.

## 1942

After a good summer the vines around the Côte de Beaune were damaged by hail. The harvest began the following day on September 13 but was intermittent, taking four weeks to complete.
**Red**☆☆☆ Good, stylish, little-known and underrated wines.
**White**☆☆ Mediocre, light wines, not often seen.

## 1941

Healthy vines, but a cold autumn prevented full ripening.
**Red**☆☆ A little-seen wartime vintage; few wines remain though the reds can still be good.
**White**☆☆ Better, crisper wines, some still surviving.

## 1940

Good growing season spoiled by mildew.
**Red**☆☆ Some good wines made but few remain.
**White** ~ All consumed during the war.

## DECADE OF THE 1930s
**Red Burgundy**

A decade witnessing some excellent vintages.

**1939**☆☆ and **1938**☆☆ were both mediocre years of little interest, few now remain; but the mid-decade produced some far more distinguished wines. **1937**☆☆☆☆☆ was a rich, distinctive year, reported at the time to be the best since 1929 and far better than Bordeaux; the best still magnificent. **1936**☆ was a poor year of little interest.

**1935**☆☆☆☆ was a very good, abundant year, though little was shipped to the UK due to great interest in the fine, well-constituted **1934**☆☆☆☆ considered then to be the best of the decade. **1933**☆☆☆☆ another good year overshadowed by 1934. **1932** ~, **1931** ~, **1930** ~ were uniformly disastrous.

**White Burgundy**

The 1930s, like the 1920s, produced some interesting whites.

**1939**☆ and **1938**☆ were, however, not among them. But, undoubtedly the greatest vintage of the decade was the **1937**☆☆☆☆ though only a very limited amount of it was shipped before the war. Once hostilities had ceased merchants were seeking younger wines. Passing over **1936**☆ a minor and rarely seen vintage, the next-best years were **1935**☆☆☆ and **1934**☆☆☆☆ both good to very good vintages, but now of course scarce. **1933**☆☆☆ another lovely vintage in Burgundy, was still showing well in the mid-1950s but has proved disappointing more recently. **1930~**, **1931~** and **1930~** were all uninteresting.

## DECADE OF THE 1920s

### Red Burgundy

Including one of the best-ever Burgundy vintages, seven very good to excellent years, two mediocre and only one poor.

**1929**☆☆☆☆☆ was a classic vintage of immediate appeal, combining quantity with quality which, if well-cellared, lasted remarkably well. **1928**☆☆☆☆ survived the hazards of difficult weather to produce fine, firm wines. Leaving aside the dismal **1927~** the other great year was **1926**☆☆☆☆ a small vintage, the best wines of which were fabulous, though few tasted recently.

**1925**☆ a disappointing vintage; **1924**☆☆☆☆ very attractive despite the difficult weather conditions, although not as exciting as **1923**☆☆☆☆☆ which produced a small quantity of very good wines. **1922**☆ was a moderate vintage following two more very good years: **1921**☆☆☆☆ and **1920**☆☆☆☆☆ the latter despite having faced bad weather and disease.

### White Burgundy

A decade that included some outstanding wines.

**1929**☆☆☆☆ was a magnificent soft, ripe vintage, but not as crisp as the excellent, firm, nutty **1928**☆☆☆☆☆ which was certainly the best vintage between 1921 and 1937. If well kept the 1928 whites can still be excellent.

The four mid-decade vintages, **1927**☆, **1926**☆☆, **1925**☆ and **1924**☆ were generally uninspiring, as was **1922**☆; **1923**☆☆☆☆ was very good for white burgundy, and even better was the remarkable **1921**☆☆☆☆☆ a magnificent vintage for white wines throughout France and Germany, though the few remaining white burgundies are now scarce and tiring. **1920**☆☆☆ was also a good vintage.

## DECADE OF THE 1910s

### Red Burgundy

This was a decade which included three exceptional years of very high quality as well as its fair share of unexceptional years.

Favourable weather conditions leading up to an excessively hot August in **1919**☆☆☆☆☆ produced a fairly small vintage of outstandingly fruity, ripe wines, which can still be good. **1918**☆☆, **1917**☆ and **1916**☆☆☆ were three moderate years, best of which was 1916. The second first-rate vintage of the decade was **1915**☆☆☆☆☆ which enjoyed an abundant quantity of superb quality grapes that made full, fruity wines.

Passing over the three years preceding **1915,** the other great year was **1911**☆☆☆☆☆ a magnificent classic burgundy vintage, the perfect summer and early harvest yielding a small crop.

## DECADE OF THE 1900s

**Red Burgundy**

The first decade of the 20th century included some remarkable
vintages, although, inevitably, scarce now.

**1909** ~ mediocre. **1908** ~ was generally a poor year due to
unpredictable weather; **1907**☆☆☆ was a good year, producing
light wines, few of which are now seen. The best vintage was
**1906**☆☆☆☆☆ an ideal growing season and early harvest, perfect
wines, the best can still be lovely; and even better than those of
**1904**☆☆☆☆ the other good vintage of the decade. Again, the
conditions were perfect, resulting in stylish, soft wines. **1905** ~,
**1903** ~, **1902** ~ and **1901** ~ of no interest. **1900**☆☆ was not as
good as its counterpart in Bordeaux, but did produce an abundant
yield of moderately good wines.

## 1900 TO 1919

**White Burgundy**

**1919**☆☆☆☆ was one of the three great vintages of the 1910s. The
other two being 1911 and 1915. **1906**☆☆☆☆ was the outstanding
vintage of the preceding decade. Those well cellared remained
more than just interesting for a considerable length of time.

## PRE-1900s

**Red Burgundy**

The best vintages were **1898**☆☆☆, **1894**☆☆☆, **1893**☆☆☆ an
interesting year which produced some extremely good wines
made in conditions of great heat, **1865**☆☆☆☆☆ and **1864**☆☆☆☆
magnificent and can still be lovely to drink.

# Rhône

Looking rather like an apple on a string, the narrow strip of
vineyards along the banks of the Rhône eventually opens out
across a broad plain. The division between the wine areas of the
north and south is distinct: the microclimates differ, as do the
vine varieties grown, and styles of wine produced.

## Red Wine

The vineyards to the north are on steep slopes flanking the river.
The two principal red wine districts being Côte-Rôtie, adjacent to
Vienne not far south of Lyon, and Hermitage. Two lesser districts,
St-Joseph and Cornas, are on the right bank of the Rhône, more
or less opposite Hermitage; the vineyards of Crozes-Hermitage
above and behind Tain L'Hermitage. In the key northern districts
high quality, sturdy, long-lasting reds are predominantly made
from one grape variety: Syrah. Vintages are important. The best
repay keeping.

Châteauneuf-du-Pape is a small town just north of Avignon.
Its vineyards, some of the most important of the southern Rhône,
are on a wide plateau of stony soil upon which up to 13 permitted
vine varieties are grown. It is a hot district. The grapes are literally
sunburnt, the pigment extracted from their thick "tanned" skins

resulting in deeply coloured wine. The hot sun, supplemented by heat-reflecting pebbles which act like night-storage heaters, produces a naturally high sugar content which converts into a proportionally high level of alcohol. Wines of power rather than finesse result, but with richness, softness and depth of fruit.

Wines designated Côtes du Rhône tend to be lighter in style, best drunk young. Even the best, like Gigondas, should be consumed within two to four years of the vintage. They are not individually commented on in the notes that follow: a good year in Châteauneuf will generally also be good in the Côtes du Rhône.

## White Wine

The three principal districts are Condrieu, south of Côte-Rôtie, Hermitage and Châteauneuf-du-Pape, all of these producing only relatively small quantities of dry white wine.

A tiny amount is made in Condrieu from one grape variety, Viognier. Its most famous vineyard, with its own official appellation, is Château Grillet. Most are best drunk young, within, say, three years of the vintage.

The white wines made in Hermitage, from Marsanne and Roussanne grapes, combine delicacy with sturdiness and the best keep well. White Châteauneuf-du-Pape is relatively rare, it often has a distinct touch of sweetness and, lacking high natural acidity, should be drunk relatively young.

The weather conditions in the north and south of the Rhône can be taken as the same for white as for the preceding red.

## 1997

**Red**☆☆☆to☆☆☆☆☆ **White**☆☆☆ A rather split result for the Rhône Valley this vintage. The north enjoyed perfect conditions and a straightforward, uniformly successful harvest. Conversely, further south unfavourable weather presented various problems and a far less consistent growing season.

In both areas the year started favourably with early budding. Flowering was also very prompt, when the south experienced some April frost and localised hail damage. This did not cause as many problems as feared but did reduce the yield slightly. Conditions were cooler during summer which slowed down the maturation process. A heatwave then hit the region at the end of August, causing drought. There were a couple of sporadic thunderstoms before harvesting began and thereafter the harvest enjoyed three perfect, sun-filled weeks.

The north started picking white grapes on September 15 and red on September 25. The grapes ripened slowly and evenly, but producers reported that the extreme heat had burnt some vines, causing some damage. But on the whole the red wines are excellent and show great longevity.

In the south picking started on September 8. A problem still remaining in this area is that many producers do not have temperature controlling equipment – vitally important when the grapes are harvested very hot. Both reds and whites have good colour and aroma, but slightly lack acidity as a result of the heat.

*After decades in the doldrums top Rhône wines, particularly Côte-Rôtie and Hermitage are now fashionable and expensive. Massive when young they keep as long as great claret but are rarely given the opportunity. Whites soon. Reds worth cellaring.*

## 1996

**Red**☆☆to☆☆☆ **White**☆☆☆ An inconsistent year and a difficult vintage, mainly due to rain during the summer and harvest time. The start of the year saw a successful flowering, and producers who thinned out their crop in July greatly improved their chances of success. The beginning of August was cool and wet which hampered the natural sugar development. The weather then followed two different routes in the north and south.

In the north, late August became sunny and conditions were good until the end of the harvest. October 5 saw the start of the harvest, with the Mistral wind providing a cooling influence for the next three weeks. As a result the crop was healthy, rot-free and abundant. Syrah found it harder to ripen so the reds are austere in style, but good for slightly earlier drinking. Meanwhile, producers in Condrieu rejoiced after harvesting their Voignier grapes at 15 per cent potential alcohol, with complementing acidity levels. Some even made Vendange Tardive wines, after harvesting as late as November 10.

The south suffered more as the rain continued into September, causing dilution in the reds. In mid-September the Mistral wind rescued the area from potential rot disaster, but a hard ripening had produced only a light and early-drinking vintage. As in the north, whites had better results – great acidity.

*Condrieu and the other white Rhônes almost invariably best drunk young, around three to four years after the vintage. Reds, from the north and south for early to mid-term drinking.*

## 1995

**Red**☆☆☆☆☆ **White**☆☆☆☆ A good, clean and consistent vintage for the Rhône. January was dry with average temperatures, resulting from the effects of the longer than usual Mistral wind. February was dry and mild, then March turned fresh and windy. April was warm and rainy, notably during the final ten days. These conditions helped strengthen the vines. May was very warm promting rapid bud burst, but then June brought cool nights and things slowed down again. Flowering commenced on June 7 without too many problems. July and August were hot and dry and the vintage started early on September 4. Ideal conditions prevailed and continued until the end of the harvest.

In the north yields were down by 20 per cent, due to *coulure* and *millerandage* problems during flowering. The reds are elegant and charming while the whites are more delicate than 1994s with good acidity. Some excellent Marsanne and Roussanne wines.

The late September Mistral wind had a drying and concentrating effect in the south giving super-ripe reds with high sugar levels. Balanced with good acidity and tannin, these wines are delightful and comparable with those of the 1990 vintage.

*Clearly a highly satisfactory year for red and white. Classic Hermitage and Côte-Rôtie with good prospects, say 2000 to 2015; Chateauneuf-du-Pape sooner. Crisp whites 1998 to 2002*

## 1994

Red☆☆to☆☆☆☆ White☆☆☆ Vegetation progressed quickly in the Rhône after a very mild winter and, unlike other French regions, the summer sun was so extreme that it scorched many of the grapes. Temperatures were as high as 42˚C (107˚F). The resultant wines are varied in quality and reflect the timing of their harvests in relation to the heavy mid-September rains.

In the north, budding took place early, around March 15. The temperature rapidly fell, retarding this growth. The end of May finally witnessed the flowering which was followed by some disease related problems including a small amount of *coulure*. Grapes from steep slopes were not unduly affected by the rains that fell during the harvest, but those from the plateau lacked balance with too much acidity. The final grapes to be brought in suffered from being too waterlogged and chaptalisation was widespread throughout the region.

Further south similar problems at flowering occurred and *coulure* affected both Grenache and Syrah resulting in small bunches. The producers who harvested most of their grapes before the rains were very happy with their results. Generally, the wines tend to have less colour but more tannin than 1993.

*A "vintage of the century" dashed by heavy rain; yet the top producers, selecting only their best grapes made excellent wine, particularly in the north. We must wait to see how they turn out. The vast majority of the far less copious and important whites are best drunk two to three years after bottling.*

## 1993

Red☆☆to☆☆☆ White☆☆☆ Similarly to Burgundy in the north, conditions during spring and early summer were favourable. The Rhône Valley in its entirety benefited from a reasonably hot and sunny summer, but mounting hopes of a great vintage were washed away by rains from mid-September. These resulted in very serious flooding, most notably in the south.

Reds from the north are light early-developing wines, with the best coming from old vines or from growers who cut their vines back significantly in August. Careful selection was necessary because of the prevalence of mildew and parasites. Chaptalisation was required throughout. In the south, the red wines hold a little more promise as many grapes were harvested before the rains fell. Châteauneuf-du-Pape was the most lucky in this respect, claiming better wines than both the 1992 and 1991 vintages. Elsewhere in the south, many growers were able to get the crop in rapidly, managing to retain some fullness in the wines. The better wines have good levels of tannin and colour.

White wines fared best, due to their earlier harvest. Condrieu has good acidity, but a little less fruit than usual. Hermitage, Crozes-Hermitage and St-Joseph all produced agreeable wines.

*Selected reds from top growers will be drinking well now until the end of the century; whites, pleasant now but variable.*

## 1992

Red☆☆to☆☆☆☆ White☆☆☆ Conditions were good during winter and spring, with normal temperatures and healthy levels of rain (after several unusually dry years). May was hot and a successful flowering took place. Unfortunately, this was followed by six weeks of wet weather which caused *coulure*, mildew and eventually uneven ripening. The month of August was hot and consequently raised the hopes of the growers. Once into September dramatically wet and stormy conditions struck the region. Further rot had set in by the time of the harvest and in the north, the size of the crop was reduced by a quarter. Despite the extreme conditions, red wines from both north and south have fairly good colour and extract with soft tannins.

The white wines, although quite varied, are of satisfactory quality. Hermitage has good, rich extract and Condrieu, with higher than usual levels of acidity, needs some time to soften.

*Reds: mainly for early consumption though some leading growers, such as Gérard Chave, made exceptional wines. Whites are all ready for drinking.*

## 1991

Red☆☆ White☆☆☆ An uneven year, both climatically and for the resultant wines. Winter was unusually cold, March was mild and wet, April and May dry but cooler than usual – but, the region escaped the frost damage suffered elsewhere in France – and vegetation was delayed. Flowering was from May 25 to June 20, Grenache in the south being seriously hit by *coulure*. July and August were hot and dry, enabling the vines to catch up. However, mid-September rains in the north dashed hopes of a top-class harvest. Some rot in Côte-Rôtie but grapes were fairly healthy.

In the south the surviving Grenache grapes had ripening problems. Late summer storms and humidity in September caused some rot. A small crop of mainly light red wines in Châteauneuf-du-Pape. In the north and south white wines are reported to be good, the grapes being picked before rain set in.

*The reds from the south are lighter than usual, best for drinking soon; from Hermitage and Côte-Rôtie the reds will be middle-distance runners. Whites, with good acidity, drink now.*

## 1990

Red☆☆☆☆☆ White☆☆☆☆ Drought prevailed in many areas of the Rhône but the wines were, like those of the previous year, powerful and promising, if a little less aromatic.

Throughout the north flowering was early and, where the weather turned cold, there was some *coulure*. Rain was only very localised, but the heat was less intense than in 1989 and July enjoyed some cool nights. Most growers started to pick in mid-September and the grapes were in ripe, healthy condition. Further south there was good rainfall during May and ripening was advanced. Harvesting of whites at Châteauneuf-du-Pape, where the rainfall had allowed the grapes to ripen fully, began September 5 and for reds September 10.

Overall, these wines were slightly lower in acidity than those of 1989, particularly in the south, but tannins were firm and alcohol levels high, indicating that these wines will be slow to open up but are full of promise and staying power.

*Sturdy, long-lasting reds in north and south: Châteauneuf-du-Pape drinking now to well beyond 2000, Hermitage now to 2020, Côte-Rôtie even longer. Whites to be drunk soon.*

## 1989

Red☆☆☆☆ White☆☆☆☆☆ This was a very mixed year in the Rhône, ranging from good to very good. The long, hot summer which produced so many good wines throughout France caused serious drought in the Rhône region.

Where rain did fall it was very localised. Some areas were, however, at a greater advantage than others: the older vines with longer roots were able to draw moisture from the subsoil, vines on clay-based soil benefited from clay's capacity to retain water.

The grapes harvested late produced better wines than where growers had panicked and picked early. Potentially excellent wines were made in Côte-Rôtie – one of the few areas receiving some precious rain. Châteauneuf-du-Pape was also very successful, producing rich, complete reds. Hermitage was less reliable, though the best reds are rich and complex and the whites are deep and full flavoured. White wines from elsewhere are attractive but low in acidity.

*Châteauneuf-du-Pape drinking now to 2005, the best reds from the north now to 2000. Whites drink soon.*

## 1988

Red☆☆☆☆ White☆☆☆☆ A very good year along the length of the Rhône, the wines from the north being excellent. Hail and rain around the Côte-Rôtie during flowering reduced yields and concentrated the crop. Excessive humidity during the spring and early summer caused problems in the south. Thereafter, the weather was hot and dry with sufficient rain in August to swell the grapes. Early picking avoided problems caused by later rains.

The crop was of average size and made rich wines with good levels of tannin and fruit. The white wines are generally of good quality, possibly for long keeping.

*Top reds drinking now to well beyond 2000. The whites of both Condrieu in the north and white Châteauneuf-du-Pape drink soon, white Hermitage to the end of the century.*

## 1987

Red☆to☆☆☆ White ~ In the north of the region the weather was satisfactory and good wines were made at Côte-Rôtie. Hermitage was not so fortunate: rain fell during the spring and flowering, resulting in uneven fruit set. Stormy weather in August did not relent for the harvest (mid-October) and the vintage was less than perfect. The conditions in the south was worse – rain, storms, fog, even a mass invasion of caterpillars. Light, early-drinking wines.

*Côte-Rôtie soon. All other reds drink up. Whites: drink up.*

## 1986

Red☆☆to☆☆☆☆ White☆☆☆ Warm, dry weather during the summer. September dull, rain at the end of the month delaying the harvest which began on October 10. Those who selected carefully avoided the problems of pests and rot resulting from the wet weather. Further south the good weather held during the vintage, which lasted for one month from October 6.

*Some good, long-lasting, tannic reds from Côte-Rôtie to Châteauneuf-du-Pape. Most drinking well now but will continue developing. Whites now fully mature.*

## 1985

Red☆☆☆☆☆ White☆☆☆☆ After a severe winter and cool spring, the weather improved, with good flowering in early June. The summer was hot, dry and sunny and harvest took place in good conditions from September 16 until October 11. Outstanding reds, rich, long-lasting.

*Reds from the south drinking well now. Best Châteauneuf-du-Pape, in common with Hermitage and Côte-Rôtie, will improve over the next ten years or more. Whites: drink now.*

## 1984

Red☆☆ White☆ A small crop of moderate quality wines. A late flowering took place in good weather, thereafter conditions were unsettled, becoming increasingly cool and wet. The harvest ran from September 19 to October 15. These were not wines for keeping. However, some, mainly from Syrah, are holding well.

*Drink up the whites and most reds. However good Hermitage and Côte-Rôtie will continue to evolve to, say, 2000.*

## 1983

Red☆☆☆☆☆ White☆☆☆ The flowering took place during an unsettled June, and a magnificent hot, dry summer followed. The harvest was early and *coulure* reduced the Grenache yield to below average. The red wines from both the north and the south regions are excellent. They are rich and concentrated with hard tannins which will soften with maturity.

*Châteauneuf-du-Pape is now mature and drinking well. Hermitage and Côte-Rôtie now to 2000. Whites, drink up.*

## 1982

Red☆☆☆☆ White☆☆☆☆ A very large crop. As is often the case with such a big harvest the quality varied considerably, but the best were excellent. Summer was long and very hot; heavy rains in August continued until harvest began on September 7. These conditions led to problems: the heat reduced acidity levels, fermentation was difficult and many wines seem "cooked" as a result. Pre-harvest rain also reduced concentration in the grapes.

Growers who picked their grapes carefully, did not overcrop; and who controlled fermentation, produced the best wines. A vintage often paired with 1983: it is holding well but will not last as long.

*The best are reds, many are drinking well and will last until the turn of the century. Whites need drinking.*

## 1981

**Red**☆☆ **White**☆☆ Rain in the north during the flowering and the harvest seriously disrupted this vintage. Nevertheless some good wines were made, particularly those from the Côte-Rôtie. Further south, cold weather during the flowering resulted in an uneven fruit set and reduced quantities. After a summer drought the harvest began on September 14. This was a moderate vintage; rich, concentrated wines from Châteauneuf-du-Pape, which, like the better wines from the north, have improved with time.

*Though laden with bitter tannins the wines of Châteauneuf-du-Pape have ameliorated somewhat and should be drunk soon. The wines of Hermitage are fully developed, the best Côte-Rôties are drinking well.*

## 1980

**Red**☆☆to☆☆☆ **White**☆☆ In the north of the Rhône the year started badly with poor weather during the spring and flowering period. As a result not all the flowers set and the crop was small. The weather improved during the growing season and a late harvest began on October 8. In the south the weather was generally fine throughout the vintage. The largest crop ever recorded was harvested from September 25.

Fairly good, deep wines which have, along with the 1979s, 1981s and 1982s, always been overshadowed by the great 1978s.

*Drink up.*

## 1979

**Red**☆☆to☆☆☆☆ **White**☆☆☆ Favourable weather conditions produced wines of high quality. In the north temperatures were cool until late July; thereafter dry, sunny weather held for an abundant harvest beginning late September in Côte-Rôtie, while around Hermitage rains delayed the harvest until October 8. A good year for the south: after a late budding, flowering took place quickly in good conditions. Some variability in the wines can be found where the vines suffered from drought.

Overall, a moderately good vintage: wines from the north were concentrated with good levels of acidity and tannin, with good ageing potential; those from the south were fragrant and soft. Most whites were consumed during the mid-1980s.

*Now fully mature. Drink soon.*

## 1978

**Red**☆☆☆☆☆ **White**☆☆☆☆☆ Terrible weather conditions made this a very difficult year, yet with excellent results, the best vintage since 1911. A cool, wet spring reduced yields; flowering was late and slow; the remaining summer hot and dry, too dry for some, through to the harvest. These were big, tannic, rich reds with acidity for long keeping. Whites should still be on top form.

*Astonishing reds, packed with fruit, extract and alcohol, drinking well, the top wines from Hermitage and Côte-Rôtie with a 20 to 40 year life span. Whites fully mature.*

## 1977

**Red**☆to☆☆ **White**☆ A poor year in the north, bad weather produced thin, acidic, unripe wines. In the south, fine autumn weather allowed winemakers to produce light, attractive wines.

*Drink up.*

## 1976

**Red**☆to☆☆☆ **White**☆☆☆ A hot, dry summer produced ripe, concentrated wines in most of the north, at worst the whites lack acidity and are variable. The south enjoyed similar weather, but high hopes were dashed by rains during the harvest in late September. Here too, good wines but not for long keeping.

*Best Côte-Rôtie and Hermitage at peak now. Whites past best.*

## 1975

**Red**☆to☆☆ **White** ~ A poor year in the north and south. In the south August rains had a disastrous effect on many of the grapes which had ripened too early, while benefiting those which ripened later. Problems were further exacerbated by a hot, dry Sirocco wind blowing in mid-September. Thin, astringent wines, lacking fruit and concentration: very short-lived.

*Drink up.*

## 1974

**Red**☆to☆☆☆ **White** ~ The second of two large vintages in the Rhône. Early autumn rainfall diluted the grapes in the south. Overall, a mediocre year; the best wines coming from Hermitage and Châteauneuf-du-Pape where those made in the more traditional style were capable of ten years ageing.

*Drink up.*

## 1973

**Red**☆to☆☆☆ **White** ~ Heavy rains in early September resulted in a huge crop throughout the region. The wines from the Côte-Rôtie had good colour but were a little light; best suited for early drinking. There was some hail damage in Hermitage, but the reds and whites from this region had good ageing potential. Further south the wines were light and low in acidity, best drunk young.

*Drink up.*

## 1972

**Red**☆to☆☆☆ **White**☆☆☆ A disappointing vintage in the Côte-Rôtie where wines were acidic and hard. A better year in Cornas and Hermitage where a small crop contributed both good colour and flavour. Some attractive wines in Châteauneuf-du-Pape.

*Fully mature. Drink up.*

## 1971

Red☆☆☆to☆☆☆☆☆ White☆☆☆ A very good vintage. The Côte-Rôtie produced big, full-bodied wines with real ageing potential. Harmonious, attractive, lighter wines from Hermitage. The south also had very good results, though with lower levels of acidity they will not age quite as long as those from the north.

*Attractive reds, now fully mature.*

## 1970

Red☆☆☆to☆☆☆☆☆ White☆☆☆ An excellent year in the south, and very good in the north: a vintage with real ageing potential. Hot, sunny weather during the growing season. Many rich and well-balanced wines were made throughout the Rhône.

*Fully mature, the best still drinking well.*

## THE BEST OF EARLIER RHONE VINTAGES:

**Côte-Rôtie**

1969☆☆☆☆ 1967☆☆☆ 1966☆☆☆☆ 1964☆☆☆☆☆
1962☆☆☆ 1961☆☆☆☆☆ 1959☆☆☆☆☆ 1957☆☆☆☆
1955☆☆☆☆ 1953☆☆☆☆☆ 1952☆☆☆☆ 1949☆☆☆☆☆
1947☆☆☆☆ 1945☆☆☆☆☆

**Hermitage**

1969☆☆☆☆ 1967☆☆☆☆ 1966☆☆☆☆ 1964☆☆☆☆☆
1961☆☆☆☆☆ 1959☆☆☆☆☆ 1957☆☆☆☆ 1955☆☆☆☆
1953☆☆☆☆ 1952☆☆☆☆☆ 1949☆☆☆☆☆ 1947☆☆☆☆
1945☆☆☆☆☆

**Châteauneuf-du-Pape**

1969☆☆☆ 1967☆☆☆☆☆ 1966☆☆☆ 1964☆☆☆☆☆
1962☆☆☆ 1961☆☆☆☆☆ 1959☆☆☆ 1957☆☆☆
1955☆☆☆ 1953☆☆☆ 1952☆☆☆☆☆ 1949☆☆☆☆☆
1947☆☆☆☆ 1945☆☆☆☆☆

# Loire

A relatively northern district of France, with a maritime climate at its western end, the well spread vineyards along the meandering banks of the Loire and its tributaries mainly produce distinctly light, dry and acidic wines, best drunk young. Most are white, some are rosé, just a few are red: Chinon, Bourgueil and Sancerre Rouge. Vintages vary, some producing wine more acidic than others. Contrarily, the rare very hot summer, such as 1989, does not produce the most typical Loire wines, though the reds and the sweet wines benefit from the extra ripeness.

The dry to bone-dry whites such as Muscadet, Sancerre and Pouilly-Fumé should be consumed within one to three years after the vintage, as should Anjou Rosé whose main attractions are its pink colour and freshness. They do not feature in the notes on the older vintages. However, the semi-sweet (*demi-sec*) Vouvray and the glorious Vouvray *doux*, Coteaux du Layon, Bonnezeaux and Quarts de Chaume which, in certain years, are beneficially affected by *botrytis*, the same "noble rot" responsible for Sauternes. These all keep marvellously.

## 1997☆☆☆☆☆

A hat trick for the Loire, after the preceding two very successful vintages comes a third. Bud-break ran smoothly in relatively good conditions, although there were some patches of local frost. Flowering was complete for most areas before hail fell in mid-June. The end of June did not improve and was the coldest and wettest in 30 years. The central vineyards did suffer from some uneven development. Fortunately a long and hot summer, punctuated by thirst-quenching storms in late August, ensured successful ripening and concentration in the grapes.

Picking started in Muscadet on August 29 and very high ripeness levels were recorded. This was also the case for the Chenin Blanc producers, who achieved some record levels. The harvest for *moëlleux* wines almost lasted until the end of October.

Cabernet Franc triumphed again with a style very similar to 1996. Harvested at potential levels of 13 degrees of alcohol, the wines have dense colour and perfect balance of acid and tannins. Sancerre and Pouilly-Fumé experienced a small drop in yields and had to pick in stages after the uneven flowering. However, they did achieve very good ripeness, with matching acidity levels and fine aromas.

*Glorious wines, particularly the sweet wines which have that certain honeyed touch of botrytis. The dry wines such as Muscadet and Sancerre will come on to the market early and perhaps as well: they are much better drunk young and fresh.*

## 1996☆☆☆☆

A very successful vintage all over the Loire. The result of a dry and cool growing season and more sunshine hours than average.

Winter and spring were fairly cold, holding the vines back two weeks. The first half of June heated up, letting the vines catch up, but then cooled down towards the end, meaning that the vines were behind again. By late June a healthy and rapid flowering implied a large harvest, but drought conditions during the summer decreased this potential size. By September some welcome rain had swelled the small berries and harvest started at the end of the month. Conditions then were dry, with wind reducing the risk of rot.

Muscadet had a large crop, giving a lighter style. Chenin Blanc did very well, with a high level of ripeness. *Botrytis* found it difficult to break the thick skins and a cool, wet November did not help the sweet styles. But some very good wines were produced by grapes left to dry on the vines. The red wines had an exceptional vintage; Cabernet Franc was harvested at 12.5 per cent potential alcohol and producers declare the wines similar to those of 1989 and 1990. Sauvignon Blanc yields were down by ten to 20 per cent, however, very aromatic, vibrant and concentrated wines with great acidity were produced as a result.

*Muscadet, Sancerre and other dry, acidic whites are best drunk young and fresh. Quite the opposite for the superb sweet whites from the mid-Loire, Vouvray and Coteaux du Layon, where sweetness is gloriously balanced by acidity. Will keep well.*

## 1995 ☆☆☆☆

A most successful and promising vintage. Most of the Loire valley enjoyed a long, hot, dry summer. These conditions continued through to the harvest and an Indian summer was experienced, similar to many other areas in France at this time. The resulting wines were fine, rich and of very high quality.

Muscadet had a smaller than average crop, which produced attractive wines with good concentration. In Angers, a warm and humid autumn provided perfect conditions for noble rot and the production of stunningly deep and elegant sweet wines. Vouvray and Montlouis suffered slightly after some rain and many grapes required careful selection.

The reds fared well, giving charming wines. Top wines show firm structure and good capability to age. Central vineyards experienced optimal conditions up to harvest, and suspended picking for a few days to concentrate the grapes further. Generally, most wines are very good, especially the sweet whites.

*Superb vintage, better than usual Muscadet for early enjoyment. Sauvignon Blancs untypical. Wonderfully ripe mid-term reds, say 1999 to 2010. Sweet whites: long lasting classics.*

## 1994 ☆☆

The conditions were favourable throughout the region during the winter months but the frosts of mid-April were more devastating than elsewhere in France. Touraine was the worst hit and in Chinon the crop was half that of the previous year.

May ended on a cool note but the extreme heat from mid-June to mid-August consolidated the healthy, advanced state of the vines. Along with other parts of France, the Loire believed itself to be on course for a great vintage. The national pattern continued with the weather taking a downturn and Touraine in particular was unseasonably cold from mid-August until the heavy rains of mid-September.

Harvesting in the Loire took place very quickly due to the reduced size of the crop and was unprecedentedly completed in the main by the end of September. September 26 saw the return of fine weather offering ideal conditions for the development of *botrytis*. Generally this vintage in the Loire will have produced some reasonably good wines, not the great wines many had hoped for earlier in the summer. On the other hand, it was not the disastrous year some had proclaimed.

*Dry white: drink soon. Sweet whites had better potential, though overtaken by the 1995 and 1996.*

## 1993 ☆☆☆

In contrast to regions south of the Loire, the different weather patterns allowed growers here to produce satisfactory wines.

Along with the rest of France, the growing season began with early budding, but this was followed by a period of cold weather that delayed flowering until mid-June. Adequate conditions followed for healthy ripening apart from hail which affected certain vineyards around Saumur-Champigny. Most of the central and western districts were able to complete most of the harvest before the rains fell in October. Sancerre and Pouilly-Fumé were the only areas affected as their harvests started on October 8.

In general, the growers were satisfied with their results – wines of modest to reasonable quality. The reds have good colour and structure and very few sweet wines were made.

*Dry whites – drink now whilst comparatively young, fresh and pleasantly acidic. Sweet white, few to be seen. Early drinking.*

## 1992☆☆

A productive vintage after the enforced rest imposed by the severe frosts of 1991; careful selection was, therefore, vital.

The growing season started well and vines advanced quickly. Prospects were good by the end of July; however unfortunately, variable weather followed throughout the ripening season, and periods of rain and humidity were interspersed with warm, dry conditions. This resulted in the grapes swelling and induced rot.

Dry whites from all along the Loire were a reasonable success and a few sweet wines were produced from grapes picked as late as early November. Chinon reds are also good, notably those resulting from careful vat selection that concentrated colour and structure. Bourgueil was less successful.

*Except in exceptional hot ripe years (rare enough along the banks of the Loire) both reds and dry whites are best drunk whilst young and fresh. The 1992s – a case in point.*

## 1991☆

A disastrous year climatically. Of all the French regions, this was the worst hit by April frosts which decimated the well-advanced shoots after an enticingly mild spring. Chinon and Bourgueil were virtually wiped out. Flowering in late June, was also hampered by cold and, adding to frost losses, *coulure* and *millerandage* reduced the potential crop. A hot and dry summer raised hopes which were finally dashed by rain and rot-causing humidity at the end of September. By dint of careful selection, however, some good wines were made, albeit in small quantities.

*Light and acidic, most should have been consumed. A small amount of the sweeter Quarts de Chaume for drinking soon.*

## 1990☆☆☆☆☆

The drought of 1989 continued into 1990; results were good but, as for many areas in France, acidity levels were a little too low.

Extremely mild weather during winter and spring which, with the exception of a very hard frost in Muscadet at the beginning of April, encouraged an early flowering (mid-May), but cold weather in some areas, including Anjou, in early June meant uneven ripeness. The desert-like heat scorched many of the grapes, especially in Vouvray, but the late summer rain then swelled them slightly. Picking began August 29 in Muscadet, September 24 in the central Loire and Sancerre, and October 8 in Vouvray.

In Muscadet the wines were better-balanced than those of the previous years, although quantity was down. White wines from

Sancerre were rich but low in acidity, making them suitable for early drinking. In Anjou the crop was larger than the preceding year's, and this is destined to be an excellent year for the sweet whites of Coteaux du Layon, thanks to early morning October mists which encouraged the development of *botrytis* on the grapes. Also good for Vouvray.

*Muscadet, Sancerre and Vouvray sec drink up soon, Vouvray demi-sec, doux and Coteaux du Layon now to 2000.*

## 1989 ☆☆☆☆☆

An outstanding year for Loire wines; one which might well become the vintage of the century.

A mild winter and exceptionally hot summer encouraged very early growth. Budding was in February and flowering three weeks ahead of normal in perfect conditions. Picking in Muscadet began in late August and Vouvray on September 20.

The sun-ripened Cabernet Franc grapes in Chinon, Saumur and Bourgueil produced beautifully rich, powerful red wines with high natural alcohol – perfect candidates for long keeping.

Growers from the Muscadet, Sancerre and Pouilly vineyards produced plump, rich wines lower in acidity than normal, making this an untypical vintage, close to 1959 and 1964 in style.

Chenin Blanc in Vouvray and Anjou came into its own this year, especially *demi-sec*. Sweet whites, with age, will be classics.

*Muscadet and Sancerre drink up. The demi-secs soon, the magnificent sweet wines of Vouvray and Coteaux du Layon from now to 2020. The reds, usually dry and over-acidic, are well-constituted and will keep well, say now to 2000.*

## 1988 ☆☆☆☆

An abundant vintage of very good quality wines throughout the Loire; for the sweet whites, it was an excellent year.

A mild, wet winter developed into a warm, sunny spring, pushing bud-break and flowering about ten days ahead of normal. Good weather continued throughout the summer and the harvest continued from mid-September into October for the Cabernet grapes around Chinon and Bourgueil. These were rich, well-balanced wines with soft tannins.

Grapes for sweet whites thrived during the mild autumn and developed good levels of *botrytis*. Some growers harvested as late as November, producing wines of 14 per cent alcohol. Coteaux de Layon, Quarts de Chaume and Bonnezeaux stand comparison with the great 1959s. *Demi-sec* and *moëlleux* will keep.

*Dry white: drink up. Classic sweet wines: now to 2005.*

## 1987 ☆

A very mixed vintage which does not on the whole stand comparison with the years on either side.

A cool, damp spring led to late and protracted flowering and uneven fruit set. The weather improved, with plenty of sun between July and September, but broke during the harvest, necessitating careful selection of the grapes.

Those who picked early and whose grapes had ripened fully produced good wines; elsewhere grapes were picked unripe and swollen by the September rains. This was particularly the case for the red wines of Chinon, Bourgueil and Saumur which produced attractive, but light, acid-deficient wines.

The dry whites, in particular Muscadet, were the exception this year. Picking was completed before the rains came and good, though variable, wines for early drinking were made. Vouvray's *méthode traditionnelle bruts* worth watching for.

*Drink up.*

## 1986☆☆☆☆

After a cool, wet start to the year, the weather improved and flowering took place only one week later than normal.

Overall, this was a good year for the reds. Some good Cabernet Franc wines were produced in Chinon, Bourgueil and Saumur where there was enough sun to fully ripen the grapes.

The fine summer provided ideal growing conditions for the dry white wines. The Sauvignon grapes were fully ripened, yet maintained a good level of acidity. A good year for Sancerre, and Pouilly-Fumé was reputed to be the best of the decade.

A year of above average quality for the sweet whites from Vouvray: they were elegant wines with a flowery fragrance. Some very good Vouvray *mousseux* was made late in the year.

*All at peak now though the relatively few demi-sec and doux will keep a while longer.*

## 1985☆☆☆☆

A highly satisfactory year, particularly for the reds and the sweet whites. After a wet spring the weather picked up and remained hot and dry right through until the end of the vintage. The grapes were harvested in ideal conditions from September 30 until November 10. Pickers were able to go through the vineyards several times, enabling them to harvest the grapes at their optimum ripeness.

The reds were big, ripe and attractive; well-suited for early drinking. In the districts where sweet wine is made, growers who waited were rewarded by the development of noble rot and produced some excellent Chenin Blanc wines.

The Vouvrays were soft and dry with a perfect balance of sugar and acidity; they have excellent ageing potential.

*The dry whites and reds need drinking though the botrytis-affected sweet wines will keep longer.*

## 1984☆

A poor vintage throughout the Loire. A wet spring developed into a poor, cloudy summer, which was followed by a wet September.

The wines on the whole were harsh, acidic and out of balance. As the acidity fades some of the sweeter wines may show more style but, with the exception of some good Vouvray *mousseux*, this is not a vintage to look out for.

*Drink up.*

## 1983☆☆

A large crop of good wines. Spring and summer were wet and humid with some August hailstorms, but conditions improved mid-October in time for the harvest. The poor start to the year produced slightly light, acidic, dry wines. The sweeter styles benefited from the good October weather; some were judged to be slightly too acidic but, for the Vouvray, this meant wines with good ageing potential.

*Drink up, though demi-sec can still be pleasing.*

## 1982☆☆☆

Good weather prevailed throughout the summer but there were some violent storms during the harvest. On the whole this was not a memorable year, although Vouvray produced some good, dry wines. Drinking well in the mid-1980s but not worth keeping.

*Drink up.*

## 1981☆☆

A very small, modest vintage. Late spring frost damaged the buds and consequently reduced the crop, but the weather was fine thereafter. Good, fragrant wines were made around Vouvray; they were worth keeping but are now very scarce. Some lacked acidity.

*Drink up.*

## 1980☆☆

A good spring but protracted, wet summer. The harvest in Anjou, Touraine and Vouvray took place under snow from October 11 to November 11. Some pleasant wines nevertheless.

*Drink up.*

## 1979☆☆☆

A good year. Budding was late after a slow, wet spring; July was dry and August wet; September started warm and dry but saw some rainfall towards the end of the month. Dry, fairly well-balanced whites and light, balanced reds. Best for early drinking.

*Drink up.*

## 1978☆☆☆to☆☆☆☆

A cold, damp spring caused delayed flowering and *coulure* and *millerandage*. July hail caused further damage but late summer and autumn were sunny. A small crop, and a vintage which developed slowly, the sweet whites revealing themselves as remarkably well built. Particularly good for Sancerre and Pouilly-Fumé and the dry whites of the mid-Loire. Reds for long life.

*Reds now fully mature. Drink up few remaining whites.*

## 1977

A poor year. A long, wet winter and spring with an exceptionally cold spell in April when temperatures sank to –8˚C (18˚F). This led to a long, laborious flowering with *coulure*, then patches of mildew during the summer. Thin, dry whites and light reds.

*Few seen. Drink up.*

## 1976☆☆☆☆

The best vintage of the decade. A cold, dry winter and early, warm spring. Flowering was advanced; summer was very hot and dry, but temperatures cooled down in September. The harvest was, nevertheless, much ahead of normal, beginning early September. Unusually powerful wines; Pouilly-Fumé was more like Burgundian Chardonnay. Reds were well-built with long life.

*Reds and sweet whites fully mature. The dry whites should have been drunk by now.*

## 1975☆☆☆

Spring was late but warm, thereafter a very normal growing season with the harvest starting in early October. An average sized crop of good wines. Fresh supple whites which were slightly superior to the reds. The richer wines have life yet.

*Sweet wines still drinking well.*

## 1974☆

A large crop, after normal growing season, produced mediocre wines: the best reds and whites had quite good ageing potential.

*Few if any remain. Drink up.*

## 1973☆☆

A mild winter and spring encouraged a large crop. But, cold wet weather in July, with occasional hail, caused some damage. Mediocre wines, although a good year for Sancerre and some well-structured reds.

*All consumed by now.*

## 1972

A cold year. Spring frosts and rain persisted well into the summer; picking was late as a result. The crop was of average size. Mediocre wines, some good whites and light reds but on the whole a year to forget.

*Avoid.*

## 1971☆☆☆

A warm but short spring, followed by a stormy summer with very damaging hailstorms. A small crop of balanced wines for keeping.

*Some good Vouvrays and Coteaux du Layons still drinking well. All others passé.*

## 1970☆☆

A long, wet spring resulted in an abundant flowering. A stormy summer followed and harvest produced an abundant, pleasant crop. Soft, well-balanced wines. Not a year for dessert wines.

*Avoid.*

## OTHER GOOD/GREAT LOIRE VINTAGES

**1964**☆☆☆☆☆ produced great sweet wines, still on top form; and **1959**☆☆☆☆☆ magnificent Vouvray, Coteaux du Layon, and outstanding Moulin Touchais.

Excellent dessert wines were made in **1949**☆☆☆☆ (at their peak now) and in **1947**☆☆☆☆☆ the greatest vintage for classic Coteaux du Layon, Quarts du Chaume and Vouvray *doux* – still marvellously rich. **1945**☆☆☆☆ also produced very good, firm, sweet wines. **1937**☆☆☆☆☆ was the best vintage of the 1930s: wines with excellent acidity. **1934**☆☆☆☆ was very good too, though tiring now. And **1928**☆☆☆☆☆ another great vintage: the best sweet wines still beautiful to drink.

# Alsace

With the exception of small quantities of red wine and even rarer rosé, virtually all the wines of Alsace are white, the vast majority made to be consumed whilst they are young and fresh.

The dry whites made from Sylvaner and Pinot Blanc, and the less often exported Zwicker blend, should be drunk between one to three years after the vintage. However, when it comes to the major grape varieties, Riesling, Gewurztraminer and the too-little known Tokay-Pinot Gris, vintages are important, those of the highest quality achieving sublime heights and capable of remarkable longevity.

## 1997☆☆☆☆

Record sunshine hours, double that of 1995, were soaked up by the vines this year. After some frost during a cold, dry winter, uneven bud-break and coulure problems due to rain in June and July, producers were slightly tentative. The weather then took a turn and the sun rose to reward August and September.

The harvest began on October 1, after the vines had taken full advantage of the exceptional conditions during September. This was another vintage for Riesling which achieved very high ripeness levels, while again Gewurztraminer had been affected the most by coulure and suffered crop losses. The harvest continued until November 4 and some early morning mists in October helped achieve *botrytis*, but not much.

The grapes were harvested at levels equal to or higher than those required for the *botrytised* styles, however, without this element the wines are never quite of the same quality. And so it was to be a year for the dry wines, with only a few top quality sweet styles produced. Some compared this vintage to others such as 1949 and 1959 – rather masculine wines showing ideal sugar and acidity levels for ageing.

*Alsace has consistently produced pure, unadulterated wines of good honest quality. We should drink more of them. Let's start with this vintage. Ideal restaurant wines.*

## 1996☆☆☆☆

A vivacious and healthy success for Alsace, their third in a row. Yields were slightly higher than usual, except for Gewurztraminer which suffered some *coulure* during flowering.

The best wines produced came from the Pinot family – Pinot Gris, Blanc and Noir – which all performed very well. Winter was cold but saw a nice balance of sun and rain, spring then arrived ten days late. Bud burst started on April 19, but was uneven leading to variations in maturity during the harvest. June was warm and dry for most and flowering commenced on June 6. July and August followed similarly with warm conditions, some producers felt drought was a threat before a long, cool and dry harvest began on October 7. Picking continued until November 11 for the late harvest wines. Due to the cold, dry weather however, *botrytis* was virtually non-existent. Some producers used passerillage (drying the grapes on the vine, in the sun) to produce ripeness levels as high as those required in Sélection des Grains Nobles (SGN) wines. This is a year for the dry wines – aromatic, clean styles with high acidity and alcohol levels, which will definitely benefit from bottle-age.

*Unfortunately there is a tendency to drink Alsace wines too soon. These well constituted dry wines will benefit from age in bottle; between 2000 and 2004.*

## 1995☆☆☆☆to☆☆☆☆☆

Declared a perfect Riesling vintage; though Gewurztraminer did not experience the same fortune. Bud-break came late and a generally damp spring meant uneven flowering and problems with *coulure*. This was to limit the size of the vintage which was consequently down on average by 25 per cent. September rain and cool temperatures did not help matters encouraging grey rot to spread widely, especially in vineyards where vines had not been thinned. Producers who had resisted picking early due to the rain were blessed, along with the rest of France, as October witnessed a long Indian summer.

The official starting date for vintage was October 5. Riesling and Pinot Gris had super high sugar levels and above average acidity, with a ripeness level comparable to that of 1983. Noble rot produced very good Vendange Tardive and a few SGN wines from these two varieties. Gewurztraminer did not achieve the same ripeness or level of quality.

This vintage was very good for those who had thinned and taken a strict *triage* regime. Their wines show superb glyceral texture as a result of noble rot; depth, concentration and a high residual sugar content were particularly evident in the late harvest wines. These wines have substantial structure for ageing. Less fortunate producers' wines lacked personality and grip.

*Most are drinking well now, though the top late-harvest and SGN qualities will not only keep but positively need bottle-age. Certainly up to 15 years.*

## 1994☆☆to☆☆☆

The growing season did not advance quite as quickly in Alsace as it did further south or west in France. Generally, vegetation progressed as normal – budding took place in April, but was hindered by cold rainy weather.

This year the flowering took place soon after these wet conditions ended on June 8, and drier weather continued until early September. The rains came down in September and lasted 30 days – in that one month Turkheim experienced between 120 and 150mm (4.7–5.9ins). Grey rot rapidly became a threat to the crop, particularly to Pinot, Auxerrois and Riesling. The only crop remaining healthy throughout the deluge was Gewurztraminer.

The best wines are from growers whose patience held out until the beginning of October. Fine weather had returned and conditions were good both for harvesting and for noble rot. Some of the grapes picked at this late stage resulted in wines with a ripeness reminiscent of 1989 or 1990. The overall quality of these later-picked wines is significantly higher than 1993. The more basic wines should be carefully and thoughtfully selected but fine wines from later-picked low yields will have excellent potential.

*Hard to generalise. Clearly, the lesser wines were for quick consumption. Selected late-harvested wines for the mid-term; say now to 2000.*

## 1993☆☆☆☆

The heavy early autumn rain experienced by the rest of France had a less dramatic effect in Alsace thanks to the protection offered by the Vosges mountains. The volumes are lower, but the quality is higher than the 1992 vintage. Later-picked vines were the few to be affected by the rains. Grand Cru and more particularly, sweet wines are, therefore, in tiny quantities.

The growing season progressed healthily with an early budding. Flowering took place smoothly two weeks ahead of usual. As the harvest approached, hopes were extremely high for a classically great vintage. However, poor weather hit the region shortly before the harvest that started on September 23, the earliest date since 1976. Picking was carried out between showers.

Other than the aforementioned late-picked grapes, all varieties performed successfully with ripeness levels at times reaching those of 1988 and 1990. Dilution was not a threat due to healthy thick skins which also helped deter rot. The wines generally have good structure and ripe, round flavours.

*Satisfactory wines drinking well now.*

## 1992☆☆☆to☆☆☆☆

Unlike the rest of France, the climatic conditions in Alsace were perfect for a really great vintage. After a mild winter, budding was early and flowering was trouble-free. A warm, dry summer followed, with the hottest August since 1921, quite a contrast to more southern parts of Europe. The torrential rain that caused so much damage in the south completely bypassed the region and harvesting began on September 30.

Most growers reached the production limits imposed by the authorities, but better growers reduced their crops by as much as a quarter by green-pruning in July. If there is any criticism, it is that the acidity levels tend to be low, suggesting earlier rather than later drinking. Fine weather at the end of the harvest permitted the production of some glorious sweet wines, but overall, the wines have a full, round, opulent style.

*An attractive vintage, most wines at their best now, though the great late-picked wines of the leading producers will continue to develop and delight well beyond the turn of the century.*

## 1991 ☆

After three years of drought the rains came, but not at the most propitious moment. Happily Alsace's vineyards did not suffer from the frosts that crippled other districts and the flowering took place in good weather conditions. However, due to lack of moisture in the soil, the grapes were small. Hail in August devastated some vineyards and heavy rain hindered development. More rain in September delayed the start of picking until early October and the protracted harvest ended a month later. A small crop of moderate and variable quality.

*Drink up all but the Grands Crus and the relatively few late-harvested wines.*

## 1990 ☆☆☆☆

The second of two excellent vintages, very similar in style to 1989, but smaller in quantity. Particularly good for sweet dessert wines.

Alsace had no real winter, no frost or snow, and the vines began to grow three weeks ahead of normal in drought conditions. Budding began in late May, but cold, wet weather followed, resulting in both *coulure* and *millerandage,* particularly affecting the more delicate Muscat, Gewurztraminer and Tokay-Pinot Gris.

September onwards enjoyed a mixture of rain, fog and brilliant sunny weather. The harvest began on October 4 and quantities were down by around 25 per cent from the previous year. The grapes were beautifully healthy, but the absence of *botrytis* meant no SGN wines were made. A very high sugar content and low acidity necessitated very careful winemaking. This was, however, the third successive year in which late-harvest wines were made. An exceptional vintage.

Overall, the wines produced this year are characterised by their richness and roundness, due to a smaller crop than usual and particularly high levels of ripeness; especially for the Gewurztraminer and Muscat grapes. This vintage was considered by many to be comparable climatically, and possibly superior in quality, to the great 1961 vintage.

*A good ripe year, most of the wines enjoyable whilst young and fruity. The top quality wines made from the "noble" grape varieties from, say, now to the end of the century.*

## 1989 ☆☆☆☆

An admirable year, combining abundance and excellent quality. The vintage for late-harvest wines was the largest ever, producing extremely powerful wines, some reaching 214 Oechsle (30 per cent potential alcohol).

A hot and dry summer provided ideal growing conditions, pushing the growth well ahead of normal. Some areas suffered from drought but early September saw some relief in a little rain; an unusually early harvest followed, beginning on September 27 in fine weather. The Grand Cru wines will keep well. The late-harvest and SGN wines will need considerable time to develop. Hailed as one of the greatest vintages ever.

*The lesser wines drink up. The great late-harvest and SGN wines now to beyond 2000.*

## 1988 ☆☆☆to☆☆☆☆☆

The excellent weather throughout the spring and summer raised hopes for a good vintage. However, heavy rains before the harvest disappointed many growers: as much as 50mm (2ins) fell the weekend before picking.

For some growers, particularly those with well-drained sites, drier weather during the first week of the harvest saved the day. These areas produced some very good wines, including the top Rieslings and Tokay-Pinot Gris. Also some excellent late-harvest *botrytis* styles.

*All but the top class late-harvest wines drink soon. Wines like Schlumberger's Cuvée Anne impressive but very powerful and demanding considerable bottle-age, beyond 2000.*

## 1987 ☆to☆☆☆

Following a poor summer, the warm, sunny autumn saved this vintage from disaster. These are light wines, lacking the structure necessary to age; some of the late-ripening Rieslings will develop complexity, but on the whole this vintage is best for early drinking.

*All but the Grand Cru and special cuvée wines should have been consumed by now.*

## 1986 at best☆☆☆☆

A very good, if slightly uneven vintage. An extremely cold, snowy winter was followed by a more temperate spring, providing excellent conditions for the flowering. Late July saw hail and the bad weather continued until September. Harvesting began late October/early November in misty, sunny, *botrytis*-inducing weather.

Growers who selected grapes carefully during the harvest produced some excellent wines, particularly the Rieslings which have aged well.

*All fully mature. Drink soon.*

## 1985 ☆☆☆☆

A huge crop of good wines. After a cold, wet winter and spring, with a particularly cool spell in April, conditions were fine and dry for the entire summer. Flowering was uniform and excellent, and picking began in early October and continued into December for the SGN wines.

This vintage was very much an all-round success. Some excellent wines were produced, including Gewurztraminer: good early drinking. Those for laying down were also of fine quality, including some Rieslings and good late-harvest wines.

*Lovely results at each end of the spectrum but only the top SGN and Vendange Tardive wines warrant further bottle-age.*

## 1984☆

This was a dull year in Alsace. A mild spring was followed by a cool, wet summer and autumn. A dry October saved the day and the harvest yielded an average crop of wines, thin however, and lacking in fruit. The best were the light Rieslings and Pinot Blancs. Very few late-harvest wines were made.

*Drink up.*

## 1983☆☆☆☆☆

An abundant crop of excellent wines throughout Alsace. A very warm winter, wet spring and dry summer which lasted into November, enabled growers to pick late into the month.

These were big, rounded, opulent, spicy wines, if occasionally a little overblown. The Gewurztraminer and Tokay-Pinot Gris are delightful and the top Rieslings are worth cellaring longer. 1983 was also an excellent year for the late-harvest wines and SGN.

*Lesser wines drink up. The best late-harvest wines are perfection now, yet firm enough for another decade.*

## 1982☆☆

Apart from a cold spell in January, the weather was fine throughout the year. Picking began on October 7 and yielded one of the largest crops ever – 50 per cent up from the previous year. Results were of low quality. With the exception of some of the better *cuvées*. Flat, dull wines tending to lack concentration.

*Drink up.*

## 1981☆☆☆☆

A good year throughout Alsace. The yields were high and this balanced out stocks after the small 1980 harvest. High humidity in the earlier part of the vintage gave way to dry, sunny weather during flowering. This lasted throughout summer until a hot, humid period in early September. The harvest took place in good conditions from late September.

These were – with the exception of some light, inferior Sylvaner – well-balanced, attractive, fruity wines. An excellent late-harvest vintage.

*One of the least-known of the really good vintages. Worth looking out for. Undervalued yet at their peak now.*

## 1980☆

This year produced a small quantity of varied, but generally low quality wines. Bad weather during the flowering, reducing Muscat and Gewurztraminer, was followed by an indifferent summer. Harvest took place during early October in fine weather.

*Drink up.*

## 1979☆☆

After a cool spring, the vines flowered in warm weather. Below average temperatures in July picked up in August and fine weather continued through to the harvest. Grapes were picked from October 30 until late November.

The wines were of good commercial quality but tended to lack acidity; suitable for early drinking.

*As always with Alsace, some delightful surprises; drink up.*

## 1978☆☆

Fruit set was incomplete following a prolonged flowering in a cold June. Consequently the harvest, which took place from late October until mid-November, yielded a small crop. Some fairly good wines were produced, especially the Rieslings and Tokay-Pinot Gris from the top sites, which supported high acidity levels allowing a degree of bottle-age.

*One or two of the late-harvest wines remain and are still beautiful to drink.*

## 1977☆

A large vintage; its size was not, however, matched by good quality. Poor weather in spring delayed bud-break, and was followed by an indifferent summer. Picking began late October. At best the wines were steely and austere; the worst, thin and acidic.

*Few to be seen. Avoid.*

## 1976☆☆☆☆☆

After a cold, snowy winter, vines flowered during hot, dry weather in mid-June. The sunny, dry weather continued throughout the summer with the occasional rain shower in July and early October. Harvesting began early in October in good conditions and an average size crop was picked.

The wines are excellent with depth and concentration which, after a rather aggressive youth, have matured well: This year was also a successful vintage for the late-harvest wines and SGN, which are still superb.

*Minor wines drink up. Most Vendanges Tardives now fully mature, though the great SGN will continue beyond 2000.*

## 1975☆☆☆

After a fine spring the weather was warm and humid for flowering. Conditions were fine throughout the summer and the harvest began in late October.

This was an average sized crop which produced some good wines, particularly the Riesling and Gewurztraminer. Others, especially the Muscats, lacked acidity. The vast majority however, should have been drunk by the end of the 1970s.

*Drink up.*

## 1974☆

A disappointing year. After a mild, dry winter, bud-break took place in early April but further development was halted by freezing temperatures. The summer was mainly dry and growers forecast an excellent harvest. Hopes were dashed by non-stop drizzle for 30 days. This was the only year when October resulted in no increase in sugar levels. A small crop of poor wines.

*Avoid.*

## 1973☆☆☆
After a mild winter, a cool, dry spring with bud-break in late April and a good flowering in mid-June. A splendid summer followed with very little rain from flowering through to the harvest, which began during the second week of October. Grapes for the late-harvest wines were picked by mid-November. The huge size of the crop would now be illegal, but did, nevertheless, produce good Gewurztraminers, attractive Muscats and dry but short Rieslings.

*Even the best late-picked wines have passed their peak.*

## 1972
A disappointing year. Bud-break mid-April; a cool May and June and perfect flowering which started on June 20. Hot, dry weather from early July to early August, followed by heavy rain and cold winds, caused drought and unusually low temperatures. This inhibited maturation, resulting in a large crop of thin, acidic wines.

*Avoid.*

## 1971☆☆☆☆☆
The smallest vintage of the 1970s. Cool, misty weather in June caused *coulure* among some of the Muscats and even the Gewurztraminers. Overall the very dry weather, which extended through spring, summer and autumn, produced some excellent late-harvest wines and SGN wines – especially Gewurztraminer. High temperatures during fermentation necessitated careful control. Careful winemakers were rewarded well.

*Most now past best, but fine, rich, late-harvest wines can still be good, though only the finest SGN wines will survive longer.*

## 1970☆☆
After a late bud-break, June was wet and flowering began towards the end of the month, marred slightly by *coulure*. Thereafter the weather was generally fine, picking began in mid-October and finished during the first week of November. A large crop of very ripe, commercial wines tended to lack the acidity for long-ageing.

*Few remain. Drink up.*

## OTHER GOOD/GREAT ALSACE VINTAGES
**1967**☆☆☆☆ **1964**☆☆☆☆ **1961**☆☆☆☆ **1959**☆☆☆☆☆
**1952**☆☆☆☆ **1949**☆☆☆☆ **1947**☆☆☆☆ **1945**☆☆☆☆☆
**1937**☆☆☆☆☆ **1921**☆☆☆☆☆

Only the rare dessert whites with a high Oechsle reading, and have been well stored, will have survived.

# Europe

## Germany

The wines of Germany have many virtues: they are immediately enjoyable while young, fresh and fruity and do not require a big investment. They are light and generally low in alcohol; and even fine wines from the best estates are not expensive – about the best value in terms of price and quality of any of the world's wines.

Yet, apart from cheap, fairly innocuous QbAs – wines of lesser quality to which sugar has been added before fermentation – the finer wines do not have the following they deserve. There are several reasons: first the labels and names appear, at first sight, to be dauntingly complicated, yet they are logical and more informative than most; second, they are not, apart from the new Trocken (dry) wines, food wines, they are best drunk by themselves, not with meals; third, and most worrying, there is understandable confusion: a commercial Niersteiner Domthal sounding much like a Niersteiner Pettenthal of, say, Auslese quality from a great estate, inhibits the price that the latter can charge – a short term advantage for the consumer but, long term, not the best inducement for quality wines to be made.

Vintages are important. Indeed, being a northerly European wine region, weather conditions are by no means as reliably satisfactory as more sunny, southerly areas. There is less sunshine, lower natural grape sugars and higher acidity – factors all of which experienced growers turn to advantage, making wine of delicacy and charm, and perfect balance of fruit and acidity.

The harvest may take place in stages: early picked bunches suitable for chaptalisation, later-picked, riper, bunches for Spätlese and Auslese qualities, then, if the autumn sunshine persists, with beneficial morning mists, very ripe, sugar-laden grapes affected by *botrytis* are individually picked to make superlative sweet Beerenauslese and intensely concentrated Trockenbeerenauslese (TBA). Hopefully, in most vintages light, agreeable wines will be made for drinking soon after bottling, usually the spring after the harvest.

The vintage notes that follow are more concerned with the higher grades of wine; the better the vintage, the finer the wines and the longer they will keep. It is a mistake to think that all German wines should be drunk young. The top quality wines, Auslese and above, actually need and improve with bottle-age. Many 1971s are just approaching their peak, some of the great 1937s are still miraculously lovely.

### 1997☆☆☆☆☆

The good fortune continues for these northern producers, the tenth successive excellent vintage. It is also being compared to the vintage of 1971 and is quoted as the best vintage in 25 years.

The season did not start smoothly as much of the winter was freezing and frost in April disrupted the bud-burst. Low-lying and flatter vineyards were affected the most and Riesling proved to be the most resilient vine. Flowering was hampered by cool conditions in June and local hailstorms. By August the whole country was treated to ten weeks of perfect ripening weather, with essential rain falling on September 12 and October 13 to 15. The Indian summer brought clear blue skies and lengthened the growing season. The harvest began around the beginning of October and was complete by the second week of November, producing the most healthy grapes growers could have imagined.

Ripeness levels were high and acidity was slightly lower than previous years. The result was that no adjustments were required in the final wines. Yields were down again this year, due to the problems at the start of the season, some producers had experienced losses of up to 50 per cent. *Botrytis* was nearly non-existent meaning the sweet styles are very rare, however, some producers did manage to produce some Eiswein.

The quality generally is high, mostly at Kabinett and Spätlese levels. The wines have fine structure and will be slightly earlier maturing due to the lower acidity levels.

*At long last, the Riesling, king of German grapes, is being acknowledged as not just one of the great white varieties but arguably the greatest. It reaches its zenith in the Rheingau and the Mosel. For sheer variety of style, of sweetness unbeatable; for delight unmatched. This is the year of the Riesling.*

## 1996 ☆☆☆

By September doom and gloom hung over Germany in apprehension of a failed vintage. Luckily fortunes turned and the results were actually quite remarkable. The one downside was a drop in yields of 19 per cent as compared to the ten year average. The Mosel and Pfalz had the smallest yields, but of fine quality.

Snow in February during a long winter pre-empted a mild spring and early bud-break on April 18. May was unpleasant, but a good start to June prompted quick flowering. This weather then broke, causing delayed and uneven flowering, plagued by *coulure*. July and August were warm and a cool but sunny period from September running into October lengthened the harvest period and facilitated good ripening. A little rain in September also boosted strained water supplies.

The harvest began on October 2, two weeks later than usual and was finished by mid-November. The later-picked grapes were the best, having more ripeness to balance high acidity levels. Mosel and Pfalz producers did not pick until the end of October. This was another year of mostly QbA and Kabinett wines due to the late ripening, but they possess good concentration and depth. A Christmas vintage for the Eiswein wines, between December 24 and 26, triggered by Arctic "Tom" and freezing temperatures.

*The northern regions of Germany have had great fortune. All that is needed is for the consumer to appreciate more fully the superb wines of the great estates. even Spätlese wines benefit from further maturation in bottle. Best to drink the drier styles between five and seven years after the vintage. The richer Auslese, six to ten years and the Beerenauslese and TBA wines up to 25 years. Glorious wines, give them a try!*

## 1995 ☆☆☆☆

A labour intensive and tricky vintage, but generally it was very successful and for some even exceptional. Many good QbA wines, mostly Kabinett QmP wines and a few Eiswein wines were produced. Production was below average, approximately ten per cent down; while some producers experienced up to 50 per cent loss as a result of poor vintage conditions; requiring crop thinning, multiple *tries* and strict selection.

Summer was very warm with some refreshing showers during August which helped to control ripening. Nackenheim and Pfalz experienced some nearly disastrous summer hail. September was wet and awkward with rot causing most problems. October warmed up and with these weather fluctuations *botrytis* occurred with grapes showing extremely high sugars and acidity. Producers who picked early jeopardised the character and vitality of their wines. But those who managed well and hung on until mid-October, especially in the Mosel and Mittelrhein, made stunning wines. Vintage was finishing by the end of October, but two cold days on November 5 and 6 allowed some Eiswein production.

Riesling performed exceedingly well, with thick skins offering protection from excessive *botrytis*. A tricky vinification with stuck fermentations succeeded to produce intriguing and beguiling wines with good dry extract, very high acidity levels and suitable longevity potential.

*Some really lovely wines for drinking now. Top Mosels of Auslese quality, delectable yet with more to come.*

## 1994 ☆☆☆to☆☆☆☆☆

A good to excellent vintage and in some regions as remarkable as 1990. The percentage of Prädikat wines was surprisingly high, so much so that in some regions, such as the Mosel, better producers downgraded wines to QbA level. The sugar and acidity levels of late-picked grapes were generally very high and offer great potential for longevity.

Winter and spring were mild and fairly wet but offered favourable conditions for early budding and flowering. By June the onset of high summer temperatures confirmed the potential of a great vintage. Many of the better properties chose to green prune to avoid excessively high yields.

Heavy rains fell throughout Germany during September, although not as dramatically as those in France but failed in the main to affect the crop. Warm, misty autumnal weather in conjunction with damp conditions proved ideal for the development of *botrytis* and helps to explain why wines of Spätlese and Auslese quality were in profusion. Riesling in skilled hands performed splendidly throughout Germany at all Prädikat levels but none more so than those from the Pfalz and the Mosel.

*The consumer should be having the time of his life – if only he understood German wines. Halbtrocken and Trocken, not to be confused with TBA, really do seem to take on a flavour with food and need not necessarily be drunk when young, particularly those further qualified as Spätlese and Auslese.*

*An Auslese Trocken, confusingly, is dry but rich, with length, whereas a straight Auslese will be semi-sweet and rich, best drunk alone. Auslese and higher qualities of the 1994 vintage should be kept eight to 12 years after the vintage, Spätlese from top estates best five to eight years of age.*

## 1993☆☆to☆☆☆☆

This year came extremely close to being great, but as in the rest of western Europe, rains fell in September resulting in a distinctly varied vintage which was difficult for the grower. Those prepared to take the gamble and harvest late (benefiting from a warm sunny autumn – most notably in the Mosel) and who selected carefully, produced some great wines, with a high proportion of Prädikats, most notably at Auslese level.

The winter was mild and an early, warm spring provided optimum conditions for early budding and flowering, which took place three weeks ahead of usual. Hopes for a very fine vintage rose quickly, but were dashed by regional drought conditions and a cold August. From mid-September until the first week of October the weather was poor and heavy rains fell – three times the monthly average. These proved to be beneficial in the better-drained sites (particularly the steep slate hillsides of the Mosel Valley) but caused rot in parts of the Rhine. Many growers had started picking but decided to stop and wait for more clement weather. The better growers gambled and only started picking once the rains had passed. This paid off enormously as throughout Germany growers and vines basked in late autumn sunshine. Grapes rapidly dried out and the warmth and early morning mists encouraged widespread *botrytis*.

Vigorous and time consuming selection was required in order to retain only the most healthy grapes and when the yields were low, some very fine wines were made; generally, the harvest was about a third that of 1992. The best wines have intense fruit, healthy acidity, luscious sweetness, finesse and great elegance with the ability to age beautifully for many years.

*Minor wines, QbAs, drink up – or ignore. Take advantage of the late-harvested Rieslings which will approach their best around 1999 and continue well into the next century.*

## 1992☆☆to☆☆☆☆

This schizophrenic vintage neatly demonstrates the conflict in standards in German winemaking. On the one hand this vintage is comprised of sensationally good, long-living wines from super-ripe grapes, and on the other: weak and watery wines (even at QmP levels). Attitude, perhaps, is more the culprit than nature.

The conditions were good throughout the winter and spring; budding took place a little later than usual, but things caught up and flowering occurred two weeks ahead of the average. The summer consisted of very high temperatures, humidity, thunderstorms, even hail (in the Ruwer) resulting in stressed, unhealthy vines. Overcropping was a problem and many of the better growers chose to green prune, though many did not.

From October 20 there was frequent interruption by rain. The beginning of November was dry, but rain resumed on November 9 which had a further diluting effect. In general, the best wines were those picked before the first wave of rainfall. *Botrytis* did affect a few sites and there was even some Eiswein made, but overall, the drier wines were more successful.

*With such good vintages and wines in the years up to 1990, and some attractive wines more recently, it would be understandable to give 1992 a miss, but there are some refreshingly acidic Spätlese and food-worthy bone-dry Trockens. Few for keeping.*

## 1991 ☆☆to☆☆☆☆

After the unprecedented successes of the previous three vintages it would be easy to dismiss 1991 as a failure. This is not so, however, the results are highly variable, depending on the district and the times of picking. In any case, after so much quality wine, a large harvest of QbAs should prove useful commercially.

In the Saar and Ruwer, the severe frost of April 20/21 halved the crop. Perversely, this increased the concentration of the remaining grapes and enabled them to survive the summer drought that affected most other regions, inhibiting ripening. There was also frost as late as early June, but flowering, though delayed, was generally successful. The weather remained hot and dry until mid-September: those vineyards on water-retentive soils, such as the eastern parts of the Rheingau, survived better than those on light sandy soils, as in the Pfalz. Hail in August decimated some areas of the Rheinhessen.

Because of the weather conditions, picking time was critical. The rain was too late, and optimum harvesting conditions only lasted for one week. Those who picked before October 27 and after November 4 missed out. Nevertheless in certain districts *Botrytis* was taken advantage of, and some growers in the middle Mosel managed to make wine at every quality rung up to TBA. An Eiswein from the Rülander grape was made, for the first time, at Castell in Franconia on December 13.

*The inexpensive QbA wines, drink now (all brands of Liebfraumilch can be drunk as soon as they appear on supermarket shelves or merchants' lists). Rarer and expensive, Beerenauslesen and TBA wines to either side of turn of century.*

## 1990 ☆☆☆☆☆

An excellent vintage; never before has Germany had three consecutive years of top quality wines, although everywhere quantities were down on 1989.

Leaf development was very early but stopped for two weeks during a very cold April. May was mainly warm and dry, accompanied by occasional hailstorms and showers. Very cold and sometimes freezing nights extended blossoming over almost four weeks, particularly in the southern regions. The result was incomplete fertilisation or "blossom-drop" and an irregular development of the small berries.

Berries remained small throughout the hot, dry summer and the heavy rain in late August, followed by storms in many areas, resulted in rot reducing the crop size. Picking was advanced for the early varieties, many of which made wines in the Prädikat range. Everywhere this was described as an "ideal" autumn. Contrary to expectation, acidity was higher than in the 1989s and many growers felt that this would be the firmer, better, more consistent vintage of the trio.

A classic Riesling vintage: some estates reported harvesting only Spätlese and Auslese-quality Riesling with excellent acidity, and in the Rheingau the wines promise to store well. Growers from Baden were optimistic for excellent red wines. The only disappointments were in the Saar and Ruwer where the grapes were less ripe and *botrytis* did not develop well, consequently few late-harvest dessert wines were made.

*Minor wines drinking well now, those of Spätlese and Auslese quality from now to well into the 20th century.*

## 1989 ☆☆☆☆

A huge vintage of excellent wines, twinned with 1988: the latter being firm, and the 1989s having grace and charm. An average of 50 per cent of the crop was declared as Prädikat wine, and this increased to as much as 66 per cent in the Rheingau.

Near perfect weather prevailed throughout the year. A mild winter and warm spring prompted an early bud-break, followed by flowering in ideal conditions. The summer was warm and dry, only interrupted by occasional thunder and hailstorms, the effects of which were severe but very localised. The grapes ripened well and picking began early at the beginning of September.

Most growers selected carefully, and so avoided the usual disappointments associated with overproduction. The Rheingau enjoyed their best vintage since 1971: the grapes had benefited from elevated *botrytis* levels and made highly concentrated wines. A classic Riesling vintage.

*All can be drunk now but the better quality Prädikat wines will improve in bottle until the end of the century.*

## 1988 ☆☆☆☆

Excellent summer weather prompted hopes that this would be a classic year for German wines. However, unfortunate pre-harvest rain, fog and, in the Saar and Ruwer, hail, dampened expectations. But this did not prevent it from being a good vintage.

In the Middle Mosel the weather remained fine throughout the harvest and some classic Auslese wines were made, especially in the region between Erden and Bernkastel. Many of these will last well. Frosts during the harvest in the Nahe on November 7 enabled growers to make superb Eiswein.

Rheinhessen and Pfalz produced some good wines – top Prädikats being real classics. Perhaps the weakest wines came from the Rheingau, but even here many reached Kabinett level.

*QbA and Kabinett wines need drinking but Auslese, though delicious now, will keep well.*

## 1987

A severe winter, during which temperatures sank to -15°C (5°F) causing some damage to the vines. April was warm but temperatures fell again during May and June and heavy rain caused rot in some areas. Considerable pessimism resulted from this – one renowned Mosel grower declared that he would not be bottling his 1987s at all.

Warm, dry weather from mid-September until the harvest alleviated much anxiety. The Rieslings were harvested from October 28, although many growers held off for as long as possible so that picking continued until the end of November. The crop was quite large, but of this only 15 per cent was QmP (quality wine), the majority being only QbA.

*Drink up.*

## 1986 ☆ to ☆ ☆ ☆

Problems caused by difficult harvest conditions made this a vintage of mixed quality. An exceptionally severe winter, during which temperatures fell as low as -20°C (-4°F) was followed by a mild spring, then warm weather during May and June. Flowering was early, starting mid-June.

The hot summer gave way to a poor September but this did not dispel optimism among growers for a good harvest. However, violent storms hit in late October stripping many vines, and made harvesting particularly difficult.

Those sites which had escaped the storms produced some excellent, top-quality wines. The best of which were the Auslese, Beerenauslese and TBA produced in the Pfalz region. Elsewhere the wines were of average quality.

*Drink up all but the top quality wines, the sweetest capable of lasting a further 50 years or more.*

## 1985 ☆ ☆ ☆

Severe frosts and hail during the winter considerably pruned the eventual size of the crop, but the quality was generally high.

In the Mosel flowering took place in late June and poor weather continued until September. An Indian summer saved the day, providing good conditions for late ripening, and the harvest began on November 17. The better sites here made some excellent, well-structured, acidic wines which will last well.

After a poor start to the year the Rheingau enjoyed more even weather conditions than the Mosel; the summer was hot and dry and picking began November 4. The dry weather reduced the size of the crop and winemakers produced some excellent wines. At worst, sometimes dull, short and lacking.

*Most are delicious to drink now and really should be consumed. Only the very best are worth hanging on to.*

## 1984

A cool spring delayed flowering until mid-July. Vine growth was on average three weeks behind normal, and problems were exacerbated by poor weather throughout the summer. The harvest started in late October for the lesser grape varieties and mid-November for the Riesling. The grapes were unripe and the wines were excessively acidic.

*If you still have some, drink up, otherwise avoid.*

## 1983☆☆☆☆

The year got off to a bad start with a cool, wet spring which caused flooding along the Rhine and Mosel. Fortunately, the vines were not damaged and fine, warm weather in June accelerated the growth. The flowering took place at the end of the month, and the excessively wet spring was counterbalanced by one of the hottest, driest summers on record. Early-harvest grapes were picked in September. A period of rain followed by sun then swelled and ripened the Rieslings and their picking began later in October. Virtually no *edelfäule/botrytis*.

The wines of 1983 combine quality with quantity. Over 40 per cent of the huge crop was of Prädikat standard. The best since 1976. Those from Saar and Ruwer and the Nahe fared best.

*Take advantage of a very attractive vintage, an all round success: delicious wines, the top grades will keep.*

## 1982☆

A huge vintage – the biggest ever recorded in Germany – producing 165 million cases. The quality, however, did not match the quantity. Fine, warm weather during spring encouraged an early flowering during the first week of June. The gloriously hot summer prompted much optimism among growers, but hopes were dispelled by wet weather in early October which diluted the grapes and caused rot.

About 22 per cent of the wines were of Prädikat quality; the top sites producing some very good results, the best coming from the steep, well-drained sites of the Mosel where the Riesling grape (which resists rot well) thrives.

*Drink up.*

## 1981☆☆

A warm spring prompted early growth. Unfortunately, progress was checked by severe April frosts, damaging the newly grown shoots – most seriously in Rheingau and Saar and Ruwer.

May and June were warm and wet, and flowering began fairly early (June 8) but was interrupted by rain causing damage in all areas, particularly in Rheingau. The remaining crop ripened well in good weather during the last part of the summer, only to encounter the hazards of rains during late September/early October. Riesling was picked from October 12 and growers who held out longer and harvested later were rewarded by drier weather towards the end of the month.

This was a small crop of mixed quality wines. The best were the fresh and racy Kabinett and Spätlese from the Mosel.

*In winemaking there is life-supporting acidity and tart acidity. The 1981s have a lot of both. Better Kabinett and Spätlese quality wines can still be attractive. But drink soon.*

## 1980

A disastrous year for German wines. A cold wet winter, cool spring, lovely warm weather through May to early June; then wet weather and the latest flowering in memory, finishing at the end of July. The vines also suffered severe *coulure*. Poor weather throughout the summer prevented the grapes from ripening and picking was delayed until early November. However, this enabled winemakers to produce a reasonable amount of Prädikat wine (30 per cent of total output). But overall, this was a thin, hard vintage.

*Few remain. Avoid or drink up.*

## 1979☆☆☆

Light, easy, enjoyable wines. Severe January frosts, following a hard winter, caused widespread damage to the dormant vines. The full effects were seen only in May, especially in the Mosel-Saar-Ruwer and parts of the Rheinhessen. The Rieslings, however, did not suffer greatly and the Mosel produced some good wines.

*A largely forgotten vintage, many very attractive wines were made which, thanks to good acidity levels, can still be delicious.*

## 1978☆☆

Bad weather during the spring, a late flowering and wet summer weather finally gave way to a fine, dry, sunny September which pruned the crop, especially in the Mosel. Harvest was late. Pleasant enough wines but lacking in length.

*Drink up.*

## 1977☆

A mediocre, rather uninteresting year. The vines started well but flowering was hampered by a cold April and May. The summer was changeable but generally inclement until a delightful October. Conditions were ideal for the development of *edelfäule* (noble rot) amongst the Rieslings and a small quantity of Eiswein was made. Some passable wines from the southern Pfalz, but all past their best.

*Avoid, or drink up.*

## 1976☆☆☆☆

A gloriously ripe vintage. In northern Europe exceptional heat throughout the summer produced delightful wines. Blossoming and growth was extremely early – by as much as three weeks along the banks of the Rhine and Mosel. Late August rain swelled the grapes; September to mid-October was warm and then damper conditions encouraged the spread of noble rot among the late-ripening grapes.

This year produced a fairly small crop of fruity, well-balanced wines. The best year since 1971; perhaps less ripe than the 1971s and less fat than the 1964s and the 1959s, but very appealing. Many Auslese, Beerenauslese and TBA, all lovely, the best with time in hand, some, though, lack acidity.

*Drink all but the finest soon. Most are fully mature and will not benefit from further bottle-age.*

## 1975☆☆☆☆

Except for a cold April, the weather was warm, flowering speedy and successful, and summer was hot, culminating in a scorching August. Early September was wet but autumn sun ripened the grapes for the harvest beginning on October 17.

An undervalued year, the trade being more interested in the 1976s as soon as they came onto the market. This vintage's wines were firmer and more acidic and they have, however, eventually overtaken the 1976s. A vintage also notable for increasingly widespread use of new grape varieties and unusual crossings. The Auslese wines can still be lovely.

*Upstaged at every turn by the 1976s, yet now more than holding their own. The best are still delicious and, if you can find them, not expensive.*

## 1974

A dreary, wet vintage. Heavy rains during harvest time washed out the crop.

*Few seen. Avoid.*

## 1973☆☆

The largest crop on record. A late spring was followed by an unusually hot summer, some September rain and then more sun until November. The wines were of variable quality, ranging from some very pleasant examples which, however, lacked acidity and extract (perhaps due to overproduction), to uninteresting. A vintage for quick drinking.

*Should have been drunk in the mid- to late 1970s. Too late now except for a few perfect Eiswein.*

## 1972☆

An unexciting year that nevertheless produced useful commercial wine which restocked the trade cellars depleted after the sales of the outstanding 1971s.

*Few if any remain. Avoid.*

## 1971☆☆☆☆☆

A magnificent, classic year of great abundance. So great that traders even bemoaned the lack of commercial wines in their cellars. The vines flowered early and well, then a wonderfully sunny summer lasted right through to the autumn. The resulting grapes were small, ripe, well-nourished and immensely healthy. Best of all were the grapes from the Mosel which had absorbed the moisture from the early-morning autumn mists and achieved a most wonderful balance.

They were soft, delicious wines with a perfect balance of ripe sweetness and fruit acidity. They had none of the flaccid quality of the 1964s or the almost overwhelming richness of the 1959s, but were closer in weight and charm to the 1953s and 1949s.

*Spätlese and lesser wines are showing signs of fatigue so drink up. But Auslese and the great dessert wines are not only delicious now but will continue to evolve.*

## 1970☆☆

A mediocre year. The vines blossomed late and a dry summer followed. Those who picked late were able to make high-quality wines; some picking continued right through to December and even January, enabling Eiswein to be made. Some good wines but they were overshadowed by the 1971s. Of little interest now.

*Just a few quality wines holding on; on balance, drink up.*

## 1969 at best☆☆☆

After a satisfactory summer which prompted optimism among winemakers, a dry September failed to swell the berries, then a dense fog prevented the sun from penetrating the grapes. Those who had to pick early suffered, especially in the Pfalz and the Rheinhessen, but in the Rheingau and the Mosel the Rieslings benefited from some late autumn sun. The best were good, firm wines, especially in the Mosel. Forgotten once the 1971s arrived. Some still worth seeking out.

*Some excellent hochfeine Auslese from the Mosel, otherwise drink up.*

## 1968

An abundant quantity of poor-quality wines. The odd surprise.

*None remains, thank goodness.*

## 1967☆to☆☆☆☆

After a mild winter the spring suffered a combination of sun, rain, terrible cold, wind and thunderstorms. Summer was better but disastrous harvest rain washed out some districts. Those who delayed picking were able to enjoy some late autumn sun and made excellent TBA wines.

The results ranged from a few poor, thin wines to some excellent dessert wines. The top estates are still worth looking out for: excellent and underrated.

*Happily all the lesser wines will have been consumed by now but the TBA wines are still magisterial, Wagnerian.*

## 1966☆☆☆

Good, stylish wines. Few dessert wines were made owing to cold wet weather in early November which delayed late harvesting and limited further ripening. However, a few Eiswein wines were made with some success. Overall, pale, firm, steely wines with sustaining acidity, but lacking ripeness.

*Over the top now. Drink up.*

## 1965

With the odd exception, an unusually bad year due to uneven weather conditions.

*Happily none to be found now.*

## 1964☆☆☆☆

The best vintage of the 1960s, much welcomed and very popular, coming after four rather uninteresting years. Fine, dry weather continued right through the spring and summer pushing the growth of the vines ahead of normal. The lack of rain coupled with an increase in production in some areas caused concern among growers. An enormous crop was harvested and picking continued through to the end of November.

The finest and longest-lasting wines were those from the northerly, steep, slate slopes of the Mosel-Saar-Ruwer where the acidity counterbalanced the unusually high sweetness of the grapes. Overall, these were soft, ripe wines. The best vintage between 1959 and 1971.

*All but the very best wines from the Mosel-Saar-Ruwer tiring now. The latter, from top estates, can still be lovely.*

## 1963☆to☆☆☆

Very cold weather continued throughout the winter and spring months, giving way to delightful conditions in July. The next three months were wet, followed by an Indian summer at the end of October. Overall, there were roughly equal quantities of below- and above-average wines, which, considering the weather conditions, was a success. The Mosel did not fare well.

*Minor wines long since past best. The better quality wines drying out.*

## 1962☆☆

A year which included a long cold spell and a long period of drought. However, those who delayed harvesting were rewarded by a change in the weather. Picking continued into December and much Eiswein was made. These were the best 1962s. The rest being pleasant but very light.

*All but the Eiswein long since faded.*

## 1961☆☆☆

A moderate vintage. Following a good spring, but a poor summer, September saved the day with record temperatures and uninterrupted sunshine. A small crop of very uneven quality wines was produced, and which achieved, but perhaps did not merit, very high prices. No great sweet wines.

*Few remain. Drink up.*

## 1960☆

Large crop of raw, unripe, too-soft wines. Best came from the Pfalz.

*Few if any remain; not worth seeking.*

## 1959☆☆☆☆☆

An outstanding vintage. Rarely has such a prolific crop produced such consistently high quality wines. An exceptionally fine summer: hot, dry weather right through to October. The vines were extremely healthy and, with only a few exceptions, the grapes were gathered in successfully. Anxiety was caused by the almost unprecedented heat at vintage time, the unusually high sugar content and low acidity of the grapes, though only the less-skilled winemakers encountered problems as a result of this.

The wines produced were excellent, full-bodied, naturally sweet and ripe, which developed slowly. There were a record number of Beerenauslese and TBA made in the Mosel-Saar-Ruwer districts.

*As in Burgundy, the last of the heavy-weight vintages. Many great wines from Auslese to TBA are still superb to drink. The latter will keep.*

## 1958 ☆☆

A huge crop, in fact the biggest for 20 years, but only of moderate quality wines. Few were imported, or tasted. Rather dull and over-acid in style.

*All consumed.*

## 1957 ☆☆

Early growth was badly damaged by heavy May frosts. A good summer was followed by rain throughout September, inflicting rot problems on some areas.

Some good Kabinett wines were produced in the Mosel where the late-ripening Rieslings benefited from good weather in October. Wines mostly consumed by the early 1960s.

*Few remain. Avoid.*

## 1956

A disastrous, cold, wet year. Small quantity, very low quality.

*None tasted.*

## 1955 ☆☆

A moderate, rather uninteresting vintage. Apart from eight weeks of fine weather from mid-July onwards, bad conditions prevailed throughout the year with frosts in mid-October, a week before the harvest began. With few exceptions, a small crop of uneven, commercial wines.

*Drink up.*

## 1954

Very poor quality wines due to appalling weather conditions.

## 1953 ☆☆☆☆☆

An outstanding vintage – the result of good weather throughout the year except for some severe frosts in May which damaged the vines in the lower grade areas. Healthy grapes were harvested in excellent, sunny conditions.

Wines from the Rheingau reached perfection – elegant, firm and supple. Many which were soft and pleasant, not meant to last, were produced in the Mosel; the best coming from the Saar and Ruwer. Open-knit, easy wines were made in the Rheinhessen, the Silvaner grape producing the best. Overall, a ripe and fruity vintage which varied in character from district to district.

Note the quality of corks used in the mid-1950s was poor, some failing to withstand the test of time.

*Only the feinste Auslese to TBA have survived, the lesser wines well past best. Solitary survivors can, however, be glorious.*

## 1952☆☆☆

Fine weather prevailed throughout the summer, including scorching sun in July/August. This would have been an outstanding vintage had it not been for two months of rain in September/October.

Well-constituted wines were made in what turned out to be an underrated vintage; most were consumed by mid- to late 1950s.

*Firm wines with good acidity, some of which still retain a certain freshness as well as honeyed bottle-age.*

## 1951

A poor, thin year.

## 1950☆☆

A pleasant year of commercial quality. Inevitably it stood in the shadow of 1949.

*Very rarely seen and not worth seeking out.*

## 1949☆☆☆☆☆

A great classic year – the best Mosel since 1921 – which happily coincided with renewed post-war market demand. Apart from early spring frosts, which pruned the crop size, the weather conditions were excellent. These were firm, well-balanced, refined wines which lasted well.

*The top quality wines still delicious.*

## 1948☆☆

Sandwiched between two superior years, this average vintage did not attract much interest. Few shipped. None seen.

## 1947☆☆☆☆

Severe winter frosts hardened the soil, preventing moisture from penetrating. A warm, dry summer followed, producing an average sized crop. These conditions produced grapes which lacked the moisture necessary for full ripening.

The wines were low in acidity and short-lived. They were nevertheless soft, rich and of high quality.

*TBA wines from great Rheingau estates are still magnificent.*

## 1946☆☆

Ignored by the trade who unfairly categorised this an "off" vintage.

## 1945☆☆☆☆☆

Coming at the end of the war, the vines suffered from disease and a lack of labour to combat it. There was also much looting by released Polish and Russian prisoners. Consequently, despite the fine summer, a tiny crop was harvested. However, those that were made were excellent.

*Now drying out and tired.*

## 1943☆☆

Best of wartime vintages. Beerenauslesen still remarkably good.

## DECADE OF THE 1930s

The 1930s produced some interesting vintages, although after 1937 German wines were rarely seen abroad.

**1937**☆☆☆☆☆ was magnificent: an early flowering; hot, dry summer and September rain, swelled the grapes and made this the best year since 1921. My favourite German old classic vintage. The best can still be fabulously good. The second-best year of the 1930s was **1934**☆☆☆☆ some wines even merited five stars. Few to be found now and likely to be over the top. **1933**☆☆☆ produced an abundant crop of soft wines; some Rheingau wines were still holding well in 1978, demonstrating how natural, unsugared, well-cellared wine can still be delightful at 45 years of age. First three years of the decade were, sadly, of poor quality.

## 1920s

With the exception of a few good years, the decade was not overall as satisfactory as in the main French districts.

**1929**☆☆☆☆ was the first really good vintage since 1921. Spring frosts were followed by a hot, dry summer which lasted well into September, a small crop of healthy, ripe grapes was harvested. If cellared carefully, these wines lasted well, but now are very rare. **1925**☆☆☆ was a good, though rarely seen vintage.

The best vintage of the decade was undoubtedly that of **1921**☆☆☆☆☆ arguably the greatest of the century. Spring frosts and a summer drought reduced the size of the crop and disease-free grapes were picked in good conditions. Those from the Mosel and the Rhine were the best and even some of the minor wines can still be interesting to drink. **1920**☆☆☆ produced variable but mainly good wines. Some late-vintage wines were outstanding.

## 1910s

**1915**☆☆☆ produced a good, abundant vintage; as it was in Burgundy and Champagne. **1911**☆☆☆☆☆ was an excellent year, particularly for the wines from the Rheingau: the end of an era.

## 1900s

**1906**☆ was a modest vintage. The next best year prior to 1911 was **1900**☆☆☆☆ an excellent vintage, considered by some to be even better than 1893.

## 1890s

A decade which included moderately good wines in **1897**☆☆☆ and **1895**☆☆; and an excellent vintage in **1893**☆☆☆☆☆ probably the best of the century, after 1865 and 1811. A small quantity of very rich wines after an exceptionally hot summer.

# Austria

Mozart, Strauss, Vienna, and the Danube; mountains for skiing and *The Sound of Music*. All most evocative. And wines to match, though surprisingly little known outside Austria despite their easy-to-drink charm and reasonable prices. Apart from the over-publicised and unfortunate so-called "anti-freeze" scandal in the early 1980s, excellent wines have been made here, traditionally, in the Wachau, Styria, Burgenland on the Hungarian border and around Vienna, the only major European capital city to have such a wealth of vines on its doorstep.

Although some good red wines are now produced it is the light, dry to medium-dry white wines of Germanic style that are the best known: Riesling, Müller-Thurgau, the highly scented Muskat Ottonel, Traminer, Rülander, Weissburgunder (Pinot Blanc) and the popular, soft and fruity Grüner Veltliner, best drunk young. Excellent late-harvest wines are made, rich Auslese and outstanding "Ausbruch", the latter a cross between a five- or six-puttonyos Tokay and Beerenauslese from the Pfalz.

As with most other white wines, the lighter, drier styles should be drunk within a year or so of the vintage (though the Viennese flock out to the suburbs to drink the new wine shortly after it has finished fermenting), only the finer late-harvest Auslese to TBA-type wines having a good cellar life.

## 1997☆☆☆☆☆

With close proximity to Germany, very similar conditions and results occurred. An exceedingly cold winter and late frost, especially around the Niederösterreich area, was followed by a relatively late budding and subsequently flowering was problem free and ran smoothly. July was very wet until August when the weather improved and growing conditions were ideal right through to the end of the harvest.

A very high proportion of sunshine hours and exceptional weather in September produced healthy and balanced grapes. These were harvested between the end of September and the end of November, starting in Burgenland. Yields were down compared to 1996 and sweet styles were very rare after minimal *botrytis*, although some Spatlëse and a few Eiswein were produced. The wines, both red and dry white, are of very high quality with excellent extract and balance.

*One report claims this to be "one of the finest vintages this century in Austria", so take note! Encouragingly, more attractive wines are being made and marketed at reasonable prices. Unless you have inside information, stick with charming dry whites and the surprisingly enticing sweet whites.*

## 1996☆☆to☆☆☆

A very complicated vintage, requiring great patience and strong nerves. Producers lost around 20 per cent in yields as compared to 1995. Winter dragged on causing the growing season to start late. Most were spared frost, except near Lake Neusiedlersee. May and June were fair and flowering was over quickly. By mid-August the rain had arrived and did not relent for the harvest.

A warming *Föhn* autumnal wind raised temperatures, but yields had been reduced and quality was in doubt. This was compounded by a high incidence of *botrytis*. For those who held back from picking, 14 sunny days blessed November and late picked wines were rich, with pronounced acidity. A year more suited to dry wine production, the wines marked by *botrytis*, but acidity is high and some wines will benefit from some bottle-age.

*Dry wines now; botrytised wines 1999 to 2005. The new style and better than ever reds still do not have a track record, and are probably best around the turn of the century.*

## 1995☆☆to☆☆☆☆

Summer was inconsistent, but on the whole it was warm and sufficiently sunny to allow good development. Unfortunately, rain fell quite heavily at the beginning of the harvest which took its toll on the early ripening varieties. By October an Indian summer had settled in and created perfect conditions for the rest of the harvest. The weather had reduced yields by one third compared to that of 1994, but quality was good, with a significant production of TBA wines. The cool summer had a positive effect on the acidity and concentration of fruit in the grapes.

Regional differences did occur – the region around Vienna produced finely balanced wines; Burgenland experienced the favourable *botrytis* and made elegant Prädikatswein; while Styria's wines were highly fragrant and fresh.

*All but the late-harvest wines for pleasant early drinking.*

## 1994☆☆☆☆

A successful vintage for both dry and sweet wines, which benefited from the intense heat summer heat. Although some areas experienced drought during the summer, harvesting began early in mid-September. The fruit had excellent ripeness levels, the wines good concentration and finely balanced acidity. Some of the best examples come from Burgenland – excellent reds and dry whites, the latter having very good acidity. Styria had more balanced climatic conditions than elsewhere with frequent light showers. Many wines are of Spätlese level with a few TBA wines.

*Pleasant wines for early drinking. Austrian reds are scarcely known outside their country of origin but are currently improving in quality. Their whites on the other hand are a sheer delight and all, except the remarkable and good value TBA wines, best drunk young. The Styrian whites can have a penetratingly high acidity, a style of its own.*

## 1993☆☆to☆☆☆

An unbalanced vintage of variable quality and quantity. The best wines were from Burgenland due to severe frosts at the beginning of the year which heavily reduced the crop. The worst damage occurred east of Neusiedlersee, which in parts lost as much as 90 per cent of their yield.

Spring began early and was remarkably hot until the end of May when cooler weather followed. Ripening progressed well throughout Austria. Reds and dry whites from Burgenland are near excellent. Grüner Veltliner was more successful this vintage with the re-emergence of its enjoyable vivacious character.

*Charming, easy whites for early consumption.*

## 1992☆☆to☆☆☆

The year had a cool, dry start and favourable conditions resulted in a large proportion of healthy bunches. So perfect was their condition that when torrential rains fell in June, no detrimental effect was had. By the end of the month drought conditions had set in and remained until the harvest with the summer being one of Austria's hottest ever. By the time of the harvest at the end of September, temperatures were generally still over 25°C (77°F).

The vintage is considered perfect for red wines. Few *botrytis* wines were made due to the summer's aridity, but Spätlese are common, particularly from Wachau. Here, growers picked early to retain freshness and made some successful wines. Lack of acidity is apparent in many wines, notably from Burgenland. A little rain fell at the end of October but rot was minimal.

*The sort of vintage to tempt one to try Austria's lesser known reds – summer luncheon type wines. The whites are easy, agreeable and ready for drinking.*

## 1991☆

Bitterly cold winter and late spring. The flowering was also delayed by cool weather and a poor June. July was warm and sunny but August was heralded by torrential rain causing flooding of cellars and low lying vineyards. The latter half of August was fine but the vines were too far retarded, the harvest being delayed and hampered by wet weather and rot. Nevertheless in Burgenland, growers who waited took advantage of a late Indian summer and, around Rust, made some exceptional *botrytis*-affected sweet wines.

*Best to avoid, or drink soon. Look out for the richer dessert wines which are still drinking pleasantly.*

## 1990☆☆☆☆☆

After a normal spring, summer brought the same drought which affected large tracts of Europe. Areas of light and sandy soil suffered the most, especially the younger vines where the rootstock was unable to find sufficient water, but irrigated estates (in Wachau for example) fared well. In general, good winemakers made superlative wines but overall quality can be patchy. Quantities were good.

In the individual regions there were some excellent wines in Wachau and Kamptal-Donauland, with some good dry Spätlese from most properties. A long autumn allowed good quality including a good many high Prädikat wines. The long growing season also came as a god-send to the Styrian growers, for whom cool conditions sometimes prevent the grapes from ripening fully; Sauvignon Blancs and Morillons (Chardonnays) were particularly fine. In Burgenland there were many top Prädikat wines made, including some Ausbruch. In the Weinviertel one grower even picked an Eiswein on the first day of the Gulf War.

*Minor whites, Grüner Veltliner, drink now. Late-picked quality whites benefiting from a little bottle-age, drinking well now; the dessert wines will keep longer.*

### 1989☆☆

A mild winter was succeeded by a cold, damp spring. The summer was variable with frequent rain. Finally, in mid-October, a period of good sunny weather set in and lasted until the first days of November. The variable quality of the vintage put paid to hopes of another superlative "niner" (an old peasant tradition in Austria holds that the best years for wine are those ending in nine), but the patient growers who picked late made very good wines, particularly in Burgenland and Styria.

*Drink up all but the best late-picked wines.*

### 1988☆☆

This was the first year in five not to be affected by severe frosts. The result was a potentially bumper crop. A good spring was followed by a hot summer, but the rain came in September. Those who picked early may have made wines on the dilute side, others were rewarded by an Indian summer. Quality is variable.

The vintage seems to have been best in Lower Austria. One grower in the Langenlois region harvested an Eiswein as early as November 5. Many Styrian wines betray a taste of rot.

*Drink now.*

### 1987☆

After a generally abominable year in the vineyards a good autumn came to the rescue and in general the 1987s are good if occasionally on the sharp side. One or two excellent red wines were made in Burgenland.

*Drink up.*

### 1986☆☆☆☆☆

Before 1990, 1986 was considered the best vintage in Austria since 1979. One or two Austrian wine-writers even came out with that dangerous phrase "the vintage of the century".

Frost damage reduced the size of the crop to below average, but otherwise growing conditions were near perfect. Wines to look out for are the reds from Burgenland; Styrian wines; Wachau Rhine Rieslings. High Spätlese were harvested in the Weinviertel and one or two Auslese in Vienna. One grower in Langenlois even picked a Grüner Veltliner on October 5 and fermented it in new oak! The wines are high in extract and have good acidity.

*The best dry whites, from low-yielding vineyards, are firm and acidic and at their peak now.*

### 1985☆☆☆☆

Spring frosts killed up to 95 per cent of vines in parts of Weinviertel and elsewhere the damage ensured that the harvest was not even half the average. Flowering took place under exceedingly difficult conditions. The rest of the year was good, if not excellent: "a great year" as one Langenlois uttered perversely.

There were some very good reds from the Burgenland region, impressive, long-living Sauvignon Blancs from Styria; and a small amount of *botrytised* wine was produced in the Thermen region.

*An attractive vintage, but most at peak if not tiring. The reds are worth seeking out.*

## 1984☆☆☆

Originally thought of as the post-war *annus mirabilis*, but later denigrated for a lack of acidity in the wines. Near perfect weather in summer and autumn led to a large crop. Growers who ensured that their wines had sufficient acidic backbone produced wines with the best vintage potential.

In Burgenland, 1983 produced the best quality reds to emerge before the 1990 vintage. Elsewhere areas not normally noted for Prädikat wines yielded musts high in residual sugar; there were Auslesen in Styria and the Weinviertel, and high Spätlese in the Wachau. Naturally, most were vinified as dry wines.

*Drink up.*

## 1983☆☆☆☆☆

A great vintage. Outstandingly ripe wines, notably excellent TBA.

*All the soft, dry whites should have been drunk by now but the exceedingly sweet and concentrated TBA wines are still superb and will keep.*

## 1982☆to☆☆☆

The biggest crop on record for this country. An excellent summer and the early autumn was rounded off with a miserable, wet October. Those producers who picked before (or after) the rain, produced wines of quality.

Good levels of *botrytis* in the Thermen region and there were some luscious Prädikat wines from Rust.

*The top class sweet whites at peak.*

## 1981☆☆☆

Notable only for late-picked sweet wines. These were quite widespread, with wines of TBA levels in Rust and Seewinkel; good, high Prädikat levels in the Thermen region; one or two rare Ausbruch wines from Vienna; and one of the rarest of all was Beerenauslese, from Styria.

*Ausbruch and TBA wines still excellent and will keep.*

## 1980

A bad year pretty well everywhere.

*Avoid.*

## 1979☆☆☆☆☆

An excellent year which began with a perfect flowering and continued through a hot summer and a sunny autumn. The last of the great "niners". Most of the 1979s have now been consumed. The long autumn produced Auslese levels in Wachau and Krems, Beerenauslese in Styria, Ausbruch in Vienna and Klosterneuberg, and TBA in Rust and Seewinkel.

*Drink up all but the top dessert wines, which have excellent acidity and long life.*

## 1978☆
Cold, dry year; generally mediocre.
   *Drink up.*

## 1977☆☆☆☆
Excellent year with splendid weather extending throughout the growing season: particularly good Rieslings and Grüner Veltliners from lower Austria.
   *Few, if any, remain. Drink up.*

## 1976☆to☆☆☆
Variable weather which improved only in late autumn. Those who picked early made thin, dull wines. Some good TBA and Ausbruch wines from the Burgenland. which have developed beautifully with bottle-age.
   *Drink only the Ausbruch and TBA wines which are holding well and can be superb.*

## 1975☆☆
Generally average quality only. One or two surprises such as a magnificently racy Pinot Noir from Langenlois.
   *Drink up.*

## 1974
Generally very poor.
   *Avoid.*

## 1973☆☆☆☆
Very good year, especially for Riesling and Grüner Veltliner grapes in lower Austria. A long autumn allowed for some Spätlese and Auslese wines to be made in the Wachau.
   The Thermen region made high Prädikat wines and good TBA and Ausbruch wines can still occasionally be encountered from the Burgenland region. This was also to be considered one of the great Ausbruch years.
   *Few remain but the best Auslese, Ausbruch and TBA wines worth looking out for.*

## 1972
A very poor year. Now largely forgotten.
   *Forget it.*

## 1971☆☆☆☆☆
Long-lasting wines from an excellent year.
   *Some top Rieslings from Vienna and even one or two Grüner Veltliners from the Wachau still on top form; also scented, honeyed Beerenauslese from Rust.*

## 1970☆☆
Not generally a good year. One or two stylish Rieslings from the steeper slopes of Vienna.
   *Drink up.*

## MORE REMOTE AUSTRIAN VINTAGES

**1969**☆☆☆☆☆ was one of the great "niners"; some top TBA wines from Rust can still be found and are superb. **1967**☆☆☆ produced good Prädikats from the Burgenland: look out for Ausbruch and TBA wines. **1966**☆☆☆ saw fine Rieslings from lower Austria, some surprisingly good wines from Styria, and rich, fat, powerful TBA wines from Langenlois. **1963**☆☆☆☆ some very attractive Prädikat wine from the Burgenland.

Look out for the **1961**☆☆☆☆☆ *raresimme* TBA or Auslese from the Burgenland; excellent wines were also produced in **1959**☆☆☆☆☆ though all but the richest and best are drying out. **1955** was chiefly memorable only for the departure of the Allied armies, notably the Russians. **1949**☆☆☆☆☆ was a great year.

And **1945**☆☆☆☆ the year when all the old stocks of Austrian wine unfortunately disappeared down the throats of the invading Soviet troops. Older vintages are so rare – one might as well say that they do not exist.

# Hungary (Tokay)

Hungary is a surprisingly big and successful wine producing country. Its best known regions, growing red and white table wines, are around Eger and on the slopes bounding Lake Balaton. Until the final disintegration of the Iron Curtain, basically only two qualities were produced, everyday inexpensive quick-consumption wines, and wines of slightly superior quality for the many excellent restaurants.

On the export market, these, now frequently, well made wines (often by "flying winemakers") are rapidly gaining in popularity. To produce higher quality wines was contrary to Communist Party thinking, for it introduced an exalted price factor linked with privilege. The better known wines such as Badacsony Riesling and Egri Bikaver (Bull's Blood) in good years are sound, but essentially for early consumption. Several other local grape varieties are used, making passably appealing wines for a mainly local market.

The odd man out is Tokay. Indeed Tokay is the odd man out amongst the great classic wines of Europe. Happily, there has recently been a renaissance with an influx of outside investment and influential winemakers. Tokay makes not only an unusual style of wine, it has quite remarkable ageing potential. Indeed, in common with madeira, the finest and the richest Tokays have an almost limitless cellar life. For this reason this section of the pocketbook is devoted solely to Tokay vintages.

However, Tokay appears in various guises. Szamorodni or natural table wines can be dry or sweet in style; both, in good vintages, will keep though the dry is something of an acquired taste – as are Portuguese mature white wine and Château-Chalon.

The Aszú wines, to which measures of a concentrate made from overripe grapes are added, range from medium-sweet three- puttonyos to a very sweet, Sauternes-like, five-puttonyos. Following exceptional years intensely sweet and long-lasting

Aszú-Eszencia will be produced (the pure Eszencia or Essence – it has various spellings – is rare and very expensive, but it has an almost limitless life span).

## 1990s

**1997**☆ a bad vintage, average quantity. **1996**☆☆☆☆ very good, ripe, round and balanced wines. **1995**☆☆☆to☆☆☆☆ good to very good, average yields. **1994**☆ poor.

**1993**☆☆☆☆ excellent year for Aszú. **1992**☆☆ average, but small vintage. **1991**☆☆ average wines. **1990**☆☆☆☆ a good all round vintage.

## 1980s

**1989**☆☆☆☆ very good. **1988**☆☆☆☆☆ one of the two best vintages of the decade. **1987**☆☆ moderate. **1986**☆☆ average.

**1985**☆☆ average. **1984**☆☆ average. **1983**☆☆☆☆ excellent. **1982**☆☆☆☆ very good. **1981**☆☆☆ and **1980** ~ altogether a wretched vintage.

## 1970s

**1979**☆☆☆☆ **1978**☆ disappointing. **1977** ~ poor. **1976**☆☆☆ **1975**☆☆☆☆ **1974** ~ poor. **1973**☆☆☆ good Aszús. **1972**☆☆☆☆☆ wonderful Aszús: excellent, will keep. **1971**☆☆ **1970** ~

## 1960s

**1969**☆☆☆ **1968**☆☆☆☆☆ The Aszú-Eszencia is lovely, but will develop further. **1967**☆☆ **1966**☆☆☆ **1965** ~ **1964**☆☆☆☆ the first post-war vintage of Aszú-Eszencia imported and marketed in the UK. **1963**☆☆☆☆☆ the best dry and all the sweet wines drinking well. **1962**☆☆☆☆ **1961**☆☆☆☆ **1960** ~

## 1950s

**1959**☆☆☆☆☆ dry Szamorodni tired but all the sweet wines perfect now. **1958**☆☆☆ **1957**☆☆☆☆☆ **1956**☆☆☆☆ **1955**☆☆☆ **1954** ~ **1953**☆☆☆☆ **1952**☆☆☆☆☆ **1951** ~ **1950**☆☆☆☆

## 1940s

**1949**☆☆☆☆☆ **1948**☆☆☆ **1947**☆☆☆☆☆ a perfect Aszú crop; magnificent concentrated Eszencia. **1946**☆☆☆ good. **1945**☆☆☆ Eszencia. **1944** ~ **1943**☆☆☆ **1942**☆☆☆☆ **1941** ~ **1940** ~

# THE BEST PRE-1940 TOKAY VINTAGES

**1937**☆☆☆☆☆ **1936**☆☆☆☆☆ **1935**☆☆☆ **1934**☆☆☆☆☆ **1932**☆☆☆☆☆ **1931**☆☆☆☆☆ **1930**☆☆☆ **1927**☆☆☆☆☆ **1924**☆☆☆☆☆ **1923**☆☆☆☆☆ **1922**☆☆☆ **1921**☆☆☆☆ **1920**☆☆☆☆ **1919**☆☆☆☆☆ **1916**☆☆☆☆ **1915**☆☆☆☆☆ **1914**☆☆☆ **1912**☆☆☆☆☆ **1910**☆☆☆ **1907**☆☆☆ **1906**☆☆☆☆☆ the last great vintage of the Austro-Hungarian Empire. **1905**☆☆☆ **1904**☆☆☆☆ **1901**☆☆☆

**Great Tokay Vintages** (only the Ausbruch and Eszencias will have survived): **1889**, **1865**, **1834**, **1811** – the most renowned vintage of all time.

# Italy

For sheer volume of wine produced, and for variations of style and quality, Italy is unmatched. It is also an impossible country to deal with in a general way as climatic conditions vary widely: from Sicily, with its North African influence, to the foothills of the Alps. Classic French grape varieties are starting to intrude, changing the nature of some wines, though winemaking methods alternate between primitive and highly sophisticated.

Undependable, less so; unpredictable, perhaps. But enormous strides were made in the 1980s. A combination of new attitudes, much improved winemaking and amenable weather conditions have enhanced the quality of Italian wine out of all recognition.

Two major districts have long been, and still are, regarded as the homes of the great Italian classics: Tuscany, with its famous Chianti region, between Florence and Sienna, and to the north, Piedmont, producing sturdy long-living Barolo and stylish Barbaresco in the hills around Alba and Asti. These two districts not only set the standards but, amongst Italian wines exported, are the best known in the quality field, which is why they are featured principally in the vintage notes that follow.

## 1997☆☆☆☆

Shouts of jubilation from producers all over Italy after their most successful vintage in 50 years. Growing conditions ran in near text book fashion, with a mild winter and spring giving clear and temperate days. The only small upset resulted in slightly reduced yields after premature budding and flowering were affected by late frosts in April and May. Conditions then became warmer during August and continued until October, with cool nights and rain falling at the required times.

By harvest time most vines were around one week ahead of their growing cycle and producers were ready to start picking up to two weeks earlier than scheduled.

**Piedmont** The only area to experience an increase in yield, mainly due to Dolcetto which did not achieve such high quality. Harvesting did not start early but was rapid and nearly over by late September. Nebbiolo ripened before Barbera – almost unheard of. The grapes were small and of optimal weight and size, providing complete harmony and balance of every constituent. This has only occurred in four other vintages this century. The main difference was slightly lower acidity, beneficial as sometimes this can be too prominent.

**Tuscany** Quality was exceptional after grapes had developed almost identically to those in Piedmont, and comparisons were made to the 1947 vintage. However, more directly affected by irregular flowering, yields were significantly lower – 20 per cent compared to 1996. This has not helped the continuing price rises for these wines.

*A vintage to buy and keep – the reds of course. Alas top growers' wines are now expensive, but quality is very high. Barolos 2005 to 2025; Chianti and the fashionable vini da tavola (vdt) 2003 to 2015.*

## 1996☆☆☆☆

A vintage following in the footsteps of the previous one. Comparatively, yields were up by five per cent, this is nevertheless ten per cent below that of 1994 – again a result of the grubbing up programme eliminating many quality vineyard sites.

The first two weeks of June witnessed extremely high temperatures of 30°C and above, causing a quick and uniform flowering. The summer then saw temperatures slightly lower than the Mediterranean average, but conditions were constant and the ripening was slow and even. September and October were wetter but low temperatures protected vines from rot. The harvest started at the beginning of October and ran smoothly and quickly in favourable conditions.

**Piedmont** Good results in Barolo and Barbaresco. Thick skins and late-picked grapes gave lush, opulent wines and quality comparable to 1990. Quantity was down, due to the vines still recovering from hail damage in 1995. Asti: great results with good, early ripening Dolcetto. Barbera: not achieving such high quality.

**Tuscany** Fluctuating temperatures during September gave high quality and fine aromas to the wines. Chianti and Montalcino produced wines of deep colour and great ripeness, Montepulciano experienced a few problems. Producers are undecided as to whether quality is better than that of 1995 – it is a close call.

*One of the encouraging truths is that winemaking in Italy has improved out of recognition, starting in the mid-1980s. The reds of the leading producers in Piedmont and Tuscany can match up to the level of the finest Bordeaux in quality, if not style. Classic Barolos, as always need cellaring for seven to 15 years. Chianti being more approachable at four to ten years.*

## 1995☆☆☆to☆☆☆☆☆

Another unpredictable year, becoming typical of the 1990s and possibly one of the most fickle of the last 30 years. A warm spring raised hopes only to be dashed by rain at bud set and during flowering, resulting again in decreased yields. A hot July followed by a cool August upset the vineyard cycle further, with rot causing problems. The bad weather continued into September, changing to Indian conditions from mid-September through to mid-October.

A small vintage is reinforced by new EU grants available to producers for grubbing up vines, introduced in an attempt to reduce overstocks of wine.

**Piedmont** After the rain at flowering, hail hit in August causing extensive damage. Some producers, especially in Barolo, lost between 50 and 70 per cent of their crop. For those that survived, a long growing season ended with vintage, one of the latest in two decades, at the end of October. Barolo was particularly successful.

**Tuscany** With similar tumultuous growing conditions to Piedmont, skies cleared on September 15 commencing 45 rain-free days with temperatures up to 27°C (80°F). This continued into October and patient producers, especially in Chianti Classico, harvested slowly ripened grapes with deep colour and firm structure. This vintage can be compared with 1990.

*There is a tendency to drink even the top Italian reds too young.
Restaurants often list merely what their suppliers offer, vintages
succeeding vintages as they are quickly consumed. Private
buyers are advised to buy early and give the better red wines of
Italy the respect, and ageing, they deserve.*

## 1994☆☆to☆☆☆☆

**Piedmont** Spring conditions were good with precisely the correct
level of rainfall. Severe frosts struck fairly late into flowering,
reducing the harvest by ten to 30 per cent. In July Barbaresco was
badly hit by hail. Summer was dry and hot and the grapes ripened
healthily two weeks ahead of usual. The ripening process slowed
down in mid-September when heavy rains fell for 17 days.
Harvesting went ahead in reasonable conditions with favourable
results. Medium-bodied wines, but in reduced quantities.

**Tuscany** Climatic conditions were particularly good, almost
certainly the best seen in Italy this vintage. The ripening season
started early and temperatures were consistently high. Summer
was long and hot with uniform, light rain during June and July.
Chianti Classico had the best results – a high proportion of Riserva
wines. Montepulciano and Montalcino produced concentrated
and characterful wines. Conditions also proved ideal for Cabernet-
based vdt wines and even more so for rarer Merlot-based wines.

*Not a great vintage for Barolo or Barbaresco. Agreeable
medium-term wines, the former likely to open out around the
turn of the century, Barbaresco somewhat earlier. Clearly some
attractive Tuscan wines will be coming onto the market for early
drinking, the best developing well into the next century.*

## 1993☆to☆☆☆

**Piedmont** Considering the torrential rain that fell during the
harvest, the condition of the fruit was good due to the heat and
aridity of August. The quantities are small and the quality is
reasonable. The sugar levels are unfortunately outweighed by the
acidity, as a result of the rainfall, producing early-maturing wines.
Barolo and Barbaresco have very pleasant fruit and aroma and
have a similar character to the 1988s.

**Tuscany** The further south, the more satisfactory the results –
seems to be the trend in this sodden vintage. Tuscany, therefore,
fared much better than Piedmont. More rain fell in the two weeks
before harvesting than during the previous 11 months. The hot,
dry summer resulted in very small grapes with thick skins that
withstood the rain beautifully. Quality was good to very good.

*The above summary tells all, or nearly all. From both north
and south – wines for early consumption, not laying down,
though top producers will, as always, provide nice surprises.*

## 1992☆☆

Throughout Italy the weather had been satisfactory during the
growing season, despite a cool and wet early-summer. What
eventually dashed all hopes of a fine vintage were the storms and
torrential rains of late September lasting until mid-October.

**Piedmont** Ripeness is the main problem in this region. The earlier-ripening Dolcetto fared much better than Nebbiolo and only relatively light-weight and generally early-drinking Barolo and Barbaresco were produced.

**Tuscany** Here growers were able to make more successful wines due mainly to the earlier harvest and selective picking. A tiny quantity of Riserva wines was made in Chianti after October 16, once the rains had finished. Further south in Montalcino and Montepulciano, where picking started earlier, weightier wines were possible. Some interesting Brunello and Vino Nobile di Montepulciano were made. In the main, the wines from this vintage in Tuscany are sound and early-drinking, with some very good examples also made.

*Easy, early drinking wines. A useful restaurant vintage. Not for long cellaring.*

## 1991 ☆

**Piedmont** Cold spring; late and irregular flowering; long hot and very dry summer followed by heavy rain at vintage time. An average crop, variable in quality, mainly light wines.

**Tuscany** Poor spring, cold and wet with damaging frosts; dismal May to mid-June alternating rain and too little sun. The summer was hearteningly hot and dry but the rains returned for the late harvest. Variable quality, lower than average production.

*The light dry whites should have been drunk now. Chianti Classico and Chianti Rufino more quickly developing than the previous three vintages. Barolo, also drink soon.*

## 1990 ☆☆☆☆☆

The hot, dry summer produced grapes of exceptional quality. Yields were very low everywhere and the small bunches of concentrated fruit encouraged growers to predict a top class vintage, ranking beside those of the best in the postwar era.

**Piedmont** The third year of almost perfect weather conditions in Barolo and Barbaresco. Rainfall was better distributed than in 1988 and beautifully healthy grapes were picked two weeks ahead of normal. The quantity, however, was around ten per cent down, promising well-balanced wines which will age well. A good twin with the 1989 vintage.

**Tuscany** The weather was perfect here too, providing intense heat, light rain to nourish and ripen the grapes, and cool evenings to conserve their acidity. Showers during early September helped to produce healthy fruit, and as in Piedmont the grapes were brought in early. Even the late-ripening Sangiovese had been harvested by the end of September; the last of the reds were in by mid-October. Full, deeply-coloured, flavoursome wines with round tannins and good acidity.

*The white wines are ready to drink now. Chianti Classicos, which tend to be drunk too young, are delicious from now to well beyond 2000. Barolo and Barbaresco need bottle-age, the latter at its best between 2000 and 2010, and the finest, classic Barolos between 2010 to 2020 or beyond.*

### 1989☆to☆☆☆☆

The exceptionally good weather throughout much of Europe was not experienced in Italy. Wet, often tempestuous conditions characterised the summer and disastrous rain fell intermittently during the harvest. This was the smallest vintage of the decade.

**Piedmont** Apart from a violent hailstorm in June which damaged vines around Barolo (some growers lost as much as 60 per cent of their crop), Piedmont largely escaped the bad weather. Conditions were satisfactory and sound red and white grapes were gathered. Overall, the yield was down by 15 per cent. Perhaps the best reds of the decade.

**Tuscany** A very mixed year. Some areas had too much rain while others had too little and suffered drought. The Chianti was better than the Chianti Classico and few Riservas were made. Best wines came from Montalcino and Montepulciano. Overall, light wines and early developers.

*Drink up the dry whites. Barolo and Barbaresco from 1999 to well after 2020. Chiantis, say, now to 1999.*

### 1988☆☆☆☆☆

Generally, an excellent vintage for Italian wines. The yield was very small – Tuscany brought in its smallest crop for 25 years.

**Piedmont** Cold and wet weather during flowering resulted in an incomplete flower set. Then warm, damp weather followed, encouraging the development of mildew in late June. Thereafter the summer was hot and dry, aiding the development of ripe and healthy grapes. However, rain during the harvest caused problems, especially with the Nebbiolo and the later-picked grapes in Barolo and Barbaresco. The Barbera, however, was picked just before the rain and made wine of good quality.

**Tuscany** As in Piedmont, a cold start to the year impaired the flower set, and yields were further reduced by severe heat and drought. However, the harvest, which began on September 22 for the Cabernet grapes and October 1 for the Sangiovese, produced high quality wines. Riservas were fruity with firm tannins. The best wines came from Montalcino where weather conditions were less severe. The harvest was early; the crop above average size.

*Whites drink up. It is a shame to drink the great classic reds too soon: they usually need at least ten years bottle-age. To be realistic: Chiantis and the good vdt now to 2005, Barbaresco 2000 to 2020, Barolo and Brunello di Montalcino 2003 to 2030.*

### 1987☆☆to☆☆☆

Variable quality, overshadowed by the superior 1988 vintage.

**Piedmont** A cold winter was followed by a cool but dry spring. Conditions were generally fine throughout the summer, with the exception of a rather cool July. August and September saw some welcome light rain and the harvest began in early October. The crop was of average size.

**Tuscany** The vines flowered under excellent conditions but their progress was then hampered by a long, dry spell which lasted from July until late September. The harvest, which began on

September 23 for Cabernet grapes and October 3 for Sangiovese, took place in many areas during damp, rot-inducing weather. In Montalcino, however, the grapes were picked earlier and a large quantity of excellent quality wine was produced. Overall, these were light and enjoyable wines, but not likely candidates for Riserva status.

*Most whites should have been consumed by now. All but the very best reds drink up.*

## 1986 ☆☆☆

A good year which provided better drinking than the 1987s but shadowed by the tiny but excellent crop produced in 1985.

**Piedmont** The winter was unusually cold and spring was wet. All of Italy sizzled under a heatwave during May which broke at the end of the month with unsettled weather and sometimes violent localised hailstorms. Some growers lost their entire crop, while others escaped miraculously altogether. Unfortunately and sadly, affected areas included the top sites, including Barolo where growers lost up to 40 per cent of their crop. The rest of the summer was hot, dry and humid.

Rain during the first ten days of September fleshed out the grapes which were then fully ripened by two weeks of hot weather. The harvest began during the last week of September and a small quantity of good quality grapes was picked. Forward wines for mid-term drinking.

**Tuscany** Here a large crop was harvested after a hot summer which, with the exception of the odd burst of rain in July, was mainly dry. Picking began on September 22. Some good, fruity Chiantis were produced, but few Riservas. The Brunello and Vino Nobile di Montepulciano were of average quality but the top vdt now showing elegance.

*Most reds are drinking well now.*

## 1985 ☆☆☆☆

An extremely good vintage throughout Italy but, perhaps even more importantly, the year that a shift of attitudes was perceived and a new era of more serious winemaking began, particularly in Tuscany.

**Piedmont** An exceptionally cold winter gave way to a warm, dry spring. A rather uneven summer followed, yet superb wines were made, particularly by the best individual producers in the best districts. Those from Barolo were very successful, making deep-coloured, richly tannic, long-lasting wines.

**Tuscany** Even better than Piedmont. Similar weather conditions. Superb estate wines can be found, some full of fruit and ready for drinking, some tannic and needing bottle-age. They are worth buying and drinking.

*Wonderful wines. Great depth of fruit. Mouthfilling without being coarse. The big Barbarescos, Barolos and Brunellos though delicious, are still developing. They will be at their best from 2000 to 2020, or beyond. Chiantis drinking well now but the top wines need more bottle-age, say, now to 2005.*

## 1984☆☆

A poor year throughout Italy, with the possible exceptions of Sicily and Sardinia and northern Piedmont.

**Piedmont** Cold, wet weather in May and June led to a late and incomplete flowering. The weather was cool and unsettled throughout the summer and the grapes were not fully ripened in time for the harvest. The wines were thin and unripe.

**Tuscany** A similar story to Piedmont, with almost continuous September rain. Ironically, this was the year in which Chianti was promoted to DOCG status.

*Drink up.*

## 1983☆☆to☆☆☆☆

An uneven year: disappointing for some, excellent for others.

**Piedmont** The vines flowered during rain, July was hot and humid and some growers experienced problems with rot. Uneven weather in late summer improved in time for the harvest in October. The crop was of average size and the best growers, who selected their grapes rigorously, made very good wines. Elsewhere the quality was often poor.

**Tuscany** A good year. Spring was mild and the vines flowered in early June. Summer was fine with just the required amount of rain. In Chianti the weather continued unbroken until the harvest which began on September 22. Riserva Chiantis made delightful drinking. In Montalcino the weather deteriorated during harvest, and careful selection was needed.

*Drink up, though the "new wave" of Chiantis are still delightful and Barolos, as always, will keep longer.*

## 1982☆☆☆☆

An excellent vintage throughout Tuscany and Piedmont.

**Piedmont** Mild, dry weather during the spring pushed growth ahead of normal. Some vineyards were damaged by hail in late April but overall there were few problems. Summer was hot and dry with some rain in late September/early October prior to the harvest. An average crop: rich, ripe, flavoursome wines.

**Tuscany** A long, cold winter relented with a sudden change in the temperature in May. Apart from the odd wet period and hail in early September, the weather was hot and sunny, approaching drought conditions. Picking began on September 20 and the quality of the wine was consistently good for all of Tuscany. The top Riservas were outstanding.

*A most attractive year. Highly regarded Sassicaia excellent, with life in hand. Classic Barolos still laden with tannin.*

## 1981☆☆☆

An uneven and generally disappointing year.

**Piedmont** Winter was long and cold. Vines then suffered rot during a hot, humid June and July. Apart from a wet patch in late August/early September the weather was cloudy but dry until the harvest, beginning in late September. Careful selection of grapes was essential. The best wines were the Barbarescos.

**Tuscany** Overall, a much better year for this part of Italy. Spring was late but hot and the good weather continued almost without interruption through the summer. The harvest, beginning on September 20, was staggered thanks to rain midway. As a result the wines made from grapes picked before the rain are of superior quality to those made later. They were elegant wines with good ageing potential.

*Some very rich wines but overall variable. Drink up.*

## 1980☆

A moderate year, although inevitably there were the good, if not outstanding exceptions.

**Piedmont** A mild winter ran into a cool spring which lasted until June. Growth was retarded until July when the weather suddenly became hot and dry. These conditions lasted until late September when rain fell until early October. The harvest started extremely late and was interrupted by snow on November 4. An average sized crop was picked.

**Tuscany** Tuscany saw very similar weather conditions to Piedmont. Picking started in early October but was delayed by rain and many growers found that they did not finish until November. On the whole the grapes were ripe and healthy and some very good wines were made.

*Drink up.*

## 1979☆☆☆☆

**Piedmont** Nearly equal in size to 1980 but of better quality. Very good early-maturing wines from Barolo and Barbaresco, while further north the wines were well-structured, with better-than-average life expectancy.

**Tuscany** Here too a huge harvest of good to very good quality: particularly the Montepulciano and Brunello di Montalcino; not, however, for long keeping.

*Chiantis at peak. Can still be superb. The great producers' Barolos are magnificent and will age further. Sassicaia is perfection, yet will keep another five to ten years.*

## 1978☆☆☆☆

The best all-round vintage of the 1970s.

**Piedmont** Damp, cold weather in spring and early summer brought the vintage near to disaster. A warm, dry autumn saved the day: small crops of fine Barolo and Barbaresco, for ageing.

**Tuscany** Similar conditions to those in Piedmont produced a small vintage with some outstanding, long-lived wines, especially the Brunello di Montalcino, Carmignano and Chianti Classico.

*Superb reds, the best perfection now, yet with time in hand.*

## 1977☆to☆☆☆

**Piedmont** Not a good year: small crop, generally poor wine.

**Tuscany** Warm spring; dry summer. Some very good Brunello di Montalcino, Vino Nobile di Montepulciano; some good Chiantis.

*Drink up.*

## 1976☆

**Piedmont** A vintage of uneven quality in Asti/Alba but a fine harvest in Novarra-Vercelli; the Gattinara was excellent, others were sturdy wines to be drunk quickly.

**Tuscany** A disastrous year: wet spring and summer weather.
*Drink up.*

## 1975☆to☆☆☆

**Piedmont** A mediocre year, yet some delightful wines.

**Tuscany** A fair year. A rainy spring was followed by a very dry, sometimes stormy summer. Particularly good for Brunello, Vino Nobile and Chianti from the Sienna area.
*Even the best reds fully mature. Drink up.*

## 1974☆☆to☆☆☆☆

**Piedmont** An excellent, abundant vintage for long keeping.

**Tuscany** Except for some excellent Chianti Rufina, this was generally a poor, unreliable year.
*Only the substantial reds, Barbaresco, Barolo and the top Brunello worth looking out for. Drink up.*

## 1973☆☆

**Piedmont** An uneven year, mostly only fair but some excellent wines from Ghemme.

**Tuscany** As Piedmont; some excellent wines from Carmignano.
*Fully mature. Drink up.*

## 1972

**Piedmont** A disastrous year: both Barolo and Barbaresco were declassified as DOC. Further north the wines were fair to good but only ever short-lived.

**Tuscany** Again, a poor year with wet weather through spring and summer. The exception was Sassicaia.
*Generally avoid.*

## 1971☆☆☆☆

**Piedmont** For Barolo and Barbaresco this was possibly the best year since the war.

**Tuscany** Overall, a very good though uneven vintage. The best wines were from Chianti, some disappointments in Montalcino and Montepulciano.
*The better Barolos and Barbarescos at peak; Brunello has more to come. Top Chianti Classicos are perfect now though some on decline. The "new reds", Sassicaia, Tignanello, Rubesco Torgiano all superb, fully mature.*

## 1970☆☆☆

**Piedmont** A large sized crop of excellent wines, standing somewhat in the shadow of the 1971s, sometimes unfairly.

**Tuscany** A good year: excellent Brunello and Vino Nobile.
*Fully mature. Only the top Barolos have time in hand. The rest, drink up.*

## OTHER OUTSTANDING ITALIAN VINTAGES
**Piedmont** Barolo: **1964**, **1961**, **1958**, **1952**. **Tuscany** Brunello:
**1967**, **1964**, **1961**, **1955**, **1945**. Chianti: **1968**, **1967**, **1964**, **1962**,
**1957**, **1947**. Vino Nobile di Montepulciano: **1967**, **1958**.

# Spain
For over a century and a half sherry was the quality wine of
Spain, table wines being indifferent to execrable, or if good,
relatively unknown. The dramatic upturn began in Rioja in the
1960s, and a decade later one family in Penedès, Torres,
experimenting – as they still are – with different grape varieties
grown at different altitudes, and superb winemaking and
marketing, carved a niche which has raised the whole conception
of what Spain can produce commercially.

La Mancha, to the south of Madrid, still produces 50 per cent
of Spain's total production of table wines. But wines from this
area, and nearby Valdepeñas, are not in the same league as
Penedès, Rioja, neighbouring Navarra, and the two odd-men out
from the Ribero del Duero east of Valladolid: a relative newcomer,
Pesquera, and Spain's only long-established, classic (highly
priced) red wine, Vega Sicilia. It needs to be stated that Vega Sicilia
spends up to ten years in wood, so, for drinking dates, one must
add at least 12 years to the vintage.

The white wines of Spain, sherry excepted, were once
uniformly atrocious, but tend now to range from passable to good
though few are exceptional and hardly any, in my opinion,
warrant cellaring for more than a year or two. The following
vintages notes refer mostly, therefore, to the better quality red
wines. The latter have the added advantage of still being very
reasonably priced for their quality. Really old vintages,
particularly of Rioja, can occasionally be found. They seem either
cheap for their age or wildly overpriced, but in either case are
rarely more than interesting.

## 1997☆☆to☆☆☆☆
This year saw a split between the north and south of the country.
In the south results were very good, with quantity and quality
both high. Rain at the end of 1996 and start of 1997 replenished
the previously starved water-tables. In parts of the north the rain
did not do as many favours. Producers using their own grape
production and not buying in grapes were in a better position –
especially those who have turned to new technologies for disease
control, such as "*strobilurina*" a natural toxin to control mildew.
**Rioja** Unfortunately this was not such a successful vintage as the
previous three. Heavy summer rain caused rot problems and a
drop in yields and overall quality was reduced.
**Penedès** Yields were also marginally down, five per cent against
1996. The region's microclimates were dramatically revealed in
spring as coastal areas experienced high temperatures and then
rain in July, which shortened maturation. Conversely the central
and higher inland areas had very smooth and even development.

The conditions were ideal everywhere during September and October allowing uniform ripening and great results – very good whites and excellent reds.

**Ribera del Duero** Frost in spring caused yields to fall here also. But fine weather before and during the harvest produced a later ripening crop of high quality. The red wines had good extract and longevity. Unfortunately prices are still rising for these wines.

*Whites ready soon. The better reds, when they come on to the market will benefit from two to five years bottle-age.*

## 1996☆☆☆☆

After the previous three years giving drought problems, this year was one of the wettest on record. Quality varied region to region.

**Rioja** A cold and wet December prepared the vineyards for bud burst at the beginning of April. Certain areas were affected by frost at this time, but flowering was on schedule and quick at the start of June. Summer continued favourably with storms occurring intermittently. August and September experienced rain, but by late September it had cleared up and harvest ran from October to November. Yields were good, as is quality, with especially promising Reservas.

**Penedés** Consistent rain during the summer with hail in June and August, were backed by cooler temperatures which kept rot in check. In mid-September an anticyclone brought ideal ripening conditions, and a delayed harvest at the end of September gave significant yields. The whites were good and the reds even better.

**Ribera del Duero** The largest vintage since 1990, up 40 per cent on 1995. This was attributable to frosts in late spring and during the harvest, plus rain in the second week of September. Picking began on September 26 and the grapes were found to be at optimum ripeness and maturity levels. Quality was high with significant levels of fruit.

*For quality and price Spanish wines are still unbeatable. Do not hoard the whites: drink them. The best are the reds, from Penedés (Torres superb as always), Rioja and the up and coming wines of Navarra, led by Chivite.*

## 1995☆☆to☆☆☆☆

Throughout Spain frost, drought and ill-timed rain plagued many regions. However, where this was not good for white wines, some spectacular reds were produced, with intense colour, high alcohol and acidity levels and definite structure.

**Rioja** Declared "excellent" by the Consejo Regulador, this area claimed its largest harvest of all time. Autumn and winter were mild with bud burst 20 to 30 days early in March. Late frosts in April were followed by even flowering during May and June. The summer was perfect for ripening with heat and adequate rain. Harvest began in Baja in late August and continued until late October in Alavesa, yields varied by sub-region. The grapes were in perfect health to provide for this super-ripe vintage.

**Penedés** Spring frosts, then heavy rain and hail pre-harvest reduced yields by 15 to 20 per cent. The producers of Cava and other white still wines, suffered in particular. Red wines show great character and the surviving whites are very aromatic.

**Ribero del Duero** Severe frost before flowering caused some apprehension, but with the following hot summer and perfect ripening conditions the vines recovered and as in Rioja, a high quality was achieved.

*Do not hang on to the whites. Most reds to be drunk young, top Riojas will benefit from a further five years.*

## 1994 ☆☆☆

This vintage saw Spain's hottest summer since 1982 with July and August temperatures reaching around 40˚C. As a result the vines suffered so much stress that many simply stopped growing altogether, thus quantities were down in many cases.

**Rioja** A significant amount of rain fell during the previous autumn and winter which prepared the vines for the drought that was to follow. Frost struck the region on April 16, but the health of the vines remained excellent. The overall results of the vintage were good, with many age-worthy wines. Volumes were down by only ten per cent.

**Penedès** Here, the results ranged from good to very good, but with greater reduction in yields – losses of around 20 per cent.

**Ribero del Duero** The vines suffered even more ripening problems in this region and volumes were reduced by 30 to 50 per cent. The resultant wines though, are of excellent quality.

*Dry whites for early consumption, but many reds worthy of, indeed needing, ageing. The quality of wines now made by the top producers is such that in a year like 1994 they vary only between good fruity reds for early consumption, say around three to four years of age, yet many with a firmness and balance worthy of eight to 12 years' cellaring.*

## 1993 ☆☆

For the purposes of this book, only the wines of Ribero del Duero, Rioja and Penedès are significant. It was precisely in these northern areas that rain was the spoiler. Downpours during the spring delayed flowering and, after a warm summer, even heavier rain from the middle of September had a further effect on the final size and quality of the harvest.

Nevertheless, although the quantities are down, wines of useful commercial quality were made. This is particularly the case with Rioja where the demand for easy, early-drinking wines has increased dramatically.

*Quick drinking whites and reds.*

## 1992 ☆☆to☆☆☆

After a dry winter, what began as normal spring rain became unusually heavy during May and June; by well into the autumn it had escalated into a serious threat to the vintage. There were a few problems with frost, but the major initial complication was that of delayed ripening. This took place in the north and east, provoked by the continuation of the rainfall into the summer.

**Rioja** The uneven ripening here resulted in reduced Tempranillo yields; no bad thing, but after a warm, fairly dry summer, hopes for the vintage had risen. The harvest began on September 24 under perfect conditions but on October 10 excessive rainfall set in. Only the Baja sub-region went relatively unscathed, being warmer and able to harvest earlier. Elsewhere, the harvest was considerably delayed, with some growers picking until early November. Unfortunately, those who did wait saw their grapes go rotten on the vine. There are some exceptional results from earlier-picked grapes and the yields are of average proportions.

**Penedès** The pattern here was similar to other parts of northern Spain. Fortunately, most of the grapes had been harvested in this region before the onset of the rains. Some of the results are very good and in normal volumes.

**Ribero del Duero** Again, rain was the problem in this region at the time of harvest. The better properties gambled and waited for the weather to clear and, consequently, produced wine of reasonable quality.

*Whites for early drinking. Agreeable reds.*

## 1991 ☆☆☆☆

Variable but mainly very good quality, production in general down 20 per cent from 1990, but of approximately the five-year average level. The only disaster of interest was in Jerez where "industrial action", a prolonged strike, resulted in much acrimony and loss of grapes for the production of sherry.

**Rioja** Autumn rain, wind and cold weather delayed the picking of fully ripe grapes by a mere week or so.

**Penedès** Severe spring frosts caused worrying losses but from then on weather conditions were well-nigh perfect. The final crop was around 30 to 40 per cent, half that originally feared, but of extremely high quality. All grape varieties were picked in perfect conditions.

**Ribero del Duero** The quality was good but quantity down.

*Good reds, drinking well now*

## 1990 ☆☆☆☆

After two years of troublesome weather conditions, Spain enjoyed a dry but relatively normal year and produced, in many instances, some excellent wines.

**Rioja** A very dry winter was followed by an exceptionally hot summer and a harvest which began two weeks ahead of normal. The sizzling heat affected mainly the lower areas of the Rioja, while Tempranillo grapes from the higher slopes were of excellent quality; benefiting from the cooler, moister summer nights. Disease was not a problem at all this year. Late refreshing rains were an advantage but the extreme heat may mean that the wines have less body than those of the previous year. Overall, the reds should be better than the whites, which are rather low in acidity.

**Penedès** The summer here was not excessively hot, and cool nights and rains during June and July were beneficial. The main harvest began in mid-September and the white grape harvest was large. In the Alta Penedès a few violent hailstorms affected the finest white grapes but not the overall volume, which was higher than usual. Miguel Torres predicted this to be a great year for his Milmanda Chardonnay: a spring frost had reduced yields, concentrating sugars and consequently increasing the potential alcohol levels of these wines. The same can also be said for Merlot, Sauvignon Blanc, Pinot Noir and Cabernet Sauvignon.

**Ribero del Duero** Despite a very dry summer, yields here were up by more than 35 per cent: good news after the two previous years, particularly as this is likely to be a high quality year.

*Most Riojas made pleasant early drinking; Ribero del Duero reds will be excellent: Pesquera doubtless on best form around now to 2000, whilst Vega Sicilia, as mentioned in the introduction, will have a longer life span, probably being marketed in 2002 and reaching its zenith around 2020. Most dry white wines are best drunk now; only the scarcer Chardonnays and the like, will improve with a little bottle-age.*

## 1989☆☆☆

After the appalling difficulties in 1988, the main problem for growers this year was drought, cutting total yield by 11 per cent.

**Rioja** Despite drought conditions, the harvest was reasonably bountiful. A slightly better vintage for the reds than the whites, which tended to be high in alcohol and low in fruit. The reds are well-structured and the best will be the Crianzas and the Reservas. The whites are rather heavy.

**Penedès** Good conditions throughout the summer were spoiled by two hailstorms, in late August and early September, which reduced the size of the harvest considerably. As with Rioja, this was a better year for the reds than the whites.

**Ribero del Duero** Dry weather reduced yields here by around 20 per cent. The quality, however, was excellent.

*Reds now to 1998, the exception, as always, being Vega Sicilia which will not be put on the market for another decade.*

## 1988 at best☆☆☆

Spain experienced more than its fair share of disastrous weather this year. The wettest spring on record was followed by a poor summer. This was made worse by the development of rot on the vines, a rare situation which left Spanish growers unprepared. Widespread, heavy hailstorms then followed. To an extent, the quality wine regions of Spain escaped the worst effects of the weather, partly thanks to better management of the problems.

**Rioja** A wet start to the year resulted in a late flowering and uneven fruit set, but this was compensated for by excellent picking conditions (October 24 to November 2). A fair size crop was harvested and the quality was satisfactory.

**Penedès** The growers who best controlled the spread of mildew produced the best wines. The harvest began on September 10 and continued in the high Penedès into the second half of October. With some rainfall during picking, cool temperatures and dry soil prevented the spread of *botrytis*. Some very good wines.

**Ribero del Duero** Rain, hail and mildew reduced the crop by 50 per cent; some desperate growers requested that this area be declared a disaster zone.

*Reds of better producers drinking well now and will keep.*

## 1987☆☆☆to☆☆☆☆

**Rioja** A very good year. The mild winter and hot, dry spring resulted in an early flowering. A cool, period followed, with some slight frost in May, but summer arrived rapidly and held out for the harvest which lasted from October 14 to 23.

**Penedès** As with Rioja, favourable weather conditions made this an excellent year. After an exceptionally hot summer the harvest began during the third week of August for the Muscat and continued until the end of October for the Parellada grapes. Here, heavy rains during the late harvest resulted in the development of *botrytis* on the broken grape skins. Damage, however, was minimal and the grapes produced pleasant, if light, wines.

Miguel Torres declared that this was his best vintage in 15 years for red wines, especially those from Cabernet Sauvignon, with deep colour, excellent tannin, and good ageing potential.

**Ribero del Duero** A mild winter and wet spring was followed by exceptionally hot weather from May until August, which caused the vines to overripen in some areas. September rain caused rot and diluted the level of acidity in the grapes. The quantity was high for this vintage but the quality was variable, ranging from average to no more than good.

*Riojas, drink soon; the Cabernet Sauvignon from Penedès from now to beyond 2000; all other reds drink soon.*

## 1986☆to☆☆☆

A successful year throughout much of Spain, although weather conditions caused problems in Penedès.

**Rioja** Spring was late after a cold, dry winter, delaying bud-break and flowering. Warm, dry weather continued throughout the summer, broken only by rain in April and October. Harvest took place from October 20 to 28 in good conditions and the crop was below average size. The wines have good ageing potential.

**Penedès** The initial problem in this region was the drought which ran from May until August. When the rain did eventually fall it swelled the sun-dried grapes, causing the skins to split, and the rapid spread of *botrytis*. Growers were therefore forced to pick quickly and selectively. Miguel Torres reported that his Cabernet Sauvignon and Tempranillo had been severely affected by the rot, causing him to reject 40 per cent of the latter. However, where the grapes had been picked early, the wines were of better quality.

*Drink up.*

## 1985☆☆☆☆

One of the driest years for some time in Spain, although a few areas, including Rioja, suffered less from drought than others.

**Rioja** The drought in this region started during a cold, dry winter and continued throughout a good flowering, an extremely hot summer and held through the harvest which started October 20. Fortunately, the soil had retained much of the moisture from the previous wet autumn and so the region harvested a huge crop and made many very good, tannic, long-lasting wines. The best came from the high areas.

**Penedès** Conversely, the drought did reduce yields in this region. However, the growing season was cooler with warm days and cool nights. This was a small vintage of healthy grapes with good sugar levels which produced very good wines, especially the reds.

**Ribero del Duero** Classified as a "good" year.

*Even the most tannic reds have softened and drinking well. Possibly at best now to 1999.*

## 1984 ☆☆

The end of a four-year drought in Spain.

**Rioja** A mild, humid winter, frost in May, hail in September, and the appearance of hurricane Hortensia in October, all made this a problematic year. The yield was consequently small and the wines of average quality – not suitable for long keeping.

**Penedès** Flowering took place successfully after a fine spring. Growth was retarded by the mild, damp conditions which prevailed throughout the summer and the harvest started late in October. A good vintage; Miguel Torres noted this as a year for white wines, the reds have also shown much promise.

**Ribero del Duero** Classified as an "average" year.

*All should have been consumed by now.*

## 1983 ☆☆☆

Despite weather problems a passably good year, though standing very much in the shadow of its two predecessors.

**Rioja** Cold winter; heavy frost in early spring; hail in May around Nájera, Cenicero and Lapuebla and very hot weather during the harvest – all conspired to damage crops. Uneven quality: some disappointments yet some promising wines with good colour.

**Penedès** A cold, snowy winter was followed by a hot spring. A summer-long drought – the worst for 150 years – broke in September. Thereafter the grapes ripened perfectly and the harvest began during the first week of October. Both the reds and the whites were good, fruity wines.

*Drink up.*

## 1982 ☆☆☆☆

As with Bordeaux, this was an outstanding year which many felt would rank alongside the classic vintages of the century.

**Rioja** A warm, dry winter was followed by a hot, dry spring. Drought conditions prevailed, causing a loss of around 20 per cent of the yield, but some much-needed rain arrived in August. The harvest ran from October 22 until November 3. These are wines with great ageing potential; many, especially the Gran Reservas, will reward long keeping.

**Penedès** A wet spring was followed by a very hot summer – July was the hottest for 100 years – caused by warm winds blowing off the Sahara. The heatwave eventually broke and harvesting began during the first week of October. Impressive wines which, again, have good potential.

**Ribero del Duero** Classified as "excellent".

*One of the rare vintages to provide red wines which not only keep but benefit from long cellaring – well into the 21st century.*

## 1981 ☆☆to☆☆☆☆

**Rioja** A long, cold, frosty winter, with snow in April, eventually gave way to warmer weather. Flowering was early and thereafter hot, dry weather held throughout the summer until the abundant harvest at the end of October. The wines were officially classified as "good" and thought by some to be excellent. For the wines of Navarra, this was undoubtedly the vintage of the decade.

**Penedès** Flowering was delayed by a cold, showery spring. Conditions improved later with a warm, dry summer during which gentle, beneficial rain fell in mid-June and late July. An early harvest started in the last two weeks of September. A small crop of good wines – some were classified as excellent – but they are mainly past their best.

*Drink up.*

## 1980 ☆☆☆

**Rioja** A mild, wet, frostless spring was followed by a cool but humid summer. The harvest, which ran from October 5 to November 12, took place during very cold but sunny weather and yielded a large crop. This was an elegant vintage, classified as "good" by the Consejo, but the wines tended to lack body and were not for long-keeping.

**Penedès** A long, wet spring delayed flowering which, despite heavy rain, was successful. The temperatures were moderate throughout the very dry summer, but rose in August and the weather remained fine for the harvest. A successful year for Torres wines, particularly the reds.

*Drink up.*

## 1979 ☆

**Rioja** A mild, wet winter was followed by an early, frostless spring and fine summer. Hopes for an excellent vintage were dashed by heavy pre-harvest rain which caused rot. A large crop of average quality wines.

**Penedès** After a wet spring the vines blossomed and matured well. Hot summer weather continued until the end of August when light rains fell. September was initially wet but warm and the harvest was completed during a very rainy October. This year had shown promise but the quality was affected by the summer drought and autumn rain. Average sized crop of average quality.

*Few to be seen. Drink up.*

## 1978 ☆☆☆

**Rioja** Wet winter weather continued into spring. Severe night frosts affected flowering, which in turn reduced the potential crop.

However, conditions improved, with a dry, sunny summer and autumn. The harvest, which took place from October 20 to 30, produced well-balanced, fruity wines which aged excellently.

**Penedès** A wet, fresh spring was followed by a mild but dry and sunny summer. There was some light, timely rain in early September and the harvest began at the end of the month in warm, dry weather. A below average crop of good wines.

*Worth looking out for. Reds now fully mature and the very best are drinking well.*

## 1977☆to☆☆

**Rioja** A year of difficult weather conditions. Persistent, although not intense, spring frosts were followed by heavy rains and a very cool summer. The autumn was mild but this was not enough to save the vintage. Mediocre wines.

**Penedès** Also a cool summer but, fortunately, warm, sunny weather during September and October enabled the grapes to ripen well, resulting in very satisfactory wines; the best made very exciting drinking.

*Now well past best.*

## 1976☆☆

**Rioja** A variable year. Winter cold and dry, budding delayed by a very cold March, summer was hot and wet. Consequently vines matured unevenly and the wines were variable.

**Penedès** A cool, wet spring followed by a warm, sunny summer moderated by some timely storms. But good wines.

*Drink up.*

## 1975☆☆☆☆

**Rioja** A very dry winter delayed budding. Spring was wet, followed by a hot summer which continued into the harvest. Many of the white grapes developed *botrytis*. On the whole a very good vintage for the red wines which had good ageing potential.

**Penedès** The weather conditions proved ideal. Warm, sunny days throughout the summer with the occasional shower early on. The grapes ripened well and picking began early October.

*Fully mature and the very best still drinking well.*

## 1974☆

**Rioja** A damp, very cold winter; followed by heavy rains at the beginning of spring. Summer was hot and dry. Mediocre vintage.

**Penedès** Moderately good.

*Drink up.*

## 1973☆☆☆

**Rioja** Winter was cold and dry followed by a mild, dry, frostless spring. Summer was hot with only the occasional shower, leading to a warm autumn. Generally a good year.

**Penedès** A mild, cool spring preceded a dry, sunny summer. The grapes were then freshened by light pre-harvest rain and picking began in early September.

**Ribero del Duero** A short vegetative cycle, late blossoming, and summer of hot days and cool nights. A good harvest.

*Pleasant wines now past their best except for the rare Vega Sicilia, drinking beautifully.*

## 1972

**Rioja** The second of two poor years in Rioja. A very cold winter delayed budding and conditions worsened with a cool, wet spring and summer. Growers experienced great problems with oidium.

**Penedès** Not a good year.

*Avoid.*

## 1971

**Rioja** A very wet spring followed a cold, dry winter. Late frosts in May and wet weather throughout the spring resulted in widespread attacks of oidium which greatly reduced the size of the crop. Thereafter the weather was hot and dry. A poor year.

**Penedès** Excellent.

*Fully mature now.*

## 1970☆☆☆☆to☆☆☆☆☆

**Rioja** A cold, wet winter delayed budding and some vines were damaged by hail in June, but otherwise a warm, moist summer and a moderate autumn. Very good wines.

**Penedès** A legendary year which provided ideal conditions for the red wines. The crop was small but the quality excellent. The Torres Gran Coronas Black Label 1970 came top in the Cabernet Sauvignon class at the 1979 Gault Millau "Wine Olympics", beating even the Châteaux Latour and La Mission-Haut-Brion.

*Best, particularly Torres Gran Coronas Black Label, still lovely.*

## EARLIER SPANISH VINTAGES

**Rioja** The following were all regarded as excellent years: **1968, 1964, 1962, 1959, 1955, 1952, 1948, 1947, 1942, 1924, 1922, 1920, 1906, 1898, 1897 and 1894**.

**Penedès** Excellent years: **1964, 1958, 1955, 1952, 1934, 1924, 1922**. Very good years: **1968, 1963, 1959, 1954, 1949, 1948,, 1947, 1942, 1935, 1931, 1928, 1925**.

**Vega Sicilia** (from recent tasting notes) Excellent: **1966, 1964, 1960, 1957, 1953**. Good years: **1969, 1965, 1962, 1948, 1942**.

# Portuguese table wine

Vintages matter in Portugal more than most people seem to realise. There are few catastrophic years but, in spite of the warm climate, there are considerable variations between different harvests. This is especially true in the north of the country where the best years for table wine often correspond closely to "declared" port vintages. In the newer wine producing regions of southern Portugal, excessive heat and drought is often a problem. But, with modern equipment in their *adegas*, winemakers are now learning to make the best use of these extreme conditions.

Most of the Portuguese table wines currently on sale come from vintages since the early to mid-1990s. However, two principal exceptions are: Barca Velha from port producers Ferreira, and Buçaco from the unique Palace Hotel deep in the heart of the country; both of which reward long keeping. The cellars at the Buçaco Palace house wines dating back to the 1940s and even older bottles occasionally turn up for auction. There are other well-made reds which keep well, notably those from Bucelas and the Dão and Bairrada districts: some of the best can be found dating back to the 1960s. On the other hand, matured (*maduro*) white wines are something of an acquired taste, but with improvements in vinification a number are becoming more acceptably international in style.

Most Vinho Verde is labelled without a vintage date. These wines should always be drunk while young and fresh. Varietal Vinhos Verdes, however, made exclusively from the Alvarinho grape, are usually from a specified year and may benefit from maturing in bottle. The Palacio de Brejoeira makes one of the finest examples.

What all Portugal's wines have in common is good value.

## 1997☆☆to☆☆☆

Unfavourable growing conditions at the start of the year gave way to perfect harvesting weather. Temperatures were above average during February and March accelerating the growing cycle. Then, humidity caused irregular ripening which was not helped by a damp June and July. The progress made earlier in the year was lost. Yields fell on average by 30 per cent and rot problems caused losses of up to 50 per cent in Vinho Verde and Dão.

Under clear blue skies harvesting ran smoothly all over Portugal. Some producers reported extended growing seasons of up to 150 days between flowering and harvest (the average is usually around 110 days). Excellent results were recorded in Alentejo and Douro. Unfortunately, the coastal areas did not fare quite so well. The red wines are expected to be of the highest quality, with above average pH levels and good extract yielding age-worthy wines.

*Apart from the light, acidic and mainly uninteresting Vinho Verdes and pleasantly commercial Dão reds Portuguese table wines are undeservedly little known. The Douro reds are now making a distinctive mark and the Bairradas are excellent value. Not for keeping; for inexpensive drinking.*

## 1996☆☆to☆☆☆

After four years of drought conditions the weather broke during the winter. Heavy rainfall replenished thirsty water tables, especially in the south. By the time flowering started it was evident that the crop would be very large, careful producers decided at this point to thin their crop, to enhance quality. Autumn was cool causing the vintage to be delayed by two weeks. Alentejo producers started picking at the beginning of September, those in the north did not start until the final week of the month.

Many growers were picking for two months or more because of the quantity of grapes. Crops were enormous, two to three times larger than 1995s, so much so that some cooperatives could not keep up with the volumes. Diligent producers made red wines of very good quality, others have suffered from dilution. White wines fared even better.

*Best drunk on the spot and soon.*

## 1995☆☆☆☆

A very successful vintage throughout Portugal, most regions produced excellent wines. On the whole, spring time was mild, while the beginning of July became overcast and some rain fell during the summer. However, this was to be a saviour to the vines, as a heatwave struck in August, sending temperatures rocketing for four weeks.

The south was hit hardest as drought caused problems, especially in Alentejo where yields were significantly reduced. Further north in Dão yields were also small. In contrast, Bairrada on the west coast produced some of the finest wines, especially reds, from well ripened grapes. The top wines will age very well.

*The whites which all tend to be dry will make attractive early drinking. The better reds are being drunk now, but will benefit from two or three years bottle-age.*

## 1994☆☆☆

Wet conditions were a problem during winter and spring. In May, some places experienced highly localised frost which almost completely destroyed the crop. The ripening season progressed well without excessive summer heat. A couple of short bursts of rain in the Douro in August and early September helped re-establish a healthy and even ripening, resulting in good sugar levels. In this region, production was down by about 45 per cent, dramatically affecting the availability of grapes for table wine.

Throughout Portugal the harvest took place successfully and under fine conditions. The volumes are drastically reduced, but the quality is high. In the south, growers were particularly happy with their results.

*The whites are early drinking. Most reds drinking well, but top Alentejo reds are still tannic and unready.*

## 1993☆

This was an extremely unsettled vintage. Drought affected the country during the winter and early spring, followed by rains from late April until June. By the end of this dismal period, flowering was just beginning and clearly not in ideal conditions.

The summer months were warm, but rarely sufficiently hot to enable healthy ripening. As September approached, the weather became increasingly unsettled, the only respite being a dry but cool week at the end of the month. The weather barely improved and the harvest started alarmingly late. The rains returned on October 2 causing even more difficulties than already existed.

*Not a vintage to keep.*

### 1992☆to☆☆

Portugal experienced one of its driest winters on record followed by an intensely hot summer. Fortunately, heavy rains fell at the end of August, saving the vintage as the grapes were now able to ripen. By the time of the harvest, conditions had turned cold and wet. The general lack of rain resulted in crops being frequently reduced by at least 25 per cent. In the south these conditions delayed the ripening process and many wines taste unbalanced, green and hard. The weather was less extreme in the north and the wines are, consequently, of a higher quality.

*Drink up whites. Reds now ready.*

### 1991☆☆to☆☆☆☆

After a wet winter, warm weather in April and May encouraged early growth. June was unusually cool and wet but this was more than compensated for by hot weather which lasted uninterrupted until the end of August. In the north, a large crop looked likely; however, rain in early September led to rot. Some Vinho Verde growers lost 15 per cent of their crop. In the south, three weeks of extreme heat undoubtedly caused a set back and, for the third successive year, a lack of water kept yields down below average.

With financial help from the EU, wineries all over Portugal are becoming even better equipped to cope with climatic extremes. Although most producers seem pleased with the quality of their wine, some southern reds (especially those made in the old-fashioned *adegas* where temperature control is lacking) tend to be unbalanced and over alcoholic.

*Whites drink up. Middle quality reds drink now, high quality until circa 2002.*

### 1990☆☆☆

Heavy winter rains around Christmas 1989 replenished the water-table in much of the country, but a prolonged period of dry summer weather, combined with searing heat, quickly brought on a drought in some regions. Yields were down by about ten per cent in Alentejo and on the Setúbal Peninsula, though this was more than compensated for by some high quality wines. In the north, two short bursts of rain in August and September helped to swell the grapes. Growers in Bairrada, Dão and the Douro harvested an average sized crop of well-ripened grapes.

*Whites drink up. Lighter reds ready now; sturdiest reds soon.*

### 1989☆☆☆

As in so much of Europe, July and August were blisteringly hot throughout Portugal. After the previous year's extremely low yield, a large crop was badly needed. In the event, drought in some parts of Portugal retarded development of the grapes and reduced average yields by as much as 20 per cent. The early harvest produced ripe fruit, though some wines suffer from a lack of acidity. In Bairrada they tend to lack colour and depth.

*Red wines should be drunk soon, particularly the southern reds which are drinking very well now.*

### 1988☆☆☆☆

Disasters are not frequent in Portugal's mild Atlantic climate, but in 1988 vineyards in much of the country came close to catastrophe.

An uneven flowering was followed by rain which continued until the end of June. Many small growers in the north had never experienced such conditions and mildew set in before anything could be done to prevent it. The Minho was particularly badly hit; yields were in some cases 80 per cent below the average. Low yields often mean high quality and the 1988 vintage was saved by a warm, dry summer lasting until the end of the harvest.

Outstanding wines were made in the Dão, Bairrada and Alentejo regions. In the Douro, which suffered the effects of the poor spring, most of the production was used to make port.

*The better reds drinking well.*

### 1987☆to☆☆

An uneven year. In the north, high temperatures during early summer brought on a drought which slowed down the maturation of the grapes. Consequently, many wines from Bairrada, Dão and Setubál were light, astringent and somewhat lacking in colour. The best wines were produced further south in the Alentejo.

*Drink up.*

### 1986☆☆

For many winemakers in the north this was a year to forget. A warm summer was followed by torrential rain at the time of the harvest. Rot set in quickly, badly affecting vineyards in Bairrada, Dão and parts of the Douro. The south fared better; some excellent, well-structured wines were produced in the Alentejo and on the Setúbal Peninsula.

*Most need drinking up. Well-structured Alentejo reds drinking quite well.*

### 1985☆☆☆☆

In many ways, the reverse of 1986. After a wet spring, the late hot summer and warm sunny autumn ripened the grapes and provided perfect harvesting conditions. The Dão, Bairrada and the Douro in the north of the country produced intense, concentrated wines which have the potential to mature well.

In the south, however, the piercing sun shrivelled grapes in many of the vineyards before they were picked. Theses high temperatures also caused problems during fermentation in the less well-equipped *adegas*, and many of the resulting wines suffered from excess acidity.

*Top reds from the northern and southern garrafeiras have excellent depth of fruit and are well-balanced; they are lovely now and will keep.*

### 1984☆☆☆

Rain in early October followed a cool summer and many growers were caught out waiting for their grapes to ripen. As a result, Dão and Bairrada made thin, astringent red wines. The best came from the Douro. Further south, vines benefited from a relatively cool vintage and good, well-balanced reds were made in the Alentejo and Setúbal regions.

*All now fully mature. Buçaco drinking well.*

## 1983☆☆☆☆☆

The second of two excellent vintages. Good weather throughout the spring and summer months ensured a crop of ripe, healthy fruit. However, some winemakers found fermentation difficult in the increasingly hot weather.

Overall, the north produced classic, firm-flavoured reds. To the south, where the use of modern equipment is less common, the wines were somewhat less balanced, many having stewed aromas and flavours.

*Drink up all but the top quality reds, such as Barca Velha, which have a ten to 15 year life span.*

## 1982☆☆☆☆☆

After hot summer conditions growers harvested early. The Douro, Dão and Bairrada regions made robust wines with plenty of ripe fruit. Ferreira's Barca Velha has a chocolatey intensity and Buçaco produced some intensely ripe full-flavoured reds.

Further south, this year was seen to have the edge on the 1983s, particularly in the Ribatejo, where some excellent, ripe and flavoursome *garrafeiras* were made.

*Drink soon.*

## 1981☆

A year which many growers would prefer to forget. A cold spring retarded growth, and rain in September encouraged rot. Picking began late. The wines were often thin and astringent, lacking fruit and depth. The eastern Douro escaped the worst of the rain and produced a good spicy Barca Velha from Ferreira – the high note of the year.

*Drink up.*

## 1980☆☆☆☆

For many winemakers throughout Portugal this was the best vintage of the decade. A late flowering was followed by a warm summer and a dry autumn, and the grapes were harvested in perfect condition.

The Dão and Bairrada regions made fruity, well-balanced wines and further south in the Ribatejo some excellent *garrafeiras* were produced. Curiously, Ferreira did not make a Barca Velha in this year, preferring to declassify its wine as Reserva Especial.

*Fully mature now but the best reds will keep.*

## EARLIER PORTUGUESE VINTAGES

Notable earlier vintages include: **1978**, **1975**, **1974**, **1971**, **1970**, **1966**. Barca Velha: **1978**, **1966**, **1965**, **1964**. Buçaco: **1978**, **1977**, **1975**, **1970**, **1966**, **1965**, **1962** and, particularly, **1959**.

# New World

## California

It is roughly 700miles (1126.5km) from the most southerly vineyards of California, near San Diego, to Mendocino in the north; and in terms of average temperature the range varies considerably between the near coastal districts and the broad, hot Central Valley. It is therefore difficult to include weather reports and quality assessments for such widely differing areas. Similarly it is no reflection on the quality of wine made in and around Santa Barbara, Monterey or Santa Clara if the following vintage notes concentrate almost solely on the two major wine districts, being the Napa Valley, with its almost continuous string of premium quality vineyards and wineries, and the broader, but equally vine-clad, Sonoma County.

It we take into account the vines planted by Spanish missionaries, the history of wine in what is now California, though not as ancient as that of the Cape, pre-dates all other "New World" wine cultures. The business of vine growing was revived in the second half of the 19th century and, after the blight of Prohibition, took off again seriously in the 1940s, gaining momentum in the 1950s, making tremendous strides in the 1970s and climaxing, both in terms of volume and quality, in the 1980s.

Virtually every variety of *Vitis vinifera* has been cultivated in California, but, by process of elimination, Cabernet Sauvignon and Chardonnay stand supreme. Merlot has fully emerged; Zinfandel ploughs its individual furrow; Sauvignon Blanc (Fumé Blanc) fills an important niche; Pinot Noir is achieving distinction and the once dull Rieslings have found their apotheosis in late-harvest dessert wines. Perhaps even encouraging, "new" (old world) varietals such as Viognier, rather a cult grape, are being supremely handled by a small number of brilliant winemakers.

Like most light dry white wine, Sauvignon Blanc is best drunk young – indeed it does not age at all well. However, the best Chardonnay, pleasant drinking at three years of age, can be consumed with equal enjoyment some eight years after the vintage. The best reds, like Bordeaux and burgundy, need bottle-age though California Cabernets and "Zins" have an innate flesh and fruitiness which enables them to be drunk when "released" (put on the market) by the producer. Those of high quality, with a track record and from a good vintage, can develop well for 20 years or longer. California has certainly come of age.

## 1997☆☆☆☆☆

After the run of small vintages this year witnessed a bumper result. Yields were up by 24 per cent compared to 1996 and the proportion of premium wines is also high. This has helped to relieve the inflating prices for these wines.

January was unusually warm and damp. Spring came early and the weather continued favourably, providing a long, dry and not overly hot ripening period. The harvest started extremely early with grapes for sparkling wines ready for picking by the end of July. At this point things changed. In Sonoma and Napa August and September both saw tropical storms which triggered rot problems. These were intensified due to the preponderance of tight bunches on the vines. Chardonnay, Sauvignon Blanc, Pinot Noir and Zinfandel were most affected as were the lower situated vineyards. Rigorous vineyard management commenced and, as a consequence, some producers suffered stuck fermentations due to residual fungicides in the grapes. Ripening schedules were also disrupted, causing problems at the wineries during crushing.

Monterey County was spared the late storms and was rewarded with a perfect harvest, free from rot problems, and with finely balanced wines. Santa Barbara further south experienced a certain amount of rain, but is more influenced by microclimates.

Nevertheless, this year, the overall quality and quantity was excellent everywhere.

*Impossible to generalise. Whites and commercial reds not for cellaring; the top wineries are a different matter. The standard of Pinot Noir is now astonishingly high, though most are normally best drunk quite young. The Cabernet Sauvignon, Merlot and Zinfandels though attractively fruity when first released, benefit from a further two to five years bottle-age.*

## 1996 ☆☆☆

Another variable year for the west coast, growing conditions not always working favourably. This is unfortunate for the consumer as prices continue to rise due to shrinking stocks.

Winter was warmer than usual which shortened the dormancy period, this then reduced the amount of fruit setting on the vine. By spring time the temperatures had cooled slightly and rain brought bud-break two or three weeks early. Further rain in May caused the vines to "shatter" while flowering, compounding the decreased fruiting problem. A heatwave struck during July and August, bringing the onset of harvest sooner and causing it to be potentially rapid.

In the Napa Valley, a dramatic cooling in late August slowed down the ripening process, allowing more "hang time" for the grapes. A stop/start harvest dominated, which some say has added complexity to the wines. The concentration and balance of the grapes benefited most, but quantities were still down. Sauvignon Blanc and Chardonnay yields fell anywhere between 20 and 50 per cent. Pinot Noir varied according to area and Cabernet Sauvignon and Merlot were least affected.

Going south, the weather was more consistent giving better results. Santa Barbara saw an increase of around 15 to 20 per cent and yields of very high quality. Throughout the region, quality is good but there may be a shortage of premium wines this vintage.

*No doubt about it, California – a huge, straggling state of contrasting wine regions – requires a major study of its own. Impossible to generalise save to drink Sauvignon Blanc young; Chardonnays between three and six years of age; the now excellent Pinot Noir say five to eight and the best Cabernets perhaps a little longer.*

## 1995 ☆☆ to ☆☆☆☆

This year experienced similar misfortunes to the 1994 vintage. Torrential January rain, March floods and cold weather during flowering resulted in the harvest being delayed by between two and four weeks and yields being reduced.

The coastal vineyards were hit hardest with Monterey and Santa Barbara experiencing losses of up to 23 per cent of total production. Yields of early-ripening varieties such as Pinot Noir and Chardonnay fell 80 and 50 per cent respectively. Central Valley was not hit so hard and the extended growing season gave wines with added concentration as a result of good sugar levels and retained acidity. Napa and Sonoma took a hard knock after flooding, and continuing *phylloxera* problems reduced yields by around ten per cent. Mendocino was spared most of the unfavourable conditions, enjoying a rise in yields of between 24 and 29 per cent, plus inflating grape prices.

White wines suffered most losses with Chardonnay yields falling six per cent. However, red varietals triumphed as Zinfandel jumped 46 per cent and Merlot 33 per cent. Overall this was a light vintage, but the best wines can show impressive depth.

*Most whites best consumed soon. Cabernets and Zinfandels benefit a further five years. Pinot Noir best say 2000 to 2010.*

## 1994 ☆☆ to ☆☆☆

A mediocre vintage and the result of somewhat un-Californian weather – rain and unusually cool temperatures at crucial points during the growing season.

Initial problems were caused by spring rains resulting in uneven flowering and budding. For most varieties the bunches and the grapes themselves were unusually small. The harvest was drastically reduced and yields were markedly varied from site to site. The ripening process had progressed uneventfully until cool autumnal weather arrived which, in some areas, was accompanied by heavy rains. Napa Valley and Sonoma County were fortunately not affected by the rains as much as the more southerly districts, most notably, the Central Coast.

The main concerns were the reduced yields of Chardonnay and Zinfandel. The former was down by 15 to 20 per cent, with many examples suffering ripening deficiencies, and the latter, by as much as 50 per cent. Pinot Noir was reduced by about 20 per cent, but with excellent results as it was generally harvested before the rains arrived. Fortunately, Sauvignon Blanc, Cabernet Sauvignon and Merlot all had healthily proportioned yields with good to excellent quality levels.

*A roller coaster of a year. Sauvignon Blanc ready now, Chardonnay soon, the Bordeaux-varietal reds from "release" to 2000, or beyond for the top Napa Cabernets.*

## 1993 ☆☆

If there are those who still think that "the Sunshine State" makes life easy for grape growers, 1993 must surely correct this inaccurate impression.

The weather, from spring to harvest time, was bizarre, erratic and unpredictable. The early summer had unusually cold and rainy periods interspersed with strong winds. Summer ripening was alternately advanced and retarded by heatwaves and cold spells right through into October. Crops were reduced by the poor flowering, amounting to an overall loss of around ten per cent; Merlot, Pinot Noir and Chardonnay were the worst hit. All the white varieties suffered from burned and frequently "raisined" grapes because of the severity of the heatwaves. In southern California yields were closer to normal.

The results were very uneven and it remains to be seen how the top winemakers have coped in such a difficult year when not even lower yields implied an increase in quality.

*Best to drink whites early. The reds are enormously variable, most for early drinking.*

## 1992 ☆☆☆☆

The growing season started well. For the first time in six years there was adequate winter rainfall to ease drought conditions. Flowering went well two weeks ahead of usual; much sun and mild temperatures were the rule. Early summer was a little unsettled but by mid-July normal warmth resumed, heating up rather alarmingly in August. But the pattern of warm days and cool nights returned leading to an early and perfect harvest.

Overall a very satisfactory vintage. All the varieties behaved well, classic Cabernets with good fruit, for mid-term drinking, (which in Californian terms means about four years after the vintage). Well-structured wines will keep for considerably longer. The harvest for white varieties started early and the results are good to excellent. Chardonnay has a slightly higher level of acidity than usual – no bad thing.

The main problem affecting growers in the Napa area at this time was phylloxera. Of the 13,500 hectares of vines in the valley, nearly 2000 were already affected by this year. Uprooting and replanting is an ongoing and costly business: estimates vary from $40,000 to over $60,000 per hectare.

*The drinking period for reds – summarised above. Whites all ready for drinking now. Sauvignon Blanc almost invariably best when drunk young, they do not age well. Chardonnays probably best between three and seven years of age.*

## 1991 ☆☆☆☆☆

A worrying year which ended satisfactorily. Weather conditions were similar in the Napa Valley and Sonoma County: record low temperatures in the winter and an ominously dry New Year and early spring. Happily, before bud-break in March, there was exceptionally heavy rain. The spring was cool but the flowering successful, promising an abundant crop. However, the summer was also cool, by Californian standards, and extended. Leaves were removed to enable the sun to penetrate and crops thinned to encourage concentration and maturation – the latter finally concluded by an excellent unbroken Indian summer.

Ripe, well-balanced grapes were picked before late October rains and the long cool growing season resulted in good natural levels of acidity, vital for life and development. Levels of alcohol were conducive to finesse rather than massive structure, yet with enhanced concentration and flavour for all varietals and intensity of colour for the reds. The only cloud on the horizon at this stage, particularly in the Napa, was the spread of phylloxera (Type B) which was devastating whole blocks of vines on the valley floor, necessitating extensive and expensive replanting. There are good reasons therefore, for keeping track of – and buying – wines of this potentially excellent vintage.

*Chardonnays drink soon, depending on their weight and quality; Pinot Noirs now to 2000. Cabernet Sauvignons and related blends drinking to well beyond 2000.*

## 1990☆☆☆☆

A smaller crop than the previous year's, but one which was harvested in near-perfect conditions, particularly in the Napa Valley, promising an excellent year for California wines.

**Napa Valley** Another dry winter, temperatures were below average which led to a late bud-break. However, a long heatwave in mid-May speeded growth up. Flowering and berry-set were affected by heavy rains in late May, resulting in a smaller than average crop. Picking began relatively early in mid-August; cool mornings and evenings with gradual warming during the days characterised the harvest; making this, some say, one of the most ideal harvests in recent history.

Overall, the grapes were in good condition; fruit was mature and acidity and sugar levels were well-balanced to give intense, characterful red wines and rich whites.

**Sonoma County** Normal bud-break, followed by moderate weather, led to a good set in the Chardonnay grapes, but the Cabernet Sauvignon and Sauvignon Blanc did not set well due to heavy rain in June. Thereafter the summer was fine, interrupted by short two-day heatwaves. Harvesting proceeded normally in near-perfect conditions, with many Sauvignon Blancs being picked early at the same time as the Chardonnay. As in the Napa Valley, small yields of high quality, intense, deep-coloured wines.

*The Sauvignon Blancs and Chardonnays should have been consumed. Classic reds now to 2000.*

## 1989☆☆to☆☆☆

A year which will be remembered for the devastating earthquake which struck in mid-October, causing thousands of bottles of the previous vintage to be shattered.

**Napa Valley** After several drought years, rain in March was much welcomed by growers in California. The vines flowered in ideal conditions which held throughout the summer, encouraging high expectations for this vintage.

However, towards the end of September, with 40 per cent of the grapes picked, the harvest was interrupted by widespread, torrential rain. Unfortunately the weather thereafter was cold,

foggy and stormy, encouraging the spread of rot on the remaining white grapes. Picking resumed later; those who picked quickly and selectively produced good wine. Yields were considerably larger than those of the previous dry years; but, quality was low.
**Sonoma County** Similar conditions prevailed here. However, near-perfect harvesting conditions produced some fine wines. Cabernet Sauvignon had deep colour and good tannic structure.

*Whites drink up. The best reds need considerable bottle-age.*

## 1988☆☆☆

Described as one of the weirdest years on record because of the unusual weather conditions.
**Napa Valley** Winter was dry; February and March were hot, and encouraged early bud-break. Cold, rainy weather in April then continued through the flowering, accompanied by heavy winds. The summer was very hot and harvesting began on August 24.

The drought and erratic weather conditions affected berry and bunch size, massively reducing the size of the crop. Growers reported that the tonnage of Pinot Noir was down by as much as 60 per cent and the Sauvignon Blanc by 50 per cent. Quality, however, was high and the best, made from grapes picked early and selectively, were good, concentrated wines.
**Sonoma County** Bud-break was delayed by a dry winter but growth caught up during a warm spring and the vines flowered in early April. Summer was initially cool and wet and thereafter the growing season was alternately very hot or very cool. The vintage was early: picking began in late August and yields were low, quality high. Some finely flavoured, well-balanced Chardonnays and Sauvignon Blancs resulted.

*The Chardonnays and Pinot Noirs are ready now; Cabernet and Cabernet blends up to or beyond 2000.*

## 1987☆☆☆

A small but healthy crop with great potential.
**Napa Valley** Soils, made dry by low rainfall at the end of the previous season, produced vines with small berry and cluster size: factors which promised an excellent vintage. The growing season enjoyed fine, warm weather and the arrival of coastal fog cooled the grapes and protected acidity levels.

Picking was early: grapes for sparkling wines were picked in late July and the harvest was fully under way for all grapes by mid-August. The white wines combined a good balance of acidity with high sugar levels, the red wines were of exceptional quality.
**Sonoma County** Warm, dry weather held throughout the winter and spring; flowering took place early during hot weather. High temperatures in May caused some berry shatter, especially in Cabernet Sauvignon and a consequent drop in the yield. Thereafter the weather was generally cool and dry and the harvest took place early in mid-August. These are flavoursome wines, though slightly less ripe than the 1986s and 1988s. A fine Cabernet Sauvignon vintage.

*Whites, drink up. Cabernet Sauvignon, drink soon.*

## 1986☆☆to☆☆☆

**Napa Valley** A cold, dry winter ended with torrential storms in mid-February. Flowering was early but protracted. The summer was dry and one of the coolest on record, but was followed by hot weather in August and September. The main harvest began early, around the beginning of September, but continued into October. Soft, round wines.

**Sonoma County** Despite heavy storms in February and a mild summer, the quality of the grapes by early September in the Russian River Valley was very good, with perfectly balanced sugar levels and acidity. Rains from mid- to late-September encouraged the development of rot among the last grapes to be picked. Otherwise, yields were high and the grapes had good tannin levels. Some excellent Cabernets.

*The Pinot Noirs and Merlots drink now, the better Cabernet Sauvignons to the end of the century.*

## 1985☆☆☆☆☆

**Napa Valley** Undoubtedly an excellent vintage – one of the best ever in this region. Apart from some stormy weather in February, the weather was fine throughout the early spring and the summer. September saw some heavy rains which interrupted the main harvest, but good weather returned at the end of the month to ripen the remaining grapes.

A broad range of superbly balanced, supple, well-knit wines with excellent ageing potential.

**Sonoma County** A wet winter and early spring resulted in early bud-break. Apart from a few hot spells in June and July, the summer was mainly cool. The grapes ripened slowly and evenly, developing good concentration of fruit. Picking began around September 17; the Cabernet Sauvignon harvest was interrupted in some areas by heavy rains. A small crop of good quality wines – promising Cabernets.

*Whites should have been consumed. Pinot Noirs will be reaching their peak, but the Cabernet Sauvignons are drinking well, the best will continue to develop beyond 2000.*

## 1984☆☆☆

**Napa Valley** A very wet winter was followed by hot weather throughout the growing season. The summer was exceptionally hot – temperatures, sometimes well above 38°C (100°F), caused some berry shatter and consequently a reduction in crop size.

The harvest was the earliest ever in the Napa region, all the major varietals ripening together, making picking extremely busy from as early as the first week of August. Clean grapes made well-balanced, good quality wines with potential for ageing, although not quite up to the standard of the 1985s.

**Sonoma County** As with the Napa Valley, a short season producing small berries and a smaller than average yield. Both the Chardonnay and Cabernet Sauvignon had good, fruity, aromatic flavours; but less finesse than the wines of cooler years. Overall, these were attractive wines for early drinking.

*Generally, more of a Pinot Noir than a Cabernet Sauvignon year, but reports conflict. Most whites too old and should have been consumed.*

## 1983 ☆to☆☆☆

**Napa Valley** The wettest winter on record ran into a summer which, apart from one heatwave in mid-July, was damp and cool. These conditions caused considerable problems, including a lack of soil aeration and visibly "tired", soggy vines, as well as the inevitable rot. The best-drained sites experienced the least problems and everywhere picking was very selective.

The harvest yielded a small crop of very variable wines which ranged from poor to excellent in quality. The most successful were the Cabernets.

**Sonoma County** In this region also the year was characterised by excessive rainfall followed by one of the coolest summers on record. Picking did not begin until mid-September and was very selective. The final yield was the lowest of the decade.

*Botrytis* was widespread and helped to produce some excellent Rieslings plus some equally good Gewürztraminers and late-harvest style Sauvignon Blancs. By contrast, this was not a good year for the Cabernets.

*A distinctly uneven vintage, some reds very tannic, some soft. Hard to generalise. Best to drink up or avoid – except for the few good late-harvest wines at their peak now.*

## 1982 at best☆☆☆☆

**Napa Valley** California suffered one of its wettest winters ever, followed by a frostless spring and good weather during flowering, providing ideal conditions for a bumper crop. Mid-September rains delayed the harvest for many Cabernets and some white grapes were lost to rot, although some very good *botrytised* wines were made. This record crop produced good but not great wines.

**Sonoma County** Similar overall weather conditions to those in the Napa Valley; although flowering was later and temperatures cooler and more humid, resulting in considerable powdery mildew. September rains delayed the harvest and many white grapes were lost to bunch-rot. The Cabernet Sauvignon harvest was saved by an Indian summer, producing ripe, fruity wines. An exceptionally long harvest produced a huge crop of grapes.

*Though initially tannic, the Cabernets developed well and are probably at their peak now. Some excellent Zinfandels.*

## 1981 at best☆☆☆

The earliest harvest on record in almost all areas of California, following a summer of extreme heat.

**Napa Valley** Budding and flowering were both early and healthy, but Cabernet Sauvignon grapes suffered during the hottest June throughout the US, large crop quantities were lost as a result.

The main harvest was well underway by mid-August. The weather cooled in September, though it was followed by an Indian summer, during which some *botrytis*-affected grapes were picked and made some fine late-harvest whites. This was a fairly good year; the white wines were generally better than the reds which tended to be rather light.

**Sonoma County** Similar weather conditions to the Napa Valley plus hot, dry winds which dried out and concentrated the grapes.

This was the shortest growing season on record. As a result the Chardonnays, because of the rapid sugar accumulation, lacked fruit, while the same leanness proved to be rather more attractive in the Cabernets.

*Drink up.*

## 1980 ☆☆☆

**Napa Valley** A wet winter was followed by one of the coolest growing seasons on record. Growers feared that sugar levels might be too low but hopes were revived with warm pre-harvest weather. The wines were intense and fruity, bearing comparison with classic European wines.

**Sonoma County** A similar weather pattern to Napa. There was some localised hail damage in spring and high winds affected the pollination period resulting in a poor flowering and low yields. Acidity levels were surprisingly high, even after a week of very hot October weather, and balanced well against sugar levels, resulting in some excellent white wines. The Cabernet Sauvignon grapes dehydrated in the high temperatures and produced concentrated, powerful wines.

*Good results despite difficult conditions. Tannic, long-lasting reds, but all the best should have been consumed by now.*

## 1970s NAPA VALLEY

**1979** ☆☆☆ started hot but the cool growing season and September rain necessitated early picking. The best wines were no more than good and did not match the best 1978s. **1978** ☆☆☆☆ started with heavy rains which benefited the vines and developed into a warm growing season. A big crop; the wines were ripe and well-balanced, some were excellent. The best are drinking well but will develop further.

**1977** ☆☆ was the second of two years of drought but growers were better prepared for the associated problems. The weather was cooler than 1976; overall, some good wines were made. High sugar and low acidity characterised the wines of **1976** ☆☆☆ which ranged from poor to good: drink soon. **1975** ☆☆☆ had a good growing season with some light harvest rains; these were fine, well-balanced, elegant wines.

The star of the decade was undoubtedly **1974** ☆☆☆☆☆ arguably the best-ever vintage for California. Growing conditions were ideal: a cool, slightly frosty spring, a long cool summer and perfect harvesting weather. These were excellent, well-balanced wines; but some now starting to tire. **1973** ☆☆☆☆ also enjoyed good growing conditions and a record crop of healthy, perfectly mature grapes produced some very good wines.

The first three vintages of the decade were not of the same calibre as those of the middle years. **1972** ☆ to ☆☆☆☆ was a very variable vintage, some very good reds. **1971**☆☆☆ was better, the fruit was healthy but the wines were never better than good. Severe spring frosts destroyed half of the **1970**☆☆☆☆ crop. What was left was generally sound – the best wines were the Cabernets, some were very good – overall, though, a very mixed year.

# Pacific Northwest

## WASHINGTON & OREGON

Although conveniently twinned under the Pacific Northwest heading, the local climate and geography of the vineyard areas of these two neighbouring states could not be more contrasting. The valleys of western Oregon enjoy a mild climate, but weather conditions vary considerably over the growing season, not unlike the maritime climate of Bordeaux, whilst inland, the vineyards of eastern Washington State are in a broad, arid, semi-desert valley, the vines being irrigated by the waters of the Columbia River.

In Oregon; more northerly, more temperate, than California; Pinot Noir has – in theory at least – found a natural home, as have the more characteristically acidic Sauvignon Blanc and Riesling. However, Chardonnay, Merlot and Cabernet Sauvignon are also planted in what are relatively new wine areas. The pioneers of the early 1960s have been augmented by a host of mainly small, highly individual wineries, quality equally variable. The wines of both Oregon and Washington State are worth keeping track of.

### 1997

**Washington**☆☆to☆☆☆ Escaping the more ruthless conditions further south, yields were high and of similar quality. There were light showers during September, very unusual in this area, which caused some rot in the tight bunches. This affected Riesling and Chardonnay, but the Cabernet, Merlot and Syrah were excellent. **Oregon**☆☆☆ This season was very similar to that in California. The conditions for the growing season started well and developed into a warm summer. Then multiple storms, compounded by the region's proximity to the coast brought cold and wet weather just before the harvest. This resulted in some rot. Drying winds restored health to the vines and by picking time ripeness had been enhanced. The harvest started in mid-September and was finished by the end of October. Yields were up by 16 per cent compared to 1996, producing light and delicately balanced wines.

*A vintage to give the reds a chance to show their paces with, when released, a handful of years bottle-age.*

### 1996

**Washington**☆☆ February was pleasant, then severe frost hit, obliterating all hopes for a large crop. Essential bud development was lost, which reduced the potential harvest between 35 and 50 per cent, but this diminished crop did have greater concentration as a result. Merlot was the most affected variety – many producers resorted to buying grapes from California to boost stocks.

**Oregon**☆☆ This was a challenging vintage also. Rain hampered development and flowering fell behind. Despite warmer weather in July ripening was still slow. More rain fell in September and many grapes were unfortunately harvested while underripe. The later ripening varieties such as Riesling and Chardonnay were also affected by rot when rain continued throughout October.

*The wines from this region have not really caught on and, in my experience, quality and style are extremely variable. Worth experimenting with them, comparing wineries. Until individual track records are firmly established, drink when youthful.*

## 1995

**Washington**☆☆ A very wet and dismal vintage. The summer was consistently wet, which dramatically slowed down the development of the vines. Autumn brought a slight improvement in conditions and this assisted ripening. Producers then picked at different times when rain threatened again during the harvest. One benefit of the cool weather was to enhance the aromatic qualities of Riesling and Gewürztraminer.

**Oregon**☆☆ The season developed similarly to Washington, with rain causing problems with rot. Surprisingly the results were not as bad as expected, but the Pinot Noir grapes in the Willamette Valley did suffer significant damage from *botrytis*.

*Both Riesling and Gewürztraminer best drunk young. The Pinot Noirs, on the whole, do not have a track record and are probably best drunk from now to 2000.*

## 1994

**Washington**☆☆☆ As with California, the Pacific Northwest experienced reduced yields, particularly in contrast to 1993's enormous vintage. In Washington State the harvest was of normal proportions. The warm weather that started in June and continued through the summer caused small grapes and bunches and intensified flavours. Results were promising particularly regarding Merlot and Cabernet Sauvignon.

**Oregon**☆☆☆ The light rains that fell during flowering and budding resulted in the crop being reduced by a third compared with 1993. Similarly to Washington State, harvesting was fairly smooth and completed by the end of October. The results were exciting, especially Oregon's speciality grape, Pinot Noir, performing particularly well.

*This is a region of intriguing and challengingly attractive red wines, not only the justly admired Pinot Noirs, but also Bordeaux varietals: the Pinot Noirs, probably best at three to seven years of age, the Cabernet-based wines have insufficient track record. Probably better whilst young and fruity, though the better wines, well worth cellaring experimentally.*

## 1993

**Washington**☆☆☆ An extraordinarily cool spring initiated one of the region's most drawn-out growing seasons in history. Warm weather rescued the crop in September and October to such a degree that it was of record breaking dimensions. The quality is similar to that of the 1983 vintage – soft reds and excellent whites with good acidity levels.

**Oregon**☆☆ A much more varied vintage that was frequently dominated by overcast skies and short periods of rain. These occurred particularly during June and July and again towards the end of the harvest. The quality of the vintage is varied but the size is considerable due to many recently planted vineyards now coming into full operation.

*On the whole, wines for drinking, not keeping; though the top wines will benefit from a year or so more bottle-age.*

## 1992

**Washington**☆☆☆ A record sized harvest came as an enormous relief after 1991s reduced crop and it had many similarities to California's 1992 vintage. Flowering and budding took place two weeks earlier than usual with the rest of the season warm and dry, refreshed by just the right amount of rain. The wines have slightly lower than usual tannins, full fruit levels and good, balancing acidity.

**Oregon**☆☆☆ Further similarities with the dry, warm conditions in California resulted in the largest crop on record. Production was up by about 25 per cent, much of this is the result of new Pinot Noir plantings coming into production. This year's results have the same level of full, ripe fruit witnessed in Washington and California.

*An attractive vintage. A mass of pleasing, full-of-fruit reds for mid-term drinking.*

## 1991

**Washington**☆☆ An extremely severe winter freeze killed some and damaged many other vines, reducing the potential crop by up to 50 per cent. However, the growing season was satisfactory, the harvest taking place in balmy autumn weather, resulting in good sugar and acid levels.

**Oregon**☆☆☆☆ A cold wet spring and late flowering made up for by a virtually perfect summer and early autumn. A large, ripe harvest brought in under hot sun before heavy late October rains.

*Merlot, Cabernet Sauvignon and Pinot Noir drink soon.*

## 1990

**Washington**☆☆☆ Cool weather during the flowering cut the crop. Very high temperatures during July and August actually slowed down the ripening of the grapes and the harvest took place early, starting on September 7 running through to October 10.

September was unusually warm and those who picked quickly and promptly when the fruit peaked at optimum maturity produced excellent and balanced wines. This year witnessed the smallest yield per acre since 1985.

**Oregon**☆☆☆ The yield per acre was very low here also, although quantities were higher than in 1989 as a result of new plantations. Here too, the spring was cool, but the small crop of unusually small berries yielded some wines of great intensity and depth. Picking began in late September. This was a better year for the Chardonnay than the Pinot Noir, which is usually the most important grape in Oregon.

*Whites should have been consumed; reds soon.*

## 1989

**Washington**☆☆☆☆ The cool spring and early summer resulted in a moderate sized crop. Initially the grapes developed slowly but steadily until late August. Thereafter growers enjoyed an extraordinary period of hot, sunny days and cool nights; which provided ideal ripening conditions. The harvest began in mid-September and lasted until late October.

The wines had exceptional concentration and acidity and the reds were showing all the potential of a great vintage.

**Oregon**☆☆☆ A warm, late May and early June brought the vines into early flowering. Mid-June was wet; most vines had set by then but those on higher land set during the rain and consequently the yields were low and variable. Picking began slightly earlier than usual and took place in perfect conditions. Most Pinot Noirs were brought in at perfect maturity; if picked too late they tended to lack finesse and delicacy. Overall, the wines were of very high quality.

*The top Pinot Noirs from, say, now to 2000.*

## 1988

**Washington**☆☆☆☆ An excellent combination of quantity and quality. A smooth viticultural year with very favourable and normal weather at all times, which produced a large vintage of remarkably even quality. The harvest began on September 8 and ended on October 20. The wines had excellent fruit and good natural balance. The reds should age very well.

**Oregon**☆☆☆ A cool, wet spring and summer, but with warmer weather during flowering in May. Temperatures rose in mid-July and remained warm through to the middle of September. The yield was down by 50 per cent.

*Merlot, Cabernet and Pinot Noir drink soon.*

## 1987

**Washington**☆☆☆☆ The hottest summer in 20 years which yielded a very large vintage. The grapes were beautifully ripe and in perfect health when the harvest began on August 28. The better reds were attractive and fruity but have aged more rapidly than is typical for a Washington vintage.

**Oregon**☆☆to☆☆☆ Here too, with the exception of some cooler weather during July and August, temperatures were high throughout the growing season. Picking took place in hot, dry weather and yields were high throughout the region.

Quality varied, and the best wines were made by the growers who picked early and therefore managed to retain good levels of acidity in their grapes.

*Remaining whites drink up. Reds fully mature, drink soon.*

## 1986

**Washington**☆☆ The warm summer weather ripened the grapes and produced a large vintage. The harvest, which began on September 5, was briefly interrupted by rain. Overall the grapes were healthy but the wet weather increased yields in some areas with the result that the wines lack intensity of flavour. The grapes left unaffected by the rain, produced some very good wines.

**Oregon**☆☆to☆☆☆☆ A wet but sunny start to the year was followed by warm, dry weather through to the harvest. Heavy rain caused some growers to panic, but conditions improved in October. Yields were of average proportions; those who were prepared to take the risk, postponing the harvest until after the rains, picked mature, ripe grapes and produced the best wines.

*Some of the top Pinot Noirs, like Eyrie, still drinking well. Otherwise, drink up.*

## 1985

**Washington**☆☆☆☆ The second of two small crops resulting from unusual spring frosts. The vintage was warm enough for an early harvest, interrupted for a very short while by a cool spell in early September. The reds were big and tannic; the best wines from grapes picked early with high acidity levels.

**Oregon**☆☆☆☆ After a cool, dry start to the year temperatures rose in late May. Early June saw some rain but thereafter the weather was warm and dry, providing excellent conditions for flowering. The growing season and harvest enjoyed the same good conditions and the vintage was mainly completed by mid-October. Quantity was average and the wines showed real ageing potential. This was a vintage which increased international recognition of Oregon wines.

*Mainly fully mature.*

## 1984

**Washington**☆☆ A very uneven year. Crops were damaged by winter frost and the cool spring weather further diminished the yield. Summer saw good, sunny weather and autumn was dry but cooler than usual. Despite this the crop ripened satisfactorily and some good wines were made, although quality varied.

**Oregon**☆ As with the Washington vintage, this was a variable year. The first five months were exceptionally wet; temperatures rose in May but this encouraged mildew. Fruit set did not complete until well into July. Thereafter temperatures were low and the harvest was held back until November in the hope that conditions would improve: they did not. Large crop of light wines.

*Few seen. Drink up.*

## 1983

**Washington**☆☆☆☆ A cool year, but late summer/autumn gave warm, sunny ripening weather. Picking began on September 19. A brief frost caused damage in lower lying vineyard areas, but the other sites made exceptionally concentrated, lively wines. Very good reds: charming fruit; excellent structure; ageing potential.

**Oregon**☆☆☆☆ The vines flowered in June in perfect weather and thereafter the season was warm and dry with some benign rainfall in late August. Picking took place during the first fortnight of October. A larger than average crop; some growers waited too long before picking but otherwise these were wines with good ageing potential.

*Whites now far too old. Reds fully mature; drink up.*

## 1982

**Washington**☆☆ The vines flowered in good conditions and a warm summer was followed by a cool and extended harvest, beginning September 21 and ending November 9, with some rain. Charming but lightish wines. Many of the better reds have lasted well and shown good character, but lack intensity.

**Oregon**☆☆☆ After a cool, wet spring the weather was perfect for flowering in June. Thereafter trouble-free conditions prevailed for the remainder of the year and picking was complete by early October. These were very good wines, but will last less well than the 1983 vintage, despite having the acidity needed for ageing.

*Drink up.*

## 1981

**Washington**☆☆☆ The cool, damp weather at the start of the year held through to flowering, limiting the size of the crop, but warm summer weather helped advance development. Cool autumn nights and warm days fully ripened the grapes and picking began September 21. These were fruity, substantial wines; the reds showed great depth and potential longevity.

**Oregon**☆☆☆ The months leading to July were generally cool, then wet weather retarded flowering until mid-July. As in Washington, warm, sunny weather advanced development until late September when the rain returned. Picking began in early October and the yield was very low. These were wines which would reveal their worth with long keeping.

*The best Pinot Noirs holding up. Best to drink soon.*

## 1980

**Washington**☆☆☆ The eruption of Mount St Helens blanketed many vineyards in ash throughout this region. Fortunately this occurred prior to flowering.

This was the coolest growing season of the 1980s and the vineyards had not entirely recovered from the severe freeze of 1978 and 1979. Consequently the crop was small and the wines were light; many, though, were well-balanced, with moderate body. The best reds showed longevity.

**Oregon**☆☆☆ Cold, wet weather prevailed throughout the spring until June. Here too, vineyards were covered with large deposits of ash from the volcano, but vines were left undamaged. A late flowering finished in July. Picking began in early October producing a very small crop of excellent, concentrated, dry wines.

*Attractive, rich, root-like and earthy; the true Pinot varietal character; but doubtless peaked by now.*

## EARLIER PACIFIC NORTHWEST VINTAGES

Earlier vintages of these wines are hard to find, but the 1979 Amity and Knudson-Erath Pinot Noirs were showing well in the mid-1980s. But on the whole, the few wines that were made in the 1960s, if any exist at all, will be no more than curiosities. Times, and winemaking, have moved on.

# New York State

It will come as a surprise to most Europeans that New York is a wine producing state, so dominant is California. Wines have in fact been made in the Finger Lake District, just south of Ontario, for well over a century. However, until the early 1960s only native American varieties, not the species *Vitis vinifera*, and hybrids were grown.

Virtually the sole pioneer of classic European grape varieties was the late Dr Konstantin Frank, followed in the 1970s by one or two small wineries such as Glenora and Heron Hill, planting first Riesling, then Chardonnay. In the mid-1970s there was a revival of winemaking in the less northerly, less exposed Hudson Valley, and, even more recently, with classic whites and reds planted on sea-girt Long Island.

New pioneers, enthusiasts and state-of-the-art winemaking, particularly on Long Island, have successfully changed the New York State wine scene: Pinot Noir, Cabernet Sauvignon, Sauvignon Blanc and Chardonnay are now produced. As with New Zealand, the reds, though well made, have as yet no track record.

Wines made from the native American grape varieties such as Catawba and Concord – very much an acquired taste – and hybrids like Seibel, are not covered in these brief vintage notes that follow. The lighter dry whites, as always, should be drunk while they are young and fresh, although some of the Finger Lake Chardonnays and late-harvest whites will keep for up to five years and sometimes even more.

## 1997 ☆☆☆

A good, but uniformly average year which was better than 1996, but not as fine as 1995. The ripening period was warm, dry and sunny, resulting in the grapes ripening consistently up until the harvest in September.

Luckily the majority of producers in Long Island had picked all of their grapes before the rains came in November and quality was good. The Finger Lakes produced some fine Riesling and lighter style Gewürztraminer. This year generally gave wines of quality, but perhaps with not quite the distinction of many of the previous 1990s vintages.

*A pity that the distinctive and, in good years, excellent German-style wines are not better known. It is significant that the German varietals Riesling and Gewürztraminer, are eminently suitable to survive the cold and vigorous winters of the Finger Lakes area. Best at three to five years of age. Long Island is developing well and the reds worth watching.*

## 1996 ☆☆ to ☆☆☆

A break in the run of perfect vintages came this year as a cold and wet season prevailed. Frost in May affected some northern areas, reducing yields and resulting in winemakers requiring bought-in juice. Damp conditions throughout the summer encouraged problems of rot and reduced the size of the crop. The weather improved during the harvest and those producers who selected well made some good wines.

Yields in Long Island were significantly lower and in general styles were leaner and lighter than usual. In the Finger Lakes production was more substantial, but large berries produced less concentrated juice and the level of quality was not as good as that of 1995. Sugar levels were down in Chardonnay and Riesling leaving some producers contemplating chaptalisation.

*Clearly a vintage for early consumption, probably and mainly by the locals and enthusiasts in New York city.*

## 1995 ☆☆☆☆

The third successful vintage in a row was the result of a prolonged and warm summer which provided ideal ripening conditions. The grapes reached full maturity and ripeness levels which resulted in the red wines having great extract, colour and depth and the white wines achieving near perfect balance of fruit and acidity. The ideal weather continued throughout the harvest and no rot problems were experienced – rot is often a danger in this region during the harvest due to climatic conditions. It is worth noting that as the vines age, yield and quality are improving year by year.

*It is inaccurate to think of New York State as being a new wine region; perhaps this does apply to Long Island, but the Finger Lakes district is relatively old established, producing first rate dry whites for early drinking.*

## 1994 ☆☆☆☆

A good vintage with higher than expected yields after a harsh winter. Although the harvest was larger than the previous year's by about 65 per cent, the quality varieties relevant to this book had only average sized yields at best. Growing conditions were favourable throughout the state. Spring and summer were warm and dry with a healthy amount of rainfall. Unfortunately, frosts hit the region in the spring. Hudson Bay experienced the worst of this and many young shoots were damaged causing as much as 40 per cent losses.

Overall, results were good to excellent and the wines have good balance. Sugar levels were high, notably on Long Island, where the reds have deep colour and soft tannins. Wines from the Finger Lakes showed a great aromatic quality.

*Whites: early consumption. Reds: worth cellaring.*

## 1993 ☆☆☆☆

A very good vintage throughout the state but with greatly reduced yields. The previous year's cool, wet summer left the vines with a reduced number of buds, and in a vulnerable physical state.

Grape clusters were then small but very intense. Throughout the state, the growing season was dry, warm and long, providing ideal ripening conditions. Although the crop was on average 22 per cent smaller than the previous year's, the results were exciting. The levels of sugar and acidity were frequently ideal.

Most notable are the sweeter wines from the Finger Lakes area and Long Island produced very good Chardonnay and Merlot. The vintage resulted in many "reserve wines" with significant ageing potential.

*Dry whites, drink soon. Sweet white, probably at peak. The reds still do not have sufficient track record. Best drunk young.*

## 1992 ~

A very poor vintage. Throughout the state, conditions were cold and wet for the entire growing season. There is very little one can say about this vintage, other than that it was extremely difficult, diluted and in large proportions. Fortunately, this washout was followed by two great vintages.

*Drink up.*

## 1991 ☆☆☆

Clearly a well-above average vintage. Unlike California and the Pacific Northwest a mild winter; early spring and flowering; warm summer and early harvest. In the northerly Finger Lakes District the earliest-ever start of harvest, August 27. A large crop, Riesling and Gewürztraminer particularly successful. On Long Island the warm dry year produced wines to equal the 1988s – best vintage of the decade – a situation echoed in the Hudson River Valley

*Drink up whites . Reds soon.*

## 1990 ☆☆☆☆

A very good vintage. With the exception of the Finger Lakes where yields were good, but crop size was slightly below average. Well-timed rainfall was above average, but evenly distributed, which contributed to good berry size. Ideal ripening weather in September led to premature harvests for some grape varieties, yet with the same sugar levels as the previous year. Overall, grapes were clean and healthy, promising wines of very good quality.

*Whites drink up. Reds drink now.*

## 1989 ☆ to ☆☆☆

Following the 1988 drought, groundwater levels were low until late spring rains. Disease threatened but stopped before it was too late. This, coupled with the effects of hurricane Hugo on Long Island, made this a difficult year for many. Improved techniques and careful timing helped winemakers overcome problems.

Overall, the early-ripening varieties fared best, making this a good year for sparkling and white table wines. Those from the Lake Erie region had very good varietal character, and Hudson Valley growers considered the quality of their grapes to be excellent having fought against such difficult weather conditions.

*Drink soon.*

### 1988☆☆☆☆☆

Deemed "a winemaker's dream" – growers enjoyed dry weather and a perfect summer and autumn: warm days and cool nights. With the exception of grapes left for late-harvest, and ice-wines, the vintage was complete by mid-October. Total yield was down by 12 per cent due to the dry weather and grapes were perfectly clean and healthy. A vintage of powerful, distinctive wines; it was the best year since 1980 for the reds and the whites alike.

*Whites should have been consumed by now. Best reds still drinking well.*

### 1987☆☆to☆☆☆☆

A year which ranged from average to very good, but was overshadowed by the two superior vintages on either side. Growers experienced occasional adverse weather conditions, including strong winds in mid-September on Long Island which dampened hopes for a trouble-free harvest and wet weather throughout that month in many areas. Grapes had, however, ripened well until then and the harvest was already two weeks ahead of schedule, so adverse effects were minimised.

This was a well-structured vintage. The Long Island wineries reported better success with reds than whites, while in the Finger Lakes winemakers reported the reverse. In the end, the hybrid Seyval Blanc and red *Vitis vinifera* varieties were considered to be the most consistent.

*Reds ready.*

### 1986☆to☆☆☆

A poor year for many growers whose crops were spoilt by a wet harvest. There were, however, some exceptions. Long Island growers considered this to be a very good vintage. Their wines were typically aromatic, the whites had good colour, were smooth and had lingering finishes; their reds showed good ageing potential. A good year also for Lake Erie, a Chardonnay from this district ranked second among 223 Chardonnays from around the world in the 1987 Intervin International Competition.

*Whites too old. Reds, drink up.*

### 1985☆☆☆

Generally very good, except for Long Island where vines were devastated by hurricane Gloria which struck on September 27. Until then it had been a fine vintage; the Chardonnay had just ripened and made it to the cellars, the Sauvignon Blanc was nipped in the bud, as was the Cabernet Sauvignon. Those with skill, however, made good wines.

*Drink up.*

### 1984☆☆☆

The second of two unusually large crops. Quality of the wines varied depending on the grape variety and the region. In the Finger Lakes most early varieties had a problem-free harvest but a severe frost on October 6 virtually stopped the later grapes from ripening further. However, in the Hudson River, later varieties did well. Seyval Blanc and Chardonnay made the best quality wines.

This was also the year that marked a transition in New York State away from the dessert wines and red wines towards the dry whites and sparkling wines; and away from the native American grape varieties towards the *Vitis vinifera* varieties.

*Drink up.*

## EARLIER NEW YORK STATE VINTAGES

Long Island enjoyed an Indian summer in **1983**☆☆☆☆ and produced deeply coloured wines which were exceptionally soft when young, though were not for ageing. **1982**☆☆☆☆ and **1980**☆☆☆☆ saw good wines made, and **1981**☆ a small crop of indifferent quality. Some pre-1980 vintages of above average quality include: **1979** (Riesling), **1978** (Riesling, Chardonnay and late-harvest Gewürztraminer), **1976** (Cabernet Sauvignon) and **1975** (Chardonnay and late-harvest Riesling). All past their best.

# Australia

Australia is a continent, albeit a sparsely populated one. The wine areas are far apart, the oldest classic district, the Hunter Valley in New South Wales, being some 1,287 kilometres (800 miles) from the newest vineyard areas of Western Australia. The cooler regions such as Coonawarra and Tasmania, are in the south. Confusingly, it is quite normal practice to produce good red wine blended from different grape varieties grown in different regions.

Though vine growing and winemaking dates back to the penal colony days of the early 19th century, the demand was for fortified and, frankly, undistinguished table wines. Thanks to new attitudes and techniques, to brilliant pioneers, imaginative wine education and publicity, the past 25 years or so has witnessed a quality revolution. The results are instantly appealing giving Chardonnays; impressive reds, straight Cabernets and Shiraz and well-constructed blends; fruity Rieslings, idiosyncratic Semillons, not to mention luscious Muscats and very good sparkling wines.

However, unlike the more temperate and stable regions of Northern Europe, the weather in Australia can fluctuate between extremes of heat and drought and excessive torrential rain. Vintage variations can be correspondingly dramatic.

## 1997☆☆☆to☆☆☆☆

A definite success for premium wine production, up six per cent on last year (red wines by nearly two per cent and white wines by nearly ten per cent). These were positive results for the premium planting programme; however, unfortunately prices remain high as demand increases continually. A cool spring and early summer, with some frost problems during flowering, diminished true crop potential. Excessive heat in February caused vines to shut down and delayed the vintage by two weeks. A long Indian summer followed with warm, still days and cool nights ripening the grapes to a rich concentration.

**New South Wales** A few first-time harvests in Cowra this year, however yields were still 15 per cent down. The Hunter Valley suffered rot after rain in February, whereas Mudgee saw increased yields after a very dry year. Some excellent Semillon and Chardonnay, but not a year for red wines.

**South Australia** Adelaide Hills, McLaren Vale and the Barossa Valley harvested super-concentrated late-ripening reds, but uneven fruit set cut yields. Clare Valley made excellent Riesling due to welcome pre-harvest rain. Eden Valley produced excellent reds despite frost and storms; Padthaway harvested the ripest Chardonnay in years. Coonawarra lost 30 per cent in volume, but gained in quality, especially Sauvignon Blanc.

**Victoria** The Yarra Valley had its driest ripening in 100 years, the yields fell by up to 50 per cent – the Pinot Noir and sparkling wines were especially good. In contrast the Great Western region had a bumper crop of high quality grapes.

**Western Australia** A long and challenging late vintage yielded exceptional Semillon and Shiraz. Some had problems with bird damage in the Perth Hills, yet yields were still up 25 per cent.

*It is important to consider: this is a southern hemisphere continent, the districts are far apart and produce wines in very different conditions. Yet quality as well as variety is consistently good. Whites for drinking fairly soon as they appear on the market; most reds also best young and fruity. The best, in a year like this, will repay keeping.*

## 1996☆☆☆to☆☆☆☆

The heavens looked favourably upon this vintage in Australia. Winter rains replenished reserves and a warm spring triggered bud burst three weeks prematurely. Consequently picking started in early February in the Riverlands and finished in May with the *botrytis*-affected grapes of the Eden Valley. This produced high quality wines, in sufficient quantity to satisfy the market. Yields were approximately ten per cent higher than in 1995, providing a welcome break in the trend of rising prices for Australian wines. The largest increase was in non-premium white wines; premium red wines fell slightly short of the average.

**New South Wales** A very dry winter caused worry, but spring rain provided a good, clean vintage. Unfortunately, storms in October reduced the expected yield. In Mudgee and Cowra, later ripening Cabernet Sauvignon and Merlot had great results.

**South Australia** The Barossa Valley and McLaren Vale achieved outstanding quality in their Cabernet and Shiraz – some of which was sourced for the Grange and Penfolds Bin 707. Padthaway also saw excellent quality in all their varietals.

**Victoria** After a touch of frost in Great Western, results were very good for Chardonnay, Riesling, Sauvignon Blanc, Cabernet and Shiraz. Rutherglen also made some outstanding fortified wines.

**Western Australia** Definitely a year for the reds, especially the Cabernets. In the Margaret River region conditions were perfect allowing the grapes a slow and even development, and providing fully ripe and balanced wines.

*Remember that vintage time in the southern hemisphere is our spring. The whites are two years old this spring (1998) and are being shipped for early drinking.*

*Most reds are more amenable than their French counterparts and, with the exception of Grange and one or two "new classics", are best drunk soon.*

## 1995☆☆☆☆

This was a very difficult vintage as severe drought gripped the whole of eastern and southeastern coastal areas. Water stocks for irrigation were seriously depleted which resulted in highly stressed vines, consequently reducing the final size of the yields. Overall, the crop appears to have been reduced by 20 to 25 per cent. Nevertheless, the quality is good to excellent.

**New South Wales** Yields were severely reduced in this region, grapes used for bulk wine production were most badly affected.

**South Australia** Losses, sometimes as high as 30 per cent of the crop, were considerable throughout. Late rains salvaged the crop in many areas; but the quality, at this early stage, appears to be high, particularly for the red wines.

**Victoria** This state was much less affected by drought than its neighbouring states and the results are excellent, although slightly reduced in quantity.

**Western Australia** An ideal growing season resulted in a fine crop throughout the region. Some yields were reduced in the Margaret River area due to dry summer conditions causing the vines to become stressed, but the main – and common – problem faced by this region was damage by birds at harvest time.

*Whites, for early consumption. Reds, from mid to long term depending on district, type and quality.*

## 1994☆☆☆☆

After the disastrous 1993 vintage, 1994 turned out to be a godsend – very dry, warm conditions offering a prolonged ripening season. The response was almost euphoric with many regarding it as one of the best Australian vintages ever. Overall, the crop was large with high levels of quality, intense fruit, balancing acidity and soft, ripe tannins.

**New South Wales** Unrepresentative of this vintage, this region was beset by more problems than other parts of Australia. In the Hunter Valley the dryness and heat resulted in bush fires. In other areas heavy rains were a problem in the run up to, and during, the harvest. Overall, the results varied from disappointing to good and the volumes were reduced by ten to 30 per cent.

**South Australia** An exceptionally dry vintage and a long ripening season was the result of mild, warm weather. For many growers the harvest started two weeks later than usual. Fortunately all varieties have a great intensity of flavour, and the wines should age successfully.

**Victoria** Flowering and ripening were delayed by cold spells, the most worrying occurring half way through the summer. The weather did improve and many areas experienced an Indian summer, but the harvest was generally about a fortnight late. Results were of considerable quality, but overall quantities were down, often by as much as 30 per cent.

**Western Australia** Extremely dry conditions; the period from September to April was the driest ever recorded in Western Australia. All grape varieties ripened in optimum conditions and the lack of rot and disease was remarkable. Exciting results.

*An attractive vintage. Good dry whites for early and easy consumption. Reds of very acceptable commercial quality and some Pinot Noirs and Shiraz well worth cellaring.*

## 1993 ☆to☆☆☆

It never fails to surprise me that weather conditions in the southern hemisphere frequently mimic those in the north despite the converse calendar, their spring coinciding with Europe and California's autumn. Having said this, it is always dangerous to generalise about conditions across as widespread a continent as Australia.

With the exception of the Hunter Valley the Australian summer was marred by incessant rain, which not only hampered ripening but caused severe mildew problems. Those grapes that survived benefited from the late burst of hot weather. However, there was a 12 per cent shortfall of red grapes, Cabernet Sauvignon being worst affected, prices have consequently risen.

**New South Wales** The Hunter Valley was the only region not affected by the rains. Consequently, the results are good with healthy levels of production.

**South Australia** Cabernet Sauvignon and Shiraz production were dramatically down in Coonawarra, whereas the neighbouring Padthaway's crop was of more regular proportions. In the latter area, the white varieties posed more of a problem with losses, Chardonnay suffering the most.

**Victoria** This generally cooler region suffers particularly from damp conditions. A cool, wet summer resulted in reduced yields and many disappointing wines due to widespread rot.

**Western Australia** The Margaret River region was severely hit by hail in some areas which damaged the vines considerably. The region underwent further heavy losses while the harvest was taking place, due to birds. Meanwhile, the Swan Valley had one of its most successful vintages for years.

*A roller coaster vintage and hard to advise. Drink up the dry whites. The reds vary enormously, most are drinking well now, but the best, beyond 2000.*

## 1992 ☆to☆☆☆

This was one of the most difficult vintages in the past 20 years, making generalisations hazardous – some very good, and possibly great, wines will come out of it; but at the same time so will some very ordinary ones.

**New South Wales** A region which experiences very different weather patterns to those of southern Australia – the harvest in the Hunter Valley is one to two months earlier. This year was one to forget. A severe winter and spring drought sharply reduced potential yields and was followed by heavy rain throughout the harvest. The odd Semillon, a few Chardonnays and occasional Cabernet Sauvignon will succeed, but be careful when buying.

**South Australia** The coolest summer since records began, well over a century ago. Powdery mildew appeared on a scale not seen since 1974. Three periods of rain in early March, the end of March, and late April turned vintage time into a game of Russian Roulette. Those producers who guessed correctly have made some wonderfully intense and aromatic wines; those who got caught by mildew and/or rain have fared poorly.

**Victoria** Similar summer weather, the coolest this century, but missing the rain. From northeast Victoria (superb Muscat and "Tokay") through to the Yarra Valley in the south (great Pinot Noir), the state's 200 vignerons have a smile broadened further by the good though not excessive yields.

**Western Australia** Again with the same viticultural vexations of South Australia. Yields were high, as were expectations, but rain during the vintage caused headaches for many winemakers. It also has to be remembered that like California, most Australian regions expect (and are often blessed by) dry growing and harvest seasons. The white wines suffered most this year. Some good Cabernet Sauvignon was produced in the south and will almost certainly redeem the situation.

*Whites drink up, reds drink soon.*

## 1991 ☆☆☆☆

A generally warm and dry vintage produced smaller than usual crops and wines of power and concentration. For some regions a better year than 1990, but not for all.

**New South Wales** For once the Hunter Valley had a good growing season followed by a dry vintage, resulting in fleshy, rich wines which will give tremendous pleasure early in their lives, but not particularly long-lived – especially the white wines.

**South Australia** A wet spring followed by a dry, warm summer and autumn. Yields were down on 1990 by ten to 30 per cent, with red wines most affected. The compensation was great depth of colour and extract, although time will show whether they have the vinous heart of the best of the 1990s.

**Victoria** Much the same conditions as South Australia, with yields down by 15 to 33 per cent. All regions – of which there are a dozen – had a relatively early start in March and moved through to the end of April in benign conditions, making lush, concentrated wines which will provide a great contrast to the more elegant but lighter wines of 1990.

**Western Australia** This year the Swan Valley had a mild (relatively speaking) vintage of high quality. Ironically, the southern regions experienced a Swan Valley-like heatwave in early February which was most damaging in the lower Great Southern region, (but which did not prevent some of the top vineyards making lovely wines from yields down by 15 to 40 per cent) and which had much less impact in Margaret River.

*The whites are rich and full-flavoured wines which are fully mature. The reds are rich and concentrated and need further bottle-ageing.*

## 1990☆☆☆☆

A good growing season for most regions in Australia and a mild summer suggested that this would be a vintage with relatively high natural acid levels and therefore suitable for ageing.

**New South Wales** A wet winter followed by excellent conditions during the spring and summer. Bud-break, flowering and fruit set all took place in ideal conditions. However, around harvest time rainfall was heavy, diluting the Chardonnay and Semillon in the Lower Hunter Valley and consequently reducing the yield. The later-harvested reds were less affected, but overall, this was an uneven year.

**South Australia** A wet spring in most areas, particularly Coonawarra, was followed by a cool summer. Vines then suffered some stress due to exceptionally dry weather throughout the growing season. Picking began early in the Barossa Valley thanks to prompt ripening of Pinot Noir. On the whole, average yields. Winegrowers in the Adelaide Hills judged this to be their best vintage for three years.

**Victoria** A generally good growing season, experiencing cool temperatures and two wet spells in the western areas. Humidity caused the odd problem, particularly in the Yarra Valley, but disease was kept under control. Growers held out until the end of March for their Cabernet Sauvignon, anticipating a very special vintage. Yields were up by 20 per cent.

**Western Australia** Mild weather during the summer provided good growing conditions. Picking began around mid-March, later in the Swan Valley. Late February rains caused some bunch rot in the later ripening grapes, particularly Chenin Blanc. Yields were above average in the Margaret River, but lower in Swan Valley. Overall, the quality was good.

*Dry whites drink up. The reds, soon.*

## 1989☆to☆☆☆

After five highly successful years, this vintage came as something of a disappointment to Australian winemakers.

**New South Wales** The Hunter Valley harvested first after a wet spring, dry summer and further wet weather just before picking. In the Lower Hunter Valley rain delayed picking. The whites were no more than satisfactory. A mediocre year for Cabernet Sauvignon, better for Shiraz.

**South Australia** High rainfall in the Barossa Valley was followed by three months of dry weather from January onwards. A cool growing season produced healthy vines and a heatwave in early March reduced the yields. Where irrigation was used, the heat did not affect the wines so much.

Overall, a good but not great year. The best wines were the Rhine Rieslings and the Chardonnays. In Coonawarra growing conditions were also very good, except for some rainfall further into the vintage causing minor *botrytis* in the later ripening grapes. In general, the whites had good character, those which were late-harvested being light, but fruity and elegant.

**Victoria** This region experienced a considerably problematic year. High winds during spring in the Yarra Valley resulted in an uneven fruit set which seriously diminished crops. Apart from the odd period of hot weather the summer was mild and wet, leading to widespread rot. Some fine wines were made, in particular deep-coloured, flavoursome Pinot Noirs and attractive Chardonnays. Other wines tended to be rather unripe and light.

In Milawa a combination of better conditions and modern technology, made this a more successful vintage, with some excellent Muscats produced. There were, sadly, some casualties: bad harvest weather forced early picking and consequently no "noble" late-harvest Rieslings were produced. The Cabernet Sauvignon grapes were picked earlier than usual and tended to make finer, lighter wines.

**Western Australia** An easier year generally. A hot, early vintage in the Swan Valley turned cool, resulting in light wines. In Margaret River cool weather and heavy rainfall in mid-January and February caused some *botrytis* in the Rhine Rieslings but this was arrested by dry, warm weather in March. The white grapes generally made good wines with high acid levels, particularly in the Chardonnays and Semillons. The reds have good fruit flavours and show much promise.

*The fragrant Rieslings and Gewürztraminers and bigger Chardonnays can still be delicious. Best Shiraz delightful now.*

## 1988☆☆to☆☆☆☆

Overall, a year which produced some exceptional wines, despite difficult weather conditions.

**New South Wales** In the Upper Hunter Valley, a warm, wet winter followed by a mild growing season enabled growers to pick early before the rains came. In the Lower Hunter, however, the harvest was delayed and rain nearly ruined the vintage. Yields were above average and subtle, elegant wines were produced.

**South Australia** In the Barossa Valley the year followed a similar pattern to that in New South Wales, but included a hailstorm on October 14 which cost some growers up to 50 per cent of their crop. On the whole, a large yield of good wines was produced. Further south, in Coonawarra, the dry, warm weather meant irrigation was necessary and resulted in the earliest vintage of the decade. Yields had been slashed by September frosts but quality was correspondingly enhanced.

**Victoria** An excellent year for Milawa. The perfect weather conditions produced outstanding Shiraz, and the late harvest proved ideal for dessert wines. Some promising liqueur Muscats.

**Western Australia** Hail and high winds in the spring plus excessive heat in the summer, made this a difficult year in Margaret River. The Rieslings and Cabernet Sauvignons tended to lack acidity but, conversely, earlier ripening varieties showed good balance in their wines.

*The light, dry, fruity whites should all have been consumed by now, though the heavier Chardonnays still good. The top reds are ready for drinking, but will develop further.*

## 1987 ☆☆☆☆

An excellent vintage throughout all of Australia, for red wines and white wines alike.

**New South Wales** Apart from heavy rain in October/November in the Upper Hunter Valley, followed by cold weather which disrupted flowering, conditions were good.

**South Australia** Heavy hailstorms in the Barossa region diminished the potential yield of the earlier ripening varieties, including the Chardonnays and Pinot Noirs. Then high winds here, and in Coonawarra, pruned the crop further. Thereafter conditions were generally good and the harvest began late – mid-May in Coonawarra where quality was not up to that of the previous year. Otherwise an elegant vintage.

**Victoria** Apart from a poor fruit set in the the Yarra Valley, which reduced yields by 30 to 50 per cent, conditions were very good.

**Western Australia** Here, too, good conditions prevailed. A mild spring saw good bud-break and a cool growing season resulted in a late vintage. High yields, high quality.

*Wonderfully luscious Chardonnays, the best still delicious. The lighter Semillons, Sauvignon Blancs and Rieslings should have been consumed. Shiraz and Pinot Noir well developed; Cabernet Sauvignon can be kept longer.*

## 1986 ☆☆☆☆☆

A consistently good vintage, possibly the best of the decade.

**New South Wales** An extremely wet winter in the Hunter Valley followed by a damp, mild spring resulted in an excellent fruit set and flowering. Dry weather held until early June but mild temperatures allowed the grapes to ripen slowly. Picking began ten days late and conditions were excellent for the sweet wines. Long-lived, tannic reds and superb Semillons.

**South Australia** A mild winter and spring in the Barossa region. Temperatures during the growing season in the hills were the lowest on record, but luckily rose everywhere in time for the harvest. Unfortunately, rain around mid-April encouraged the development of *botrytis* on the later ripening Rieslings. However, overall, this area also produced some superbly balanced, powerful and stylish wines.

**Victoria** Again, a cool growing season. The summer saw the lowest seasonal temperatures on record; grapes in Milawa ripened very late so that some of the normally late varieties were ready for picking before the earlier varieties.

**Western Australia** Generally, conditions were similar to those in the rest of Australia. There were exceptions, including a tropical cyclone in the Swan Valley, making February here the wettest on record, and yields were down by 20 per cent. Heavy showers also diluted sugar levels during the harvest in some localised areas of Margaret River.

*Chardonnays of the quality and style that have put Australia right into the top league are, if coolly cellared, still drinking well. Perfect late-harvest Rieslings are lovely now. Substantial reds, such as Grange Hermitage, are superb and needing more bottle-age. Best reds will last until 2000 and possibly beyond.*

## 1985☆☆☆☆

As with 1986, this was another consistently good year throughout Australia, although it was largely overshadowed by the vintages on either side.

**New South Wales** Good growing conditions in the Hunter Valley, with high temperatures in January, brought the harvest forward to the middle of the month. In the Lower Hunter Valley a January hailstorm caused a loss of up to 30 per cent of the crop.

**South Australia** Heavy rains in Barossa during spring saw good development of the vines but a summer drought caused problems for unirrigated estates. Late March rains caused further problems with powdery mildew. Sugar levels were below normal in Coonawarra due to cool weather, but the conditions allowed the later varieties to ripen perfectly. South Australia saw its largest ever crop, due mainly to the introduction of new vineyards.

**Victoria** The coolest ripening season in Milawa for years was followed by a warm Indian summer. The harvest finished in May, producing grapes with high sugar levels. Heavy rain during the harvest in Yarra Valley reduced yields by as much as 50 per cent, but grapes brought in prior to these rainstorms made good wines.

**Western Australia** The wines from the Margaret River were the stars of the 1985 vintage. High winds damaged vines during flowering and fruit set. Cool temperatures prevailed until late February. Picking took place in ideal conditions.

*A strange coincidence that 1985s in the southern hemisphere are as agreeably fruity and balanced as the 1985s in France. Attractive, rich but easy-drinking reds. Chardonnays fully mature so drink up. The late-picked dessert wines and Muscats can be delicious.*

## 1984☆☆☆☆

The first of a run of elegant, stylish Australian vintages.

**New South Wales** Unlike most of Australia, the Hunter Valley did not enjoy a good year. Vines were damaged in the Upper Hunter by Christmas and New Year storms, then hail. Conditions were better in the Lower Hunter Valley where cool weather encouraged excellent development. Rain later on, however, caused mildew and rot.

**South Australia** Despite a wet start to the year the yield was low in Barossa which was still suffering from the effects of the previous year's drought. A cool summer and autumn encouraged good levels of *botrytis*, making this an excellent year for the late-harvest wines. Outstanding Cabernet Sauvignon and Shiraz.

**Victoria** Stable conditions in Milawa made for a trouble-free year. In the Yarra Valley cool, wet weather throughout the year delayed the harvest; some very good late-harvest wines were made.

**Western Australia** Apart from a lack of late rain in the Margaret River region, and a cooler than normal growing season in the Swan Valley, this was a trouble-free year.

*The dry whites should have been consumed by now, but those of the Lindemans' Padthaway and Tyrrell's Vat 47 quality are still surprisingly good. The reds are good, but not great. The late-harvest Rieslings are superb.*

## 1983☆☆

An excellent vintage for some, but most areas were dogged by disastrous weather conditions.

**New South Wales** The third of four years of drought in the Hunter Valley, reducing yields to below 50 per cent of normal in the Upper Hunter Valley. The Lower Hunter Valley vintage was salvaged by torrential rain at bud-burst. Some excellent reds and rich, full-flavoured Semillons and Chardonnays were made.

**South Australia** The long drought in the Barossa region ended halfway through the vintage with widespread flooding, a carpet of mud and debris covering many vineyards. In Coonawarra conditions were better, with the exception of late rains around the harvest. Variable quality.

**Victoria** An early vintage in Milawa followed a cool growing season and a hot spell in February. A year of disasters in the Yarra Valley region after frosts in October, hailstorms in November, a summer-long drought and an invasion of European wasps all caused considerable damage.

**Western Australia** In contrast to the rest of Australia, this was a near-perfect year in the Margaret River region: excellent conditions throughout the growing season which ended with two benign falls of rain in February. Yields were up by ten per cent.

*Despite dramatic weather conditions some lovely golden Chardonnays and some velvety Pinot Noirs and Cabernets. Most need drinking, many past their best.*

## 1982☆☆☆☆

Near-perfect conditions in most areas produced some well-balanced, stylish wines.

**New South Wales** Good levels of rainfall throughout the spring and summer in the Hunter Valley brought an end to the drought. Warm to hot weather followed, enabling the fruit to ripen well.

**South Australia** Good spring rains in Barossa counter-balanced high temperatures in January and February. A late harvest, which did not finish until May, produced some excellent wines. Coonawarra enjoyed a stable year and produced fine Cabernet Sauvignon with exceptional ageing potential.

**Victoria** A mild growing season was followed by rains which delayed the harvest in Milawa. An average sized yield. In the Yarra Valley the cool, dry summer enabled fruit to ripen well and an above average yield was brought in. Again, a very good year.

**Western Australia** Margaret River saw its coolest growing season for many years with much frost damage. In the Swan Valley it was a cool, stable year producing wines of good fruit.

*Buttery Chardonnays and superb late-harvest Rieslings should have been consumed. The superlative reds: Penfolds Bin 707 Cabernet Sauvignon and, the mainly Shiraz, Grange Hermitage have years of life ahead.*

## 1981 ☆☆

A difficult and generally unpopular year. The hot, early vintage produced dull reds and whites which never improved.

**New South Wales** A serious drought throughout the Hunter Valley drastically reduced yields.

**South Australia** Winegrowers in the Barossa harvested their grapes early. The yield was very small, and, as a result of the drought, the berries were generally small and of uneven quality. Coonawarra, however, missed the worst of the drought, and had a slightly better year.

**Victoria** Mild, occasionally hot weather in Milawa led to an early harvest taking place in ideal conditions. Some good reds.

**Western Australia** Poor weather disrupted the flowering in Margaret River, and yields were further reduced by high winds in late spring. But, thereafter, conditions were good. In the Swan Valley fewer problems were experienced and the grapes were harvested in excellent condition.

. *Drink up.*

## 1980 ☆☆☆☆

A stunning vintage with an excellent reputation, especially for Cabernet Sauvignon.

**New South Wales** In all parts of the Hunter Valley this was an exceptionally hot and dry year. Picking began several weeks earlier than usual, beginning January 11 in the Lower Hunter and continuing into early March. No problems with rot or mildew, but drought resulted in a very low yield.

**South Australia** In both Barossa and Coonawarra this was a trouble-free year which produced a large crop of grapes. The Cabernet Sauvignon based wines have excellent ageing potential.

**Victoria** Described as a "copybook year" in Milawa for all styles from table to dessert wine. In the Yarra Valley a severe year-long drought produced only a small crop of good, ripe fruit, which made excellent wines of all styles.

**Western Australia** A dry year for the Margaret River producers where winemaking was still in its infancy. In the Swan Valley a mild to warm year produced evenly-ripened fruit.

*All whites should have been consumed by now but the beefy, tannic Cabernets are keeping well.*

## 1970s

Prior to 1980 it is safe to say that all the white wines will be well past their best, but Cabernet Sauvignon, the best Shiraz and blended reds can still be superb.

Star ratings for top reds: **1979** ☆☆☆☆ **1978** ☆☆☆☆ **1977** ☆☆☆☆ **1976** ☆☆☆☆ **1975** ☆☆☆☆☆ **1974** ☆ **1973** ☆☆☆☆ **1972** ~ **1971** ☆☆☆☆☆

## 1960s

The decade of the 1960s was one of development, the market dominated by the bigger, well-established producers such as Lindemans and Penfolds.

The best years for Cabernet Sauvignon and Shiraz: **1967**☆☆☆ **1966**☆☆☆☆☆ **1965**☆☆ **1963**☆☆☆☆ **1962**☆☆☆☆☆ **1960**☆☆ – all fully mature.

# New Zealand

Of all the so-called "New World" wines, New Zealand's were the newest and, in relation to appeal, quality and price, most successful. Prior to 1970 New Zealand was noted for sheep, butter and beautiful, uncrowded countryside. Then vines were planted and, throughout the 1980s, dramatic advances were made.

Several things must be borne in mind. New Zealand is not a "district" but two large islands, each with its own vineyard areas. The wine zones stretch roughly 1,207 kilometres (750 miles) north to south and the variations in vintage quality are often considerable. In 1988, for example, the Gisborne wine region was devastated by a subtropical storm while, under 322 kilometres (200 miles) away in the south, Marlborough and Martinborough enjoyed well-nigh perfect conditions. New Zealand's weather is strongly influenced by the surrounding oceans. These moderate the temperature range – both the diurnal and the seasonal. However, the country is exposed to both subtropical and subpolar climatic influences, which make the weather conditions from year to year extremely variable.

## 1997☆☆☆to☆☆☆☆

Quality is again the trade mark of this small wine producing nation that cannot seem to put a foot wrong. Yields were lower this year, falling 22 per cent compared to 1996, but the wines show an intensity of fruit in a class of their own. One reason for the drop in yields is the amount of new planting awaiting its first vintage. However, Chardonnay and Sauvignon Blanc still led the way, constituting 40 per cent of the total harvest. Merlot and Pinot Noir were the success stories for the reds.

Below average rain and a greater number of sunshine hours encouraged development after poor fruit set during flowering. A favourable autumn and continuing Indian summer provided ideal harvesting conditions and allowed for optimum ripeness at picking. Small berry size also permitted greater extraction and enhanced the flavour of the wines. In the north yields were lower than 1996; whereas in the south, Nelson's crop was alone in being ten per cent higher. Marlborough produced elegant and refined styles and some especially good Riesling.

*Definitely wines for those who like a good colour; an abundant aroma and lots of flavour. The best known whites, being Chardonnay and Sauvignon Blanc, although there is considerable variation in their style and quality, deserve our enthusiastic support. But do not buy them to keep!*

## 1996☆☆☆☆☆

The second largest vintage ever in New Zealand and the largest of the 1990s. This was an increase of just over one per cent on 1995, with significant increases in the volumes of Chardonnay and Sauvignon Blanc - around 12 per cent for both. For the reds, Merlot rose seven per cent and Pinot Noir increased by three per cent. Successful flowering occurred and perfect conditions continued through to vintage time. Some vineyards even experienced the simultaneous flowering of Cabernet Sauvignon and Chardonnay, this being very uncommon.

In certain cases, serious producers had to thin crops in order to control the vines and their quality. A more successful vintage than 1995 left the green acidity, connected to that year, behind and emphasised more the regional characteristics of each wine. On the whole, a very positive vintage as a result of warm, dry and windy conditions.

*The whites - full of flavour- continue, and understandably, to be enormously popular though no longer cheap. Drink soon. The reds still do not have a track record, the best probably drinking between 1999 and 2005.*

## 1995☆☆to☆☆☆☆

A vintage of enormous proportions - as much as 39 per cent up on 1994, making it the second largest crop since 1983. Conditions were favourable during the spring and summer - very warm and dry, which resulted in grape sugar at record levels in many areas. Due to the advanced state of the vines, harvesting started in late February, clearly the earliest since 1991.

Unfortunately, after such perfect conditions, the rains fell throughout the country in April. This led to a large variation in quality between grapes picked before and during this period. Fortunately, many Sauvignon Blanc growers throughout the country had picked by this point. In Hawkes Bay picking had been completed and the Chardonnays, Cabernet Sauvignons and Merlots all look extremely promising. The later-ripening regions have experienced a certain degree of dilution.

*A popular and commercial vintage. Whites: consume early.*

## 1994☆☆☆☆

After the low yields of 1992 and 1993, this crop was very generous, as are the quality levels. This can be explained by the favourable conditions throughout the growing season and the increasing number of vines currently being planted. The general response of the growers was that the overall quality of the fruit was the highest it had been for several years.

Auckland had the highest number of sunshine hours in recent years and produced wines with outstanding ripeness and quality. The harvest was completed quickly, finishing by Easter. Similar reports came from Gisborne which produced high quality fruit and in Hawkes Bay growers were able to delay harvesting until optimum ripeness had been reached thanks to clear, warm weather which kept the vines free of disease and rot.

Meanwhile, in Martinborough, the yields were actually lower this year. Fruit, again, was of high quality with Chardonnay and Sauvignon Blanc reaching great ripeness levels. Pinot Noir was the most successful, with its finest results for about five years. Equally exciting reports came from Marlborough on the South Island where the harvest takes place later than on the North Island. Close to perfect weather resulted in some of this region's best wines for years, particularly the Chardonnay and Sauvignon Blanc. Growers are already regarding it as a great vintage.

*Best to enjoy the scented Sauvignon Blancs as soon as they arrive on retailers' shelves. Chardonnays are ready now. Treat Pinot Noir, relatively new to New Zealand, similarly – drink now or age for interest. Frankly the reds have not yet achieved a recognisable track record, Cabernet Sauvignon can be very impressive, but it is hard to judge their optimum life span. Everyone will benefit from a little experimentation – try some now and keep the best for another five years.*

## 1993☆☆☆

Unlike northern Europe, the spring was late, poor weather delaying budding and flowering. This resulted in a dramatically reduced crop in many districts. The greatest effect was on certain white varieties used for home consumption. The ever popular exported varieties were not quite as badly affected. In fact Auckland was an exception, producing a huge crop of red grapes laden with the highest ever sugar levels. Unsurprisingly, with such distances dividing the north and south wine districts of the two islands, production and quality is as variable in 1993 as it is in most other years.

Undoubtedly the New Zealand whites have dominated the market, notably the attractive and well-marketed Chardonnay and Sauvignon Blanc varieties that have somewhat unfairly overshadowed the excellent Chenin Blanc and Riesling. The reds are impressive but as yet lack sufficient track record.

*No harm in drinking up the whites, whatever the varietal or regional origin. Most reds probably best drunk young.*

## 1992☆☆☆☆

Good wines, though crops were below average in some districts. A cool, windy spring delayed flowering and caused *millerandage* so reducing the anticipated harvest. The fallout from the Mount Pinatubo eruptions brought atmospheric disturbance throughout the 1991/2 growing season, helping to reduce sunshine levels and temperatures throughout the summer.

Prior to, and during, the harvest there was some fine but cool weather – particularly in the South Island. This resulted in grapes with higher than usual acidity levels. Although, after a delayed picking, higher than ever sugar levels were recorded in the Chardonnay and Sauvignon Blanc grapes in Auckland. The red varietals have good colour and balance.

Gisbourne produced good quality wines but lower yields for Chardonnay and Gewürztraminer. Hawkes Bay quantities were also down and acidity was high, though the wines have turned out well. In Marlborough the harvest was good but delayed, the ripest grapes came from the stonier soils.

*Whites, drink up; the best reds maturing well.*

## 1991 ☆☆☆☆

A well-above average, though late, vintage following variable but generally good weather conditions. Auckland had a mild, dry spring, though humid towards its end; a windy but dry late summer and autumn provided excellent conditions for fruit ripening, especially for the late-harvest varieties.

The neighbouring districts of Gisborne and Hawkes Bay had similar climatic conditions: a windy, cool spring, good fruit set but with quite a lot of rain followed by a late summer. More rain during the harvest dictated slightly early picking of some varieties. Later varieties matured well. Rain also caused problems in Marlborough and meant some early harvesting, but overall a mainly late harvest of excellent, ripe grapes. Advantage was taken of *botrytis* to make some late-harvest Rieslings for which New Zealand is beginning to achieve a reputation.

*Whites: drink up. Reds: most ready; best to end of century.*

## 1990 ☆☆ to ☆☆☆☆

An above average yield of good wines which was rather overshadowed by the previous vintage. Sunny conditions alternated with showers, keeping winemakers on their toes, though, ultimately, most appeared fairly satisfied with their wines. Auckland winegrowers harvested their best quality grapes for many years. Summer rain followed by dry, settled conditions during the harvest resulted in good, aromatic wines. Gisborne made good Chardonnays and other later-ripening varieties. Cabernet Sauvignon and Merlot grapes were harvested late in Hawkes Bay, producing wines of good character and maturity, leaving winemakers with high hopes for their reds this vintage.

In the South Island, Marlborough's vineyards suffered damage from late frosts. But the Sauvignon Blancs and Chardonnays had high sugar levels and good fruit. Most reds were harvested early. Conversely Canterbury, particularly Waipara Valley, harvested its grapes in hot, dry conditions. Overall, this was a very large vintage of moderately good wines. Good levels of acidity in the Chardonnays give these wines ageing potential.

*The whites are more than ready for drinking. The best reds maturing well.*

## 1989 ☆☆☆☆

Declared the "vintage of the century" by several enthusiastic winemakers. This was certainly an excellent harvest throughout the country. Abundant sun and heat, near perfect ripening conditions and a bountiful harvest, produced many top wines from both white and red grapes.

Some were, unusually, almost overripe, with high levels of alcohol in the Chardonnays and intense colours and flavours in the reds. The best of both promise to age very well indeed. Martinborough produced a handful of record-breaking Pinot Noir wines, and Hawkes Bay an outstanding collection of Cabernet Sauvignons. Marlborough boasted a "best ever" vintage.

*Whites should all have been consumed. Reds fully mature.*

## 1988☆to☆☆☆☆

A notoriously variable vintage thanks to a tropical cyclone which devastated Gisborne and severely impaired quality in Auckland and Hawkes Bay. Many Gisborne vineyards were totally submerged by torrential rain and the region was officially declared a disaster area. Nevertheless, some surprisingly palatable wines emerged from even the hardest hit regions, although their quality was eclipsed by the 1989 vintage.

In dramatic contrast, Martinborough experienced one of the hottest and driest years for some time and produced some excellent wines. Marlborough had a good vintage despite some rain at the beginning of the harvest.

*Best reds, now hard to find, will keep and develop further.*

## 1987☆to☆☆☆☆

Following two abundant harvests, 1987 saw a drop in quantity and quality. Poor fruit set reduced the size of the crop and heavy rain early in the harvest caused further problems. Auckland and Hawkes Bay suffered least but quality was markedly low in the rest of New Zealand. Later varieties were more fortunate as weather conditions improved towards the end of the year.

*Some botrytis-affected sweet wines drinking superbly, the rest, drink up.*

## 1986☆☆☆to☆☆☆☆☆

Wet weather in most areas during January and February got the vintage off to a bad start; early varieties including Müller-Thurgau suffered from rot. Thereafter, the weather cleared and 1986 enjoyed mostly outstanding results from the later-ripening varieties, particularly Chardonnay. Several of the classic New Zealand wines, including Morton Estate Black Label Chardonnay, achieved new heights in wine quality and proved to have real ageing potential. The red wines responded well to the late summer, although they were not quite as good as the 1985s.

*Cabernet Sauvignon coming into its own this vintage, the best, such as Matua Valley are ready, though they will keep.*

## 1985☆☆to☆☆☆☆

A very large vintage which added to a growing wine surplus; as a result the government sponsored a vine extraction scheme the following year.

Heavy rain during the beginning of the harvest caused outbreaks of rot which encouraged many growers to pick their white grapes before optimum ripeness. Even the usually dry Marlborough suffered because of the wet weather and made few memorable wines. The Chardonnay and red grape varieties benefited from better ripening weather late-season to give good results in all areas. The best came from Auckland, the most northerly wine region, and the southern Canterbury region.

*Drink up all except some better, but scarce, long-lasting reds.*

## 1984☆

An anticlimax after the much-praised 1983 vintage. Poor fruit set and hail damage in some regions reduced the crop by one-third of the previous year; despite an increase in the number of vineyards producing wine. Due to widespread rain and humidity, quality was average in the North Island regions; slightly better in South Island, particularly in the Marlborough region. This was certainly not a great year for reds; all varieties suffered from a lack of ripeness and flavour. North Island wines from this vintage have not aged well. Overall, a below average year.

*Drink up.*

## 1983☆☆☆☆

A top vintage which combined quality and quantity. Growers everywhere reported excellent results; many claimed this to be their best ever vintage, although advances in viticulture and winemaking were no doubt partly responsible.

Particularly successful were the North Island regions where abundant sunshine and near drought conditions produced grapes with the highest sugar levels in recent memory. The best red wines were from Hawkes Bay and Gisborne, with plenty of colour and flavour intensity and real ageing potential. In the South Island; Marlborough, Nelson and, to a lesser extent, Canterbury, had a successful vintage, although quantities were lower than from the North Island.

*Drink soon.*

## 1982☆to☆☆☆

An average vintage; strong variations from region to region. Hot, dry conditions towards the end of the growing season favoured red grape varieties, particularly in Hawkes Bay and Canterbury.

This year saw the creation of two classic red wines, Te Mata Coleraine and St Helena Pinot Noir, both of which had good ageing potential. Gisborne and Auckland suffered from rain and a lack of sunshine early in the season. As the poor conditions continued, with heavy rain in February and March, some producers lost heart and picked their grapes too early and, predictably, produced poor wines, the reds lacking in colour, flavour and longevity.

*Whites long since drunk. Even best reds need drinking up.*

## 1981☆☆

A poor flowering and fruit set was followed by a fairly dry, but rather sunless, growing season. The harvest yielded a small crop of clean but rather unripe grapes. Marlborough, Canterbury and Hawkes Bay were the stars of the vintage. Later ripening varieties, especially the reds, benefited most from sunnier conditions towards the end of the harvest. Several Cabernet Sauvignons from this vintage have survived years of maturation but show green and leafy characteristics. This is typical of wines produced before the importance of better site selection and improved viticulture had been recognised.

*Drink up.*

## 1980☆

Wet weather affected most regions during the growing season, including the normally dry region of Marlborough. Canterbury and, to a lesser extent, Hawkes Bay escaped the worst of the rain at harvest time. Many grapes were picked prematurely, avoiding rot. This resulted in wines lacking ripeness and longevity.

Overall, this was a poor year for reds, but the whites fared a little better. High acidity and bunch rot characterised the worst.

*Few remain. Drink up.*

# South Africa

Cape wines can hardly be called "New World" wines. Vines were planted and wine made by the earliest Dutch settlers of this region in the late 17th century. During the next century the wines of Constantia were renowned – fashionable and highly priced – but, like madeira, fell out of favour as the 19th century progressed. Indifferent table and fortified wines were then made, the principal export until well into the 1950s being good, inexpensive sherry-type wines. The renaissance of fine table wines began in the 1960s and 1970s though was largely unnoticed or, for political reasons, ignored. Over the past two decades or so, great strides have been made in the selection of cultivars (vine varieties), winemaking and effective wine control systems.

Over a dozen red cultivars are grown in the Cape, of which Pinotage, Cabernet Sauvignon and Pinot Noir are the best known, and around 15 white cultivars, the most widely planted being the versatile Steen (Chenin Blanc), also Sauvignon Blanc, the increasingly successful Chardonnay, some Gewürztraminer and a small amount of high quality Riesling.

It might be imagined that the Cape enjoys one long hot season after another. Not so. Being the southern tip of South Africa winters can be cold and wet, the Coastal Regions having variable springs and summers. At vertical tastings in the Cape, I have noted that potentially hefty reds made with cultivars such as Pinotage are better after a long cool growing season. The ageing ability of many South African red wines, even the most commercial brands, is remarkably good. Moreover, the quality/price ratio is very favourable for the consumer.

## 1997☆☆☆to☆☆☆☆

Still struggling with a demand outstripping supply, this year did not do South Africa any favours, in fact grape prices are still rising.

Yields were five per cent below last year, although this varied by region – for instance the Paarl and Stellenbosch regions had significant losses. The season was long and cool giving low pH and high acidity levels in the grapes. The spring brought early rain which promoted growth, especially in the canopy, and a wet December caught out some growers with downy mildew borne from the humid conditions.

Then the weather became dry and continued this way throughout the harvest. Producers had to delay picking, hoping it did not rain, in order to achieve balance in the grapes. The results were of fine quality, especially the reds. The extended period on vine had allowed tannins to ripen before the sugars developed; top wines will age well. Pinot Noir produced some excellent wines and Sauvignon Blanc also benefited from a later harvest.

*Whites for early drinking. The reds of this vintage qualify for a moderately extended period in the cellar.*

## 1996 ☆☆☆

After an uncharacteristically wet December and January, the weather changed into a hot and listless February. By this stage anxieties about disease were high. Conditions then changed again, with the end of February and March turning cool and localised frost affecting a few producers. As a result, the ripening period became longer and coupled with a late flowering, meant the vintage was delayed.

A little rain during the harvest caused rot problems in certain areas. But generally the resulting wines showed a more European style due to the long, cool ripening period – displaying less up-front fruit and well-balanced, natural acidity levels. The best results came from those who harvested early from virus-free plants. Chardonnay and Chenin Blanc fared well, Sauvignon Blanc less so, while most reds show good, deep colour.

Thankfully yields were marginally up – by seven per cent, alleviating the ongoing problems of South Africa's wine shortage. The key to this country's future in wine is to adhere to quality and resist the temptation of quantity.

*A southern hemisphere region that has changed a great deal over the past 20 years. Both grapes and winemaking are of a high standard. Whites ready now, reds also best young.*

## 1995 ☆☆☆☆☆

At this early stage, reports appear promising, even hinting at some exceptional wines. The 1994/5 growing season was dominated by warm and dry conditions and vine stress became a serious problem. The situation was eased in early February with the arrival of rain followed by three hot days. The result was that grape sugars suddenly rose and acidity dropped. The harvest took place uneventfully. The fruit quality is remarkable and wines generally have fullness of body and flavour.

*Sauvignon Blanc for early consumption, the better quality Chardonnays, now to 2000. Pinotage, generally best drunk within five years; Cabernet Sauvignon, beyond. Excellent Pinot Noir from Bouchard Finlayson and Hamilton Russell. Lovely now, but will keep and develop further.*

## 1994 ☆☆to☆☆☆☆

An extremely difficult vintage for South African growers resulting in the smallest and earliest harvest for six years, due to the severe dryness and unseasonal winds. Despite reduced yields, quality was frequently good to excellent.

The wines generally have powerful fruit aromas and good balance. The red varieties have intense levels of fruit and soft, ripe tannins. In general the quality was considered comparable with the 1991 vintage which was regarded as South Africa's best vintage ever for red wines.

*Sauvignon Blanc is best consumed when it appears on the market. The Chardonnays have improved, but most are also best drunk young. Frankly, the Cape reds are very variable, only the top Cabernet Sauvignon of the best estates are worthy of, and indeed demand, bottle-age.*

## 1993 ☆☆to☆☆☆☆

Good results this year, particularly in the Coastal Region, despite cool, damp conditions and fierce sunshine. By the time of the harvest, the health of the vines was good, and this resulted in an ideal level of ripeness.

The reds are good to excellent with an impressive depth of colour and intensity, and high levels of fruit; they also possess a considerable ageing potential. The whites have good acidity and attractive aromatic quality.

*White wines are fully developed. The best reds will be drinking well from now to beyond 2000.*

## 1992 ☆☆☆☆☆

An all-time record crop: over ten million hectolitres. Cool conditions during the harvest produced juice with good acidity, excellent concentration and good colour in the reds: Cabernet Sauvignon of superb quality, Chardonnays and Sauvignon Blancs packed with fruit, and exceptional Merlots.

*Drink up the whites. Cask-matured reds drinking from now to beyond 2000, depending on quality.*

## 1991 ☆☆☆☆☆

The wettest winter on record. May and June also wet, but an early spring was followed by a cool, dry summer. Great potential.

*The lighter, drier whites, drink up; classic reds can benefit from further bottle-ageing.*

## 1990 ☆☆to☆☆☆☆

A hot growing season. Moderate whites, better reds.

*Pinot Noir and Pinotage ready now. Cabernets will benefit from further bottle-age. Whites should have been drunk.*

## 1989 ☆☆to☆☆☆☆

Passable whites, some very good reds.

*The softer reds still pleasant; "Reserve" quality Cabernet Sauvignon will develop further.*

### 1988☆☆☆☆

A hot year, some very good wines.

*Some excellent Cabernet Sauvignon, Shiraz and new blended reds, some quite tannic, all with good fruit.*

### 1987☆to☆☆☆☆

Variable weather conditions and wines. Better for reds, but some notably good Rieslings and late-harvest wines.

*Cabernet Sauvignon and Pinot Noir drinking well.*

### 1986☆☆to☆☆☆☆

An unusually hot and dry summer. A small crop of mediocre whites but good to excellent reds. Some good Chardonnays: a relatively new cultivar in the Cape.

*Late-harvest whites can still be excellent. Best reds lovely now, but will keep.*

### 1985☆☆to☆☆☆

A cool, wet summer resulted in variable quality, but good sugar/acid ratios. Whites were better than the rather light reds. Some excellent sparkling wines. A year of much experimentation with new blends of classic European grape varieties.

*Drink up.*

### 1984☆☆to☆☆☆

High temperatures during the harvest resulted in overripe whites with low acidity. A better vintage for red wines.

*"Noble" late-harvest wines still superb. Top reds, excellent with ten to 20 years life ahead.*

### 1983☆☆

A large crop, and up on the 1982 record breaking harvest, but unfortunately lacking in sugar and acidity. Overall, moderate quality, yet some very good wines: Zinfandel, Cabernet Sauvignon blends and late-harvest whites.

*Dry whites too old; sweet at zenith? Reds holding well.*

### 1982☆☆☆☆

A very good year for reds. Largest production of quality wines up to that time resulting from well-nigh perfect climatic conditions.

*The best reds (Cabernet Sauvignon) drinking perfectly and will probably keep on developing until, perhaps beyond, 2000.*

### 1981☆☆to☆☆☆☆

Cool weather from flowering to harvest resulted in white wines of high fruit and acidity. The reds less good, soft and lacking colour.
*Drink up.*

### 1980☆to☆☆☆☆

Hot, dry summer. Dry whites lacked acidity: moderate quality. Very good reds. Nederburg sweet white Edelkeur, magnificent.
*Dry whites passé. Reds passing peak.*

## 1970s

A decade of development. **1979**☆☆ had the driest and warmest winter since the mid-1920s, autumn was warm and wet resulting in much *botrytis* and some very good late-harvest whites, also some good Pinotage. **1978**☆☆☆☆ good quantity and quality. **1977**☆☆ wet harvest, passable high acid whites, light reds. **1976**☆☆☆☆ almost ideal conditions, excellent reds, good whites, Edelkeur outstanding. **1975**☆☆ a large crop of average quality, low acid whites, rain-spoiled reds.

**1974**☆☆☆☆☆ a warm, very dry year; some excellent reds now passing their best. **1973**☆☆☆ a cool vintage, small crop: Pinotage and Cabernet Sauvignon have held well but at their peak. **1972**☆☆☆to☆☆☆☆ a hot dry vintage producing high quality reds, the best still holding well. **1971**☆☆☆ a large crop, relatively light wines, yet the reds can still be good to drink. **1970**☆☆☆

## 1960s

Of the 1960s decade, **1969** and **1963** were the best vintages. The reds are now faded but they retain flavour and charm.

# Champagne & Fortified Wines

## Champagne

Champagne has something in common with port in that grapes are harvested and wine made every year but only in years producing wines of top quality is it marketed as "vintage". Champagne is a blended wine, usually, but not always, a blend of three different major grape varieties: Chardonnay, Pinot Noir and Pinot Meunier, each chosen for its different character. The grapes themselves are grown in different districts, some surprisingly far apart, but strictly classified by quality. Most Champagne is marketed under a brand name, no vintage stated. These non-vintage (NV) wines may, in turn, be of different years, blended by the chief-taster to match his house style.

Non-vintage Champagne varies in quality from passable to excellent, the best – Roederer, for instance – benefiting from further bottle-ageing. The top wines, such as Krug's Grande Réserve, being finer than many vintage Champagnes.

One generally just buys and drinks non-vintage Champagne straight away. However, as stated above, some benefit from further bottle-age. Nine months' rest in one's cellar can markedly improve a frothy, young wine.

A vintage Champagne of one of the *grande marque* houses represents a level of quality superior to even its most successful bread-and-butter "NV" brand. The proliferation of smartly dressed and high-priced de luxe Champagnes are an up-market ploy though they should, and mostly do, represent the highest and most refined quality of a major Champagne house.

Straight vintage and de luxe vintage Champagnes are not marketed until some five years or so after the vintage and, though most can be – and are – drunk within a couple of years, most benefit quite considerably from further bottle-ageing. Generally speaking vintage Champagne is best drunk between five and 15 years after it was made, depending on the weight and style of the wine – and one's personal taste. I aim for an average of 12 years.

Old Champagne has a peculiarly English appeal. After 20 years it gains colour and loses its pristine sparkle. Its bouquet and flavour becomes deeper and richer. If the bottles have been well cellared and the corks are firm, Champagne can be delicious after 30, even 50, years and, if they are lacking effervescence, can be refreshed half and half with a young non-vintage wine, the young Champagne providing zest and sparkle, the old wine character and flavour.

Older vintage Champagne disgorged in the original cellars before shipment has a different character to bottles never recorked. Bollinger "RD" is the best known: the date of disgorging/recorking usually appears on the back label. In my opinion all recently disgorged Champagne should be drunk within a year of so after the RD date.

Lastly, do not hang on to, or pay high prices for, old vintages in half bottles, in jeroboams, or in larger sizes. Stick to bottles and magnums, the latter from only the top Champagne houses.

## 1997☆☆☆☆

As the millennium rapidly approaches stimulating demand, the Champenois enjoyed another successful year. It is highly likely that this will be declared a vintage. The only bad news is that volumes are below average and sales are expected to outstrip supply – the first time since 1988. Late frost in May caused irregular flowering, and as the miserable weather continued into July, producers became extremely worried about rot.

August came to the rescue again bringing gloriously warm weather and countless sunshine hours, which promptly relieved rot concerns. These perfect conditions continued throughout the harvest and as a result many grapes were left longer on the vine. This ensured a high degree of ripeness. The harvest started on September 12 and due to the vines being rot-free, minimal sorting was required. This meant the vintage progressed quickly and was complete by the first week of October.

In some areas Pinots Noir and Meunier were picked before Chardonnay which is unusual. Together they have produced rich and full wines and another memorable vintage for this region.

*A Champagne for well into the next millennium.*

## 1996☆☆☆☆☆

Hailed as the vintage of the century, producers say that the region has not seen a result like this since 1955. Surpassing some of the more recent great vintages like 1985, 1989 and 1990; this vintage relates most closely to, then even beyond, 1988. It will be possible to open this wine for the millennium celebrations, but it will be long-lived, probably into the middle of next century.

Heavy rain in August worried producers until September brought the most perfect ripening possible. This key period for the vines has, in the last few years been disrupted by rain. But, warm and sunny days were followed by cool nights this vintage sweeping the grapes into harvest on September 15. Some rain fell sporadically during October, but by the second week the harvest was complete, with the grapes showing an unusually high level of sugar and acidity. Previous years have seen either one or other.

Results were great for all varieties, but Pinot Meunier suffered lower yields after some flowering problems. Producers found the grapes reaching ten per cent potential alcohol and over, some even chose to allow malolactic fermentation on the red grapes, due to the high sugar and acidity. Definitely a vintage to invest in.

*There will be pressure to put this vintage onto the market prematurely. Just remember that Champagne of this quality tends to be fully developed and at best between eight and 12 years after the vintage. Wait, buy, wait again!*

## 1995☆☆☆

Producers were relieved this year to achieve a very good vintage after the only average previous two years. Growing conditions were favourable throughout the summer. But when a touch of dry rot occurred due to some rain, producers did not worry as the good weather and ideal temperatures returned in time for vintage.

The resulting rot was only superficial. Harvesting commenced on September 18 at the early ripening Crus and continued until October 18. Careful selection and pre-pressing of the hand harvested grapes gave highly satisfying results. Very good potential alcohol and natural acidity was found in the still wines and this analysis encouraged many producers that there was a firm possibility of declaring a vintage this year.

On the whole, spirits were high amongst the Champenois producers, even when confronted by talk of a boycott on French wines due to the testing in the Pacific. Their minds were firmly set that Champagne would experience a substantial increase in demand for the millennium.

*Not yet put on the market, clearly a vintage to look out for. Probably at its best circa 2003 to 2007.*

## 1994☆☆

The overriding problem this year, as with the rest of France, was the rain at harvest time, dashing all hopes of a great vintage.

Climatic conditions for the growing season were favourable, permitting an even flowering of the three varieties in close succession. July was fairly warm with slightly higher than average temperatures and a small amount of rainfall. However, August was a little less settled with cooler temperatures and continued rain. By the end of the summer the prospects were good to exciting.

The harvest was due to commence around September 15 but rains had struck the region ten days earlier. More than a week of continuous rain caused widespread dilution and rot with Chardonnay being the worst affected variety. Although the sun re-emerged in time for the second week of the harvest, careful selection was the key to making wines of any quality.

*This year produced some non-vintage wines of reasonable quality, but is unlikely to result in wines of vintage status.*

## 1993☆☆

Winter and early spring were uncharacteristically clement with a reassuring absence of frost. Spring was very warm with only the occasional cool, wet spell. In May hail struck parts of the region generating some losses and providing a natural check on the size of the harvest. The temperatures were remarkably high during May and June and were, at times, almost tropical. Growth was rapid and flowering took place early around June 2, practically in the course of 48 hours. As summer progressed, despite rain in July, prospects for the vintage were good.

Unfortunately, rains hit the region just before the harvest and continued virtually incessantly. Some 140mm (5.5ins) as opposed to the usual 20mm fell and the effects were most dramatic in the Côte des Blancs. Serious widespread dilution was the obvious problem – no vintage wines were made, but non-vintage blending wines were of a fair quality.

*Some Champagne houses managed to produce better than average wines this year.*

## 1992☆☆☆☆

This year the growing conditions were highly favourable and all three varieties produced healthy, ripe and abundant crops. The harvest took place early and was completed quickly.

The vintage is a particularly interesting one to watch in that it was the first to be governed by new self-regulatory measures to control quality. This followed a spate of disappointing quality levels from the region, including some of the main houses. The industry confirmed the notion that if a wine is to marketed under the name "Champagne", it must be representative of the superlative quality associated with the region and its traditions.

The new measures aim to control the size of production at every level – limiting the quantity of grapes harvested and the number of pressings thus improving the quality of the musts. Wines produced from over 9,000kg of grapes per hectare must be held in reserve for possible future blending. However, growers can apply to formally extend their yield in certain circumstances.

Clearly, it will be fascinating to monitor the effects of these proposals and to taste the difference in the glass.

*A useful vintage for relatively early consumption.*

## 1991☆☆

This is described generally as a useful year, in which an abundance of grapes helped stabilise prices and top up depleted non-vintage stocks.

The growing year started with early problems. There were two spring frosts, the first in April destroying many of the buds, particularly in the valley of the Marne and the Côte des Blancs. The Grand Cru vineyards, particularly in the Montagne de Reims, were less affected. There was further frost damage overnight towards the end of May, mainly hitting the outlying districts of Aube and Aisne. However, when the weather improved a second wave of buds blossomed. Chardonnay flowering began uneasily around June 25 but the weather brightened up a week later for the Pinot Noir and Meunier whose flowering, ended on July 10. The grapes developed perfectly through a hot summer. However, on September 21 the weather suddenly deteriorated causing rot, though rain did help swell the grapes. The sun returned for a fairly late harvest on September 30. The wines are light, with low acidity levels, not of *grand marque* vintage quality.

## 1990☆☆☆☆☆

The third-largest vintage on record and the fifth successive above-average yield. Frost damage in April affected the crop, sometimes dramatically – as much as 45 per cent was lost in some cases. Flowering was abundant but affected by unseasonable weather, resulting in *coulure* and *millerandage* in all grape varieties.

Summer in Champagne was typical of the rest of France: hot and dry, leading to a second flowering and thereby recouping as much as 60 per cent of the crop, some of which was gathered at a second picking (the second such harvest in two years). The late summer rains and cool winds helped fill out the grapes and had the effect of significantly increasing the potential alcohol. Both alcohol and acidity levels are excellent.

Most of the *grandes marques* have declared this a vintage. "For 45 years I have lived in Champagne, and never have I seen such a year", said Claude Taittinger, president of Champagne Taittinger. Some expressed doubt though: "To say today that it is an exceptional year, that is wrong", said Bollinger's director, Christian Bizot, after the harvest. For others, however, this was undoubtedly a great year. Henri Krug considers 1988, 1989 and 1990 as the outstanding trio of the century.

*Clearly a wine to acquire, to celebrate the millennium, or even to keep until fully mature, say around 2005.*

## 1989 ☆☆☆☆☆

A large crop of superb quality. The grapes were grown and the wines made in perfect conditions, producing wines which rival 1982 for the title "vintage of the decade".

A warm spring was broken by frosts in late April. Conditions improved rapidly thereafter and flowering took place in late May. The summer was hot and sunny and produced luscious, healthy grapes ready for the harvest to begin on September 4 for Chardonnay and September 12 for the Pinots. Quality apart, this was also an exceptional year due to there being two harvests, the second taking place in October, a rare event in Champagne. The second crop produced slightly acidic wines, suitable for blending.

*Very appealing wines, tempting to drink soon but, like the 1976s, will gain depth and subtlety with bottle-age, 15 to 20 years not being excessive.*

## 1988 ☆☆☆☆

This year produced some very good Champagne. The quantity was down by ten per cent on the previous year, forcing the Champagne houses to compete for grapes at a time of high world demand for the finished product. A mild, frostless spring was followed by a good flowering in early June under perfect conditions. Progress was hampered by a cloudy July and heavy rainfall before the harvest, which began on September 19.

*Firm wines for drinking now, though the best might benefit from further bottle-ageing.*

## 1987 ☆

Not a true vintage year, but one which produced some useful wines to stock up the cellars of the trade. A poor, wet summer resulted in some grey rot, but the crop was saved, in terms of quantity if not quality, by fine weather during the harvest.

## 1986 ☆☆☆ to ☆☆☆

Following a poor spring, flowering took place in late June under ideal conditions. The summer was hot and sunny, but rain during August and early September adversely affected grape quality. This was a moderately good year except where growers did not successfully spray against rot.

*These wines are drinking well now, but the best will benefit from further bottle-age, say now to 2000.*

## 1985 ☆☆☆☆☆

The severe winter, during which temperatures dropped as low as –25˚C (–13˚F), destroyed around ten per cent of the region's vines. In some areas as much as 25 per cent of the vines were destroyed.

Wet, dull weather conditions in spring and early summer eventually gave way to a sunny July. The months of September and October were the deciding factors *vis à vis* the quality of this vintage: delightfully warm, sunny weather swelled and ripened the grapes and the harvest took place late. The wines produced have the perfect balance of fruit character, alcohol and acidity.

Growers predicted a tiny production this year. They were pleasantly surprised by a small but excellent, stylish vintage for everyone. Best of the mid-1980s.

*Beguiling now, particularly if you like your Champagne at its liveliest, though classics like Veuve Clicquot, La Grande Dame; Roederer Brut and Cristal are developing well and will be at their best around the year 2000.*

## 1984

A dull, wet spring led to a poor, late flowering. The weather did not improve during the summer and September rains caused rot. A non-vintage year.

## 1983 ☆☆☆

Initially hailed as an excellent year throughout Champagne, the wines do not in fact merit such praise, but are mainly pleasant, flavoursome and nicely balanced.

Good weather during spring and summer provided ideal growing conditions for the cultivation of a large crop of healthy grapes. September saw isolated patches of rain but October provided good harvesting conditions. The amount of grapes needed for pressing one hectolitre of must was increased by the CIVC from 150 to 160kg, resulting in more concentrated wines.

*Some assertive and potentially long-lasting wines, notably Dom Pérignon, Veuve Clicquot and the three Charles Heidsieck blends, Blanc des Millenaires, Brut and Champagne Charlie. All fully mature, some showing a touch of age.*

## 1982 ☆☆☆☆

A substantial vintage in every respect. With the exception of a bout of mildew in June and July, excellent conditions prevailed throughout the year. The grapes were ripe and healthy and rain shortly after the start of the harvest prevented them from over-ripening. The biggest crop on record. Lovely when they first came on the market. This is an elegant, seductive year for vintage Champagne. The best are still improving in bottle.

*All are delicious now but the heftier blends can cope with more bottle-age: Dom Pérignon, Krug, Pol Roger Cuvée Winston Churchill and Roederer into the 21st century.*

## 1981 ☆☆☆

Difficult weather conditions cut the size of this vintage; it produced the smallest crop since 1978. Quality was very good.

A mild spring, which encouraged the early development of the buds, was followed by frosts in April and hail in May. The vines flowered during a cold July but the hot weather in August and September ripened the fruit well before rain in late September. Picking began September 28.

Most of the wine was used for blending, but many of the vintage Champagnes have finesse, are firm and will last well.

*Drink now, though Krug and the refined Cristal Brut will be delicious until the end of the 1990s.*

## 1980 ☆

The cold, wet weather in June and July led to a poor flowering, which resulted in the vines suffering from *millerandage*. Then, last-minute sun in September saved the vintage from disaster.

A few Champagne houses, including Krug, declared this a vintage year; but on the whole very little vintage wine was made, and wisely so.

The wines were acidic and lacked body.

*Drink up.*

## 1979 ☆☆☆☆

An exceptionally cold winter which lasted through to April, followed by frosts in May; favourable conditions then continued throughout the summer and an abundant harvest of fully mature grapes was picked.

Stylish wines with acidity to provide longevity.

*The best are deliciously mature. Drink soon.*

## 1978 ☆☆

The weather brought conditions close to disaster for the vines: a very small crop was produced. Untypical wines.
*Drink up.*

## 1977

A dreary summer followed by better weather in September; the vines suffered mildew and grey rot.

*Roederer Cristal Brut, made from highly selected grapes, about the only vintage 1977 marketed. Drink up.*

## 1976 ☆☆☆☆

This year was characterised by a summer of great heat and drought. The harvest, which was the earliest since 1893, began on September 1. One of my favourite Champagne vintages, which produced firm, well-structured wines.

The best will continue to give pleasure. The top vintage and de luxe Champagnes will certainly improve further.

*Krug and Dom Pérignon living up to their exalted reputation and good for another ten years. Classic Pol Roger and Moët & Chandon delicious, but best drunk soon.*

## 1975☆☆☆

After a wet winter, snow fell in March and the weather improved at the end of April. The summer was hot but not sunny and a slightly below average size crop was picked late. A good year: the wines tended to be a bit acidic but well-balanced, rounded and full of fruit and flavour.

*Some lovely wines, notably Bollinger Brut, Lanson Red Label, Pol Roger Cuvée Winston Churchill, at or just passing their peak. Drink up.*

## 1974☆

Difficult weather conditions. Variable wines, best being average, but overall not really up to the standard of vintage Champagne.

*Drink up or avoid unless perfectly stored.*

## 1973☆☆☆

A very wet September followed a hot, dry summer and produced an appealing vintage of fairly reasonable quality. The wines had neither the body and flesh of the meaty 1970 vintage, nor the lean firmness of the 1971 vintage; but were nevertheless quite enjoyable. Most are tired now, though the best Champagnes are still pleasant to drink.

*Despite some agreeable surprises, best to drink up.*

## 1972

Not a vintage year due to a wet, sunless summer.

## 1971☆☆☆☆

This year experienced all the elements. After spring frosts, June hail, August rain and even a tornado, September was mercifully hot and dry. A small crop of irregular grapes was picked as a result. But, the wines were refreshing, lean, stylish and crisp. Champagne with finesse. The top wines can still be delightful to drink, rest were at their peak from 1979 to mid-1980s.
*Drink up.*

## 1970☆☆☆☆

After a cold spring and wet June, the growing conditions were favourable through to the harvest. Less shapely than the 1971 wines but good, substantial wines. The best with time in hand.

*All but the biggest of the classic grandes marques are well past their best, but Bollinger Vieilles Vignes Françaises is a good example of a magnificent stayer.*

## 1969☆☆☆

Moderately good. Unstable weather conditions and frequent violent storms during the summer – worst mildew since 1958. Harvest began on October 1 in good conditions. Fragrant wines with a slightly higher than average acidity. It is possible that this only moderately good vintage was released for two reasons: to make up for the two previous non-vintage years, and to supply an over-inflated market; though by its release in 1974, it had deflated.

*The wines were at their prime in the late 1970s, early 1980s, only the top marques, like Krug are more than just interesting.*

## 1968

A disastrous year due to bad weather conditions.

## 1967

Vintage not declared due to disastrous harvest weather which caused widespread rot.

## 1966☆☆☆☆

A very good vintage. Some vines killed by harsh January frosts and then further damage caused by hail from May to August. An early June blossoming, some of which was damaged by a cold spell; August was wet with some mildew. The harvest took place in fine weather. Despite the difficulties, 1966 produced a good quantity of firm, elegant, perfectly balanced, stylish Champagnes.

*One of my favourite vintages though, except for top wines like Bollinger and Cristal Brut, past their best. Drink up.*

## 1965

Bad weather damaged crops; a poor year.

## 1964☆☆☆☆☆

A first-class year which demonstrated how important it is to allow time in the bottle for big vintage Champagne: the optimum time being eight to 15 years or longer.

The vines enjoyed perfect weather conditions throughout the year. After a cold winter and early spring they flowered early, then ripened during a hot, dry summer. Gentle rain swelled the grapes during August, ready for an early harvest on September 6. Full-bodied, ripe and fruity Champagne. Broader and more rounded than the 1961s and 1962s though without the finesse of the former or the elegance of the latter.

*The best, if well kept, still drinking well despite depth of colour and loss of vigour. Salon le Mesnil and Krug superb.*

## 1963

Appalling weather resulted in a poor, non-vintage year.

## 1962☆☆☆☆

Spring was cold and the summer was fine but lacked sun. The vines flowered rapidly but growth was hampered by cool temperatures. Warm September sun resulted in the harvest beginning in conditions far better than expected in early October. These were consistently good, dry, fruity, interesting wines.

*Best to drink up.*

## 1961☆☆☆☆

A stormy April and cold May followed a mild, damp winter. Fortunately, the vines flowered in fine, sunny weather during June; after a cold July, good weather continued until the harvest on September 28. A vintage which initially benefited from the popularity of the 1961 red Bordeaux, but also had its own merit. Still lovely, though some bottle variation.

*No point in keeping longer, though still delicious, if kept well. Dom Pérignon from this vintage is still one of the greatest Champagnes ever produced.*

## 1960☆☆

Not a vintage year, but welcomed by the trade who needed to stock up on non-vintage Champagne.

## 1959☆☆☆☆

An exceptional and timely vintage. Coming after a run of bad years 1959 was, at the time, thought to be the best for decades and is now mostly consumed. The weather was wonderfully hot from May through to an excellent harvest. Well-constituted, ripe wines which held well for several decades.

*The great, full-bodied, classic marques still make a lovely mouthful – if you like mature Champagne style. The rest need drinking up.*

## 1955☆☆☆☆

A first-class vintage. Apart from a bout of May frost, good weather rallied throughout the year. Picking began on September 29 and reports noted an unusually high quality of juice from the grapes. This was an underrated vintage, the wines of which, if stored in cold cellars, can still be delightful.

*Lovely wines, though past their best; drink up.*

## 1953☆☆☆☆

Apart from a prolonged cold spell, the summer was satisfactory. Picking began early on September 14 and finished in fine weather. This was a highly satisfactory year. The wines were perhaps less firm and refined than the 1952s, but overall, well-balanced and appealing. Very popular in the 1960s and 1970s.

*Charming wines, now long past best. Few, understandably, remain, but worth looking out for if you like old Champagne.*

## 1952☆☆☆☆

This vintage enjoyed good weather conditions throughout the summer, then welcome rain fell in August and swelled the berries, causing only a very limited amount of rot. Extremely healthy grapes were harvested. This was a year of extensive variety, but, overall the wines produced made firm, well-balanced and stylish Champagnes. Still worth seeking out.

*A better bet than the 1953s, body and acidity keeping them well. Bollinger sheer perfection. Scarce. Can be delicious.*

## 1949☆☆☆☆

A small crop which prompted cautious optimism after the harvest. After a long and difficult flowering, conditions improved with an exceptionally dry summer interspersed with occasional rain and hail. This was a very good year, producing firm, fruity, elegant wines. Many gained enormously from bottle-age.

*Now straw-coloured and lacking effervescence, at best lovely old wines. Depends on storage.*

## 1947☆☆☆☆

A classic year. The vines flowered very early in June and then record hours of sunshine during August produced a small crop of wonderfully healthy grapes picked in ideal conditions. Despite their soft fruitiness, the wines have lasted well.

*Drink up.*

## 1945☆☆☆☆☆

Bud-break was early, followed by April frosts and a difficult flowering. Picking began in haste on September 6 and yielded a very small crop of exceptionally high-quality grapes. A long-lasting, elegant vintage.

*If perfectly cellared, can be delicious, Pommery for example.*

## 1943☆☆☆☆

Low temperatures and showers brought flowering problems. Oidium also attacked vines, especially on the Côte des Blancs.

This was however, a very good year: remarkable for being more successful than any other classic French district and, more importantly, for being the first major vintage to find its way into export markets after the war. Mainly drunk too young.

*Over-the-hill now. Beware of 1943s shipped in 1953 to celebrate the Coronation of HM Queen Elizabeth II. They should have been drunk at that time.*

## 1942☆☆☆

A good but little known wartime vintage.

*Can still be good, but drink up.*

## 1941☆☆

A moderately good, if rather light, wartime vintage. Rarely found.

*Now: but only for those who like old Champagne.*

## 1930s

The 1930s saw four vintage years and six undeclared vintages of very poor quality.

**1938**☆☆ was the least successful of the declared years: wines of uneven quality, not shipped because of the war. Very few have been seen in England since. **1937**☆☆☆☆☆ was excellent – turned out to be the highlight of the 1930s. These were rich wines with the acidity to give them a long life; some are still drinking well.

**1934**☆☆☆☆ enjoyed fine weather, healthy grapes and an abundant harvest. **1933**☆☆☆☆ also benefited from very good conditions. The wines were reported at the time to be possibly the best of the century. However, the trade was more interested in those of 1934. The first three years of the decade were menaced by appalling weather and did not produce vintage Champagne.

## 1920s

A decade which included many exceptional years.

**1929**☆☆☆☆ produced a large quantity of soft, charming wines but they were not of the same quality or as long-lasting as the outstanding 1928s. **1928**☆☆☆☆☆ a fine summer followed a bad winter, producing well-constituted wines which, if well kept, can still be excellent. The next vintage was **1926**☆☆☆ producing a small crop of good wines. Two non-vintage years; then a small crop of good quality wines in **1923**☆☆☆☆ the best of which were still excellent in the early 1970s and, if perfectly cellared, can still be lovely – wonderfully golden colour with a hint of sparkle.

**1921**☆☆☆☆☆ produced top-class wines, despite the difficult weather conditions. This year marked the peak of a great era for Veuve Clicquot and is probably the greatest white wine vintage this century. **1920**☆☆☆☆ subject to bad weather and mildew, but enjoyed glorious harvesting conditions. A very good vintage.

## 1910s

1910s witnessed several good years and one exceptional vintage.

**1919**☆☆☆ welcomed these refined wines, coming after three mediocre years. **1915**☆☆☆ the next good vintage. Grapes were picked early by prisoners of war and soldiers on leave. Much of Champagne was under German occupation in **1914**☆☆☆☆ a year which, nevertheless, produced some delightful and lively wines.

The best vintage of the decade was **1911**☆☆☆☆☆ probably the best since 1874. The weather was excellent; the harvest early. This year also endured Easter riots in the Champagne industry.

## 1900s

Apart from three successful years, this was not a great decade.

**1906**☆☆☆☆ suffered a drought but produced a small quantity of very good wines. **1904**☆☆☆☆☆ enjoyed perfect weather and outstanding quality: lively, flavoursome wines. **1900**☆☆☆☆ gave an abundance of very good wines following a hot summer and storms in August. Phylloxera was also progressing through the vineyards. The rest of this decade was menaced by torrential rain and disease, or, as was the case in 1907, a shortage of labour.

## 1890s

The 1890s revealed some good vintages.

They included the excellent **1899**☆☆☆☆☆ and the good **1898**☆☆☆ but not the poor and uneven period between 1897 and 1894. **1893**☆☆☆☆ was harvested in late August – the earliest harvest ever. Much wine of very good quality was made, though the grapes were perhaps a little too ripe. The finest vintage of the decade was **1892**☆☆☆☆☆☆; spring frosts reduced the crop by 25 per cent but the harvest enjoyed perfect conditions. Also noted for the advent of phylloxera. Previous two years not declared.

## PRE-1890

The best vintages recorded: **1874,** fashionable and high-priced; **1868, 1865, 1857, 1846** and **1815.**

# Port

Port, the quintessential "Englishman's wine" comes in several guises. In the old days, prior to 1960, there were "wood ports" and "vintage ports", all except for the white ports of the former category being sweet. White port, never popular in the United Kingdom, though delicious before lunch in a shippers' lodge or on a hot day up at a quinta, is made from white grapes and generally medium-dry. The other two wood ports took their names from their colour: "ruby" being a lusty young wine, undergoing relatively little maturation in cask or vat, and true "tawny" having lost its colour in cask, at the same time becoming softer, mellower, more nutty-flavoured.

Then there was the "vintage port". Up to 1970 shipped to the United Kingdom (and just a few other countries, Denmark for example) in 550-litre (110-gallon) "pipes" and bottled two years after the vintage by the importer; by a wine merchant; or even, not uncommon in the 19th century, by the butler of a big house. Since 1970 all vintage port has had to be bottled by the shipper (the producer; the company owning the brand) in Vila Nova de Gaia (this commonly referred to as "bottled in Oporto" though the lodges – warehouses where the port is matured – are all across the other side of the river Douro in Gaia).

Over the past few years the market has been greatly complicated by "late-bottled" vintage port (LBV) and, even more recently, by a rash of new "single-quinta" wines. But the quality end is dominated by fine old tawnies, still woefully under-appreciated, and the classic vintage ports, which represent the *crème de la crème*, the pinnacle of the port market.

The subject of this pocket book is vintages. Happily, despite some of the complications referred to above, port vintages are relatively easy to understand and to remember. A vintage is "declared" when the circumstances are right: that is when the year in question has produced wines of the highest quality and, at the time of considering a declaration (normally after the next vintage), that the market is ready. For example, 1931, a great year, was not declared because of the country's depression in 1932/3. Life is made even simpler if the declaration is general, i.e. that the majority of the major shipping houses agree together on quality and timing.

The only problem with vintage port is that it takes so long to mature and, though good value when first put on the market (compared with first-growth claret), requires capital to be tied up for considerable length of time, at least ten, often over 20 years. But at its zenith, it is the loveliest of wines.

## 1997☆☆☆☆

Development progressed in fits and spurts due to very unusual weather patterns this year. Spring experienced unusually high temperatures, which promoted initial growth, and flowering to occur one month early. June and July then became very cool which halted this progression. Rain and humidity caused further upset during the summer bringing problems of mildew and other rots, including *botrytis* especially at higher altitudes, to the vines. Luckily the weather then became hot and dry towards the end of August and this continued into September. This helped ripen the grapes for the harvest which started on September 15.

Yields fell dramatically due to this unsettled growth and irregular ripening – by 40 per cent compared to 1996. In some of the subzones this loss was as much as 60 per cent. Fortunately this does not cause worries in terms of overall production, as in 1996 the Douro experienced some of the highest yields of the century. This year's smaller harvest has concentrated the wines producing high quality, and very happy producers.

*This is fairly certain to be "declared" (in 1999) and a small quantity of high quality 1997 vintage port will be shipped at ever-increasing prices. Clearly with a 20 year life-span.*

## 1996 ☆☆☆

A large crop resulted, as it did all over Portugal, after heavy rain in December and January – 533mm (21ins) was recorded at Pinhão, in the mid-Douro valley. Consequently, there was some flooding and damage inflicted in certain areas, but generally this provided stocks for an impending long, hot summer.

Spring was mild which promoted good flowering and vine development. Not a drop of rain fell between June and August and ripening was behind schedule. Most houses did not start harvesting until late September and the highest quality grapes were picked right at the end, after a beneficial extension of their ripening period. Yields were larger than normal, however, producers are voicing concern about imminent stock shortages due to continuing increases in sales. The characteristics of the wines produced this year are deep colour and aroma, with wonderfully ripe fruit. Not declared a vintage.

*There is tremendous pressure, particularly on the American market for vintage port, imports now well exceeding those of the traditional UK market, so at the least we can expect LBV ports as a compromise.*

## 1995 ☆☆☆☆

This year started with a wet winter, turning at the end of February into seven weeks of fine weather. A mild spring followed, with an early bud-break in April and the vines two weeks ahead of schedule. A short frost on April 21 caused damage to some of the northern vineyards. Then a very hot July caused drought and restricted maturation. The heat continued into August and some producers in the Douro Superiore brought the vintage date forward to 23 August as they watched their vines become stressed.

Vintage started on September 4 with a short burst of rain from September 5 to 10, to rehydrate the shrivelled vines. From September 11 conditions were ideal and the finest wines were produced from grapes harvested at this time. Having reached their full maturity the grapes had greater depth of flavour and softer skins facilitating maximum extraction. This vintage was not declared by most houses due to the outstanding vintage of 1994, but Quinta do Noval (using only ten per cent of total production), Quinta do Vesuvio and Malvedos each did.

Yields were higher than expected which was good news after the deficits of 1992 to 1994. Quality was excellent: deep colour, aroma and concentrated flavours. However, not a vintage year.

*Not a classic vintage year. Those 1995s which have been put on the market will be best after 2005.*

## 1994☆☆☆to☆☆☆☆

**Widely declared** This vintage started dismally with rains right through until March, after a relatively dry December. Over 558mm (22ins) were recorded at the Quinta do Bomfim from October to the end of February and overall, there were 254mm (10ins) more rainfall than in the previous year. In April and May the weather was poor – it was damp without much warmth and humidity was a problem. The result of this was *desavinho* – an uneven ripening of the grapes. Some storms during the spring caused severe damage, but on a local scale.

Summer was satisfactory though rain fell around August 10 and 11 and temperatures rose to 40°C (100°F) briefly the following week. The condition of the grapes was excellent but the crop was relatively small. Picking started on September 8 with some growers completing their harvests quickly to avoid the problems that beset the previous year with rainfall ruining the grapes. An ideal amount of rain fell on September 13/14 that softened the skins, swelled the grapes and increased sugar levels. Those who waited benefited enormously. The results were good to excellent, although volumes were reduced.

*Widely declared as "vintage". Full bodied fruity wines that need plenty of bottle-age, the best reaching the plateau of full maturity around 2002 to 2010.*

## 1993 ∼

**Not declared** One of the worst years in recent memory. Shippers who declared their 1991 or 1992 will benefit from their foresight. In theory, demand for these and older vintages should improve. The weather pattern in Portugal was markedly different from the more northerly European areas. Autumn and winter were extremely wet, with twice the average rainfall recorded at Quinta do Bomfim. Landslides even occurred in the some of the terraced parts of the Douro. New year and spring were dry, but damp weather in May inhibited flowering. Summer was less hot than usual and was followed by unsettled weather.

Those who harvested early, such as at Quintas do Vesuvio and Malvedos, were fortunate because exceptionally heavy rainfall started on October 2 and continued consistently for two weeks, making picking difficult, uncomfortable and unsatisfactory. The rainfall was so extreme that the Douro river and its tributaries came very close to flooding.

The dramatic drop in production will, however, make up for recent years of rampant overproduction and, perhaps, help stabilise the market.

## 1992☆☆☆to☆☆☆☆

Despite a fairly curious growing season, the end results were satisfactory – good quality wine was produced. In view of the far less satisfactory 1993 harvest, the shippers, most notably Taylor's and Fonseca, who did not declare their 1991, have declared their 1992. Indeed Taylor's preferred their 1992 to the 1991, though I suspect that uppermost in their minds was the rather happy coincidence of this year being the 300th-anniversary of the foundation of the company!

What was curious about the growing season? First of all, the worst winter drought conditions since records began, with almost no rain for six months; a cold damp spell in the late spring followed by a very hot and dry early summer. Mercifully, rain at the end of August resuscitated and swelled the berries. Dry weather returned as the harvest approached which finally took place in relatively cool but showery conditions.

Overall, some good wines were made, the better wines being the result of grapes brought in during October. In comparison with 1991 the yields were down by about 20 per cent.

*Limited declaration but some very good wines.*

## 1991☆☆☆☆

**Widely declared.** A very good year resulted after a fairly sodden start. A generally dry winter sadly turned very wet in January and the rainy conditions lasted through to April, though flowering took place in May in warm, dry weather.

June through to August was hot and dry and the flower set excellent, but the heat and lack of summer rain then resulted in thick skins and reduced flesh. Light showers fell on September 10/11 which helped, with more rain towards the end of the month, the swelling of the berries. These are mostly deep coloured, ripe wines which are looking very promising.

*Needs ten to 20 years ageing, though doubtless good single-quinta and LBV port will be – should be – drinkable well before the end of the century.*

## 1990☆☆☆

**Not declared** Severe heat in July and August held back the ripening of some varieties; the Tinta Barocca grapes were particularly badly affected by *queima* or burning.

Picking began early, on September 3, but the maturity of these grapes was uneven. Instead of the super-ripe fruit that many growers had expected, sugar levels were frequently low and acidity too high; better grapes were, however, picked after overnight rain on September 19/20. A huge quantity of high quality port would have been made but for a shortage of *aguardente*, or brandy, used to fortify the wine. As a result, many reputable growers were forced to make table wine from high quality must that would otherwise have been used for port. However, it has since transpired that the "shortage" of brandy was in fact due to officially, yet not widely known, permitted overproduction of port wine.

At the time of writing there are some excellent wines from 1990, undoubtedly of declared vintage quality. However, this year was not declared, due to the recession in the UK and the US – the two largest markets for vintage port.

*Some good single-quinta wines drinking pleasantly now.*

## 1989☆☆

**Not declared** After a disastrous year, the port trade hoped that 1989 would produce a much needed abundance of good-quality wines, which would be suitable for blending. This was not to be. A summer-long drought produced only a small quantity of wines, with good vintage potential.

A dry winter and a hot, dry spring. Drought conditions prevailed throughout Portugal already, particularly in the eastern areas, except for a few very localised districts which saw rain and even the occasional hailstorm in early summer, recurring later in August. Elsewhere the drought continued throughout summer until the harvest (beginning September 6) when rain swelled the grapes, rewarding growers who picked late.

The drought led to a small crop of rather dry grapes and as a result the wines tend to lack sufficient colour and balance. The best came from the central port-making vineyards. Because of the 1988 shortfall of wines for standard blends, 1989 was not declared.

*Note regarding "drinkability" irrelevant as this wine will be lost in ruby and tawny blends.*

## 1988☆☆

A mild winter was followed by a cold, dry spring. The months from April to July were the wettest in 30 years, causing *coulure* during flowering and later mildew, reducing the crop by around 30 to 35 per cent. The wines were good but not of vintage quality. Meanwhile, the market was suffering from a severe shortage of wines suitable for blending.

*Mainly due for blending, but Martinez and any single-quinta wines drinkable between now and 2004.*

## 1987☆to☆☆☆☆

Had it not been so soon after the 1985 had been declared, 1987 would have qualified for "vintage" status. Instead, apart from one or two single-quinta wines it was declared only by Martinez.

A mild, dry winter and warm spring provided good conditions for a prolific and successful flowering. However, hopes for an abundant crop were marred by three months of uninterrupted drought and heat. This gave small, dehydrated berries which consequently reduced the potential yields.

The harvest began as early as September 7 in some areas in scorching, arid conditions which broke on September 21, when rain swelled the remaining grapes. The wines made from these grapes were of better quality than those picked earlier, which were overripe and tended to lack acidity. This was a bigger than average vintage of variable quality.

*Some good single-quinta wines to drink now to 2000.*

## 1986☆☆

**Not declared** After a cold, wet winter a long, cold spring with frosts in April followed and the weather did not warm up until early May. The vines were by now three weeks behind their normal growth schedule but warm weather during the first week of June provided perfect flowering conditions.

An uneven summer produced small, shrivelled grapes, then in the second two weeks of September heavy rainfall caused flooding in the Douro – as much as 508mm (200ins) was recorded in one weekend at Pinhão. However, warm weather followed, encouraging a rise in sugar levels and providing better conditions for the harvest.

In the Upper Douro a good quantity of grapes was gathered, but in the Lower Douro the wet weather returned in October and the grapes suffered from rot.

*Some LBV port of variable quality which ought to be drunk soon, while at their best.*

## 1985☆☆☆☆

**26 shippers declared** An unquestionably attractive vintage, declared unanimously as a vintage year; almost, but not quite, of the calibre of 1945, 1963 and 1977.

An extremely wet winter and late spring retarded the growth of the vines by around two weeks. Some localised areas saw severe thunder and hailstorms during the first days of June causing the loss of over a third of the crop. Elsewhere summer was hot and extremely dry and the healthy but too-dry grapes were harvested from mid-September.

Some winemakers experienced unwelcome difficulties during the fermentation of their grapes. This was mainly due to the very high temperatures and the resulting wines lacked freshness and bouquet. Otherwise, this was a first-rate, vibrantly fruity and concentrated vintage.

*Lovely wines, tempting to drink whilst young and full of fruit, but the classic shippers' will develop beautifully, well into the 21st century.*

## 1984☆☆

**Not declared** A cold, dry winter was followed by a wet spring. With the exception of very high temperatures in July the summer was cool. Conditions improved with a hot, dry September and harvest began on September 24. Four days later rain came, followed by high winds which dried the grapes and minimised the risk of rot. The harvest was eventually completed under ideal conditions. The wet weather had reduced high sugar levels and a large quantity of grapes made good, sound wines.

*Blends year. Variable single-quintas and LBV wines. Drink up.*

## 1983☆☆☆☆

**Roughly 10 major shippers declared** The third of a moderately good to very good trio of vintages, declared too close together and by no means generally, leading to confusion.

A dry, very cold winter ran into a cool, wet, uneven spring which did not warm up until early June. The resulting *coulure* caused the loss of around 20 per cent of the potential crop. Then, after a rather uneven summer, the September temperatures rose to as high as 30˚C (86˚F) with a few localised rainstorms at the end of the month. The harvest was one of the latest recorded in the Douro, starting on October 3 in the Upper Douro and a week later in the Lower Douro.

The best wines came from the Upper Douro; they have good colour, flavour and bouquet; some are even outstanding. They are overshadowed, though, by the 1985s and will remain under-valued until the confused market has calmed down.

*Minor shippers and quintas now; major shippers to 2015.*

## 1982☆☆☆ at best☆☆☆☆

**12 shippers declared** Some big names, including Cockburn, Graham and Warre, were not among those declared, having more faith in the 1983s. After a dry winter and mild spring, flowering took place in May in mainly warm, sunny weather. Hot, drought conditions prompted an early harvest, starting September 8, during which a light sprinkling of much needed rain freshened the grapes.

High temperatures during fermentation resulted in uneven quality and perhaps a lack of elegance, making this a currently underpriced vintage. The best wines, however, are full, firm and robust with good underlying fruitiness.

*All can be drunk now but the relatively few top shippers, such as Croft, will keep well beyond 2000.*

## 1981☆

**Not declared** A winter drought and cool spring delayed flowering until early June. Extremely hot weather followed and growth was retarded further by the lack of moisture in the soil, resulting in a reduction of the potential crop size due to stressed vines.

Heavy rain, storms and severe gales affected both the area around Oporto and the Douro, coinciding with the harvest around the middle of September. They did, however, freshen the, by now, dried-up grapes and cooled temperatures down. Eventually, the sun reappeared. The best wines were made in the Lower Douro where the grapes were picked latest. There were some reasonable LBV ports and the rest were used for blending.

*Drink up.*

## 1980☆☆☆

**Widely declared** A vintage which was thought by many to have come too soon after the superlative 1977s and the originally well thought of 1975s.

A wet winter was followed by a cold, wet spring which continued, unchanged, until flowering. The summer was hot with virtually no rainfall until September 20/21 when it rained heavily in most of the Douro. Sadly this was too late to improve the grapes, which were picked from September 22 onwards. But in the Lower Douro, where picking started later, grapes did benefit from the rainfall and made good quality wines.

Overall this was a small vintage which produced some extremely pleasant wines. Useful for drinking while waiting for the 1977s and 1985s to mature. Considered by the Symingtons as much underrated.

*Most are delightful now, the top wines will develop further, at their peak either side of 2000.*

## 1979☆☆

**3 minor shippers declared** A wet, unsettled spring was followed by a drought which ran from June onwards and eventually broke with heavy rains in mid-September.

*Drink up.*

## 1978☆☆☆

**8 shippers declared** A cold, wet spring was followed by a long drought from June to October. Heavy, coarse, full-bodied wines. A notable vintage mainly for the large number of single-quinta ports marketed.

*Most at their peak now, exceptions being Ferreira, Malvedos and, of course, Noval Nacional.*

## 1977☆☆☆☆☆

**20 shippers declared** A great vintage in the classic mould. A cold, wet winter ran into a dreary spring and a cool summer which retarded the development of the vines, but the situation improved radically with a September heatwave. Grapes were picked from September 28 and were, with the exception of those picked late in wet weather, in perfect condition.

Although there was some anxiety that the 1977 vintage had come too soon after the previously declared year 1975, this was declared as a vintage unusually early – shippers were impressed by the fresh bouquet of the wines. Notably, Martinez, Noval and Cockburn did not ship the 1977, a decision they later regretted. Generally, these were deep, consistently good quality wines. They will be worth keeping for the next century.

*Now to 2020, even beyond; well beyond for the top wines. The minor wines enjoyable now. Most will be reasonably mature from now to 2010.*

## 1976☆

**2 shippers declared** Not a vintage year. A drought ran through winter, spring and summer and ended in late August. Heavy rains fell during the harvest in late September. A small quantity of pleasant wines appearing as single-quinta and LBV ports.

*Drink up.*

## 1975☆☆☆

**17 shippers declared** A vintage welcomed by all (including shippers in Oporto where life was dominated by the revolution) and consequently somewhat overrated when it was declared.

A wet winter, followed by a long, hot summer. Early September rain swelled the grapes, but bad weather at the end of the month caused some damage in the vineyards. Doubtless the wet weather prevented the 1975 vintage from living up to earlier expectations.

*Most are, in fact, drinking very pleasantly now, and should be consumed before the 1977s and vintages of the early 1980s.*

## 1974☆

**Not declared** Grapes were ruined by heavy rain during the harvest. (Vargellas marketed, as were some single-quintas.)

*Drink up.*

## 1973

**Not declared** A wet spring, hot summer and a wet, unsettled September produced the occasional good wine.

*Rarely seen. Drink up.*

## 1972☆

**3 shippers declared** Heavy rainfall either side of heat and drought. Some flavoursome wines, but generally not declared.

*Drink up.*

## 1971☆

**Not declared** A late flowering and late harvest produced some nice wines for blending.

## 1970☆☆☆☆☆

**23 shippers declared** A highly satisfactory and underrated year. Also significant as this was the last year in which a port could be shipped in cask for bottling in the UK. After 1970 bottling at the shippers' own lodges was made mandatory.

The weather was perfectly conducive to a good vintage. After a cold, dry spring, an ideal summer and some beneficial rain in September. Harvest took place in very good conditions. Sound, healthy, well-constituted wines. Much sturdier than originally considered, and with plenty of life ahead of them. The more I taste and drink the 1970s, the more impressed I am. They are still worth looking out for for laying down, even after 20 years.

*Minor shippers now to 2000; major shippers well beyond 2020.*

## 1969

**Not declared** Bad weather conditions led to unripe wines.

*Few seen. Drink up.*

## 1968☆☆

**Not declared** Some nice wines: LBV and single-quinta ports.

*Drink up.*

## 1967☆☆

**4 shippers declared** Apart from a wet May, the summer was hot and dry. Rain in September swelled the grapes and the harvest took place under favourable conditions. Cockburn, Martinez,

Sandeman and Noval declared this vintage rather than the 1966. Those who declared misjudged the vintage and the market.

*Drink soon.*

## 1966☆☆☆☆☆

**20 shippers declared** An attractive, elegant vintage. A wet winter ran into a stormy May. July was hot but the grapes were protected from the sun by the unusually generous foliage. Some rain fell. Overall, this was an appealing, well-constituted vintage which was underrated and undervalued, but then upgraded in the 1980s. Some might even outlive the 1963s.

*Most are drinking beautifully now but have the balance to achieve fuller maturity in, say, ten years. The best are turning out to be better than the more fashionable and pricey 1963s.*

## 1965☆

**Not declared** There were nice, ripe wines nevertheless.

*Drink soon.*

## 1964☆

**Not declared** Difficult weather conditions and a labour shortage caused by the illegal emigration of workers to France made this a problematic year.

*Drink up.*

## 1963☆☆☆☆☆

**25 shippers declared** An outstanding vintage which was met with great acclaim. A wet, snowy winter and spring ran right through to April; cold and rain lasted until mid-June, thereafter the weather was fine and dry. Picking took place in good conditions, following beneficial September rain. A large quantity of vintage port was made. Well-constituted, elegant wines.

*Most drinking perfectly now. Some of the original high flyers showing a good deal of maturity. Top wines to 2020 or so.*

## 1962☆☆

**Not declared** Some good wines. Disastrous winter floods, but generally good summer. A great, classic year for Noval Nacional.

*Noval Nacional now to 2020, the rest drink now.*

## 1961☆☆☆

**Not declared** Some good wines. Undeclared largely due to its proximity to the 1958 and 1960 vintages. Some single-quinta wines and good, commercial LBV ports were made.

*Rarely seen but drinking well.*

**Prior to 1960, only "declared" vintage years noted**

## 1960☆☆☆to☆☆☆☆

**24 shippers declared** A popular and overall satisfactory vintage. Apart from two months of rain during February and March, the weather conditions were ideal: fine, hot and dry. Heat and rain which prevailed during the harvest caused some problems for the subsequent fermentation. Generally well-balanced wines.

*All are fully mature now but will give pleasure up to, and the best beyond, the end of the century.*

## 1958☆☆☆

**12 shippers declared** Good, if light wines. Uneven weather conditions included a hot June with the highest rainfall since 1896. Martinez was the most substantial port.

*Drink up.*

## 1955☆☆☆☆☆

**26 shippers declared** A very successful year – the best of the post-war vintages prior to 1963 – and greatly welcomed by the shippers and the British merchants. A heatwave throughout April and May; a good flowering; some beneficial rain during late May and June, and a hot August. Grapes harvested in good conditions.

Generally well-balanced and potentially long-lasting wines: Taylor's was a blockbuster when young but is simmering down now. Overall, my favourite vintage for current drinking.

*Mainly perfection now but most have the fruit and body to continue gloriously well into the next century.*

## 1954☆☆☆

**3 shippers declared** A good vintage but not widely declared due to the success of the 1955s. Rarely seen. Malvedos very good.

## 1950☆☆

**13 shippers declared** A generally satisfactory year weatherwise, but light, uneven wines.

*Drink up.*

## 1948☆☆☆☆to☆☆☆☆☆

**9 shippers declared** A good but partially by-passed year. The budding was early and the flowering healthy. However, intense heat throughout August reduced the size of the crop; thickened the skins of the grapes; concentrated and raised sugar levels. Deep, powerful, alcoholic port. Fonseca good, Graham excellent, Taylor outstanding, even better than the 1945.

*Perfect now.*

## 1947☆☆☆☆

**11 shippers declared** A good, abundant year. The summer was long, hot and dry with some welcome September rain. Picking began on September 22 in perfect conditions.

*Fully mature; needs drinking.*

## 1945☆☆☆☆☆

**22 shippers declared** An outstanding vintage; one of the best of the century and certainly the best since 1935. All the port was bottled in Oporto. A very hot, dry summer was followed by some September rain. Harvesting took place in great heat prompting anxiety over fermentation. Ultimately, the quality was superb but quantity small – insufficient to fill the war-depleted cellars.

*Generally, a magnificent, firm, fruity and powerful vintage which at its best can still be superb, but some wines drying out.*

## 1944☆☆☆

**3 shippers declared** Superb quality but shippers concentrated on the 1945s. Rarely seen.

## 1942☆☆☆

**10 shippers declared** A very good year which suffered wartime neglect. Not often seen. Generally good weather conditions with the exception of a stormy June.

## 1930s

The 1930s saw only two years in which vintages were declared, but some very good port was also made in other years.

**1935**☆☆☆☆ (15 shippers) Healthy, top-quality grapes which were harvested in perfect conditions. The best were from Cockburn, Croft, Graham and Sandeman; the most magnificent of all was, still is, the Taylor. The quantity, however, was smaller than that of **1934**☆☆☆☆ (12 shippers), which was the first widely declared vintage after 1927. One of my favourites: good, balanced, classic wines. Now rarely seen but worth looking out for.

**1931**☆☆☆☆ (3 shippers), though a splendid vintage, was not declared. The demand was low, the British market being in the depth of the recession, and cellars were still full of 1927s. There was, however, an abundance of good ports and this vintage was made famous by just one: the magnificent, deep, full-bodied Noval, the Everest of vintage ports.

## 1920s

This decade produced one classic vintage, two good vintages and a string of undeclared years of disappointing to good quality.

The classic year was **1927**☆☆☆☆☆ (30 shippers). After a difficult ripening, ten days of fine weather blessed the harvest. This vintage coincided with the height of the port market. Some now thin and "spotty", others still magnificent, multi-dimensional. **1924**☆☆☆ (18 shippers) produced good quality port, the quantity, though, was small due to four months of drought ending with heavy rain in September. Overall, the 1924s are still keeping well.

Prior to this, two other vintages were declared during the 1930s. **1922**☆☆☆ (18 shippers) a sorely neglected year that produced a small quantity of lightish wines, similar in style to the 1917s. **1920**☆☆☆☆ (23 shippers) the first major vintage after 1912, which produced a small crop of good, robust, long-lasting wines, which, if well kept, can still be good.

## 1910s

A decade which included one classic vintage, one very good vintage and several mediocre years. A light, elegant vintage was made in **1917**☆☆☆ (15 shippers) smooth and attractive wines, but not substantial and is now very rarely seen. The classic vintage of the decade was **1912**☆☆☆☆☆ (25 shippers) apart from rain in September which delayed the harvest, the summer was hot, and rich, now ethereal port was made. One of Taylor's greatest vintages, still good. **1911**☆☆☆ was a "coronation" vintage, shipped only by Sandeman. Still lovely when last tasted in 1964.

## 1900s

The 1900s produced three of the four great classic vintages prior to World War One, (the fourth being 1912).

**1908**☆☆☆☆☆ (26 shippers), was initially darker and fuller bodied than 1904 and 1900, and maintained its depth throughout its life. Cockburn's famed vintage is still magnificent. **1904**☆☆☆☆ (25 shippers) was indeed a great vintage, but lighter than 1900, though they have kept very well. **1900**☆☆☆☆☆ (22 shippers) was a year of exceptionally fine quality, though rarely seen now.

## 1890s

The 1890s saw several good vintages and one classic.

**1899**☆ (one shipper) was definitely not among them. Only seven shippers declared the **1897**☆☆☆☆ (known as "The Royal Diamond Jubilee Year"), fortified with Scotch whisky as all the brandy had been used for the 1896s. **1896**☆☆☆☆ (24 shippers) was the great classic vintage of the decade, but now of variable quality, thinning and tired. **1894**☆☆ (13 shippers) middling to good, of better quality than **1892**☆☆ (10 shippers) moderate, now rarely seen. **1890**☆☆☆ (20 shippers) made tough, tannic wines.

## OLDER PORT VINTAGES

**1887**☆☆☆ Queen Victoria's Golden Jubilee vintage, this is still good to drink, as are **1884**☆☆☆☆☆ **1878**☆☆☆☆☆ **1875**☆☆☆☆ **1870**☆☆☆☆☆ **1863**☆☆☆☆☆ **1851**☆☆☆☆ and **1847**☆☆☆☆☆ (the greatest of the mid-19th century).

# Madeira

At first sight madeira seems an unlikely candidate for a vintage pocket book. It is both simple to understand and enjoy, yet there are four major "noble" grape varieties: Sercial, Verdelho, Bual and Malmsey (or Malvoisie); each making dry, medium-dry, medium-sweet and sweet wines respectively. However, another and more prolific grape – the Tinta Negra Mole – is used to make the less expensive wines; as it imitates, surprisingly effectively, the four basic grape styles just mentioned. Madeira is a fortified wine. Its method of making resembles sherry in some respects, port in others. Unlike either it undergoes a heat treatment which gives it its inimitable "tang".

Most madeira is blended and marketed under a brand name. Fairly recently a leaf has been taken out the port shippers' books, by producing excellent ten-year-old blends of the major grape varieties. But the glory of madeira lies in its vintage and *solera* wines. Happily, both are still made, boding well for the future.

Madeira is a semi-tropical island in the Atlantic, off the coast of West Africa. Though there are weather variations, the climate is delightful all the year round. Vintage time is unusually long, from mid-to late August until early October, depending on the grape variety and, in this spectacularly mountainous island, on the altitude of the vineyard.

The following are the best known shippers of vintage and *solera* wines: Barbeito, Blandy, Cossart Gordon, Henriques & Henriques, Justino Leacock, Pereira d'Oliveira and Rutherford & Miles; and amongst the old vintages, Acciaioly and H M Borges.

"Vintage" madeira is a wine made from one named grape variety (they are never mixed) of one vintage, matured in cask. A "*solera*" madeira, also with a named grape, usually bears on the label the year the *solera* was started, the original wine being topped up with younger wine of the same grape and quality as the matured blend is drawn off. After sufficient maturation in cask an old madeira will be put into demijohns for an unspecified storage time until needed for bottling. It is not always clear from the label, or from a stencilled bottle, whether a dated madeira is straight (unblended) vintage or *solera*. Although the vintage madeira tends to command a higher price, the old *solera* madeira is often the finer drink.

It might be imagined that Madeira's weather is as idyllic as its setting and that vintage variations would not exist. This is not so. The decade of the 1980s catalogues many of the problems and some of the excesses. Add to this rampant inflation, exceeding 33 per cent in 1984, the cost of importing essential materials, and it is a wonder that the price of madeira can be competitive. Indeed in the lower quality range it is not. Happily, the demand for high quality island-bottled wine is increasing; and it is in top blends and, I believe, vintage madeira that the future lies.

"When to drink?" In essence, madeira is ready for drinking as soon as it is put on the market; young vintages are not bottled for "laying down". It can safely be assumed that any vintage or *solera* wine from prior to 1970 will be mature and ready for consumption. Also happily, madeira is virtually indestructible and old vintages will, with few exceptions, still be drinkable.

## 1997 ☆☆☆to☆☆☆☆

As in 1996, winter rain provided re-hydration for the vines before the onset of a hot and dry ripening period. The season was perfect and problem free, with a very uniform ripening for all varieties.

Harvesting began in the south on August 20 and for the majority picking was completed very swiftly by October 2, although for the higher vineyards – at or above 600 metres – it continued until October 10. The yields were not quite as high as compared to 1996, yet still substantial, they were only down by five per cent on the previous year's figure. Bual, Malmsey and Tinta Negra Mole were of very high quality; however Sercial, from further north, did not achieve such good results.

*Clearly a potential top solera; even, one hopes, a small amount of these grapes will be put to aside to make a vintage wine.*

## 1996☆☆☆☆

The success continues this year in both quantity and quality. Total production was up by 50 per cent compared to 1995, In common with the last vintage harvesting began fairly early on August 22 in the lower regions around Campanario and Calheta.

Winter rains had provided a good stock of water for the warm, dry ripening period. "Textbook" conditions prevailed throughout the year which provided a uniform, problem-free development until harvest. This was completed in the north by October 18. Vinification also ran smoothly, producing excellent results – especially for Bual, Verdelho, Sercial and Tinta Negra Mole.

*Very heartening to see more quality grapes and wine finding its way into the Madeira "lodges". Possibly a future vintage wine.*

## 1995☆☆☆☆

Another very good harvest with yields up by ten per cent, but this was still lower than expected. The lower and warmer vineyards around the coastal areas of Câmara de Lobos produced the highest quality grapes, especially the Bual and Malmsey. Bual was doubly successful with excellent quality in substantial quantities.

The growing season was hot and favourable with minimal rain. This encouraged rapid and consistent ripening and a very early harvest, which began on August 2 in the lower areas for the Bual, Malmsey and Tinta Negra Mole. The grapes were picked by September 20 and a week later the harvest of the later ripening varieties began. Verdelho and Sercial were the last to be picked by October 15, in the northern vineyards around Seixal and Santana. Results were fine with age-worthy wines.

*Age-worthy is the appropriate word. Madeira is basically blended, so the age of the blends is important. This year will provide a satisfactory base wine for the commercial three-year olds and, later, should develop and mature into the remarkably good and great value ten-year olds.*

## 1994☆☆☆☆☆

This was a very successful year, producing good to excellent quality but reduced quantities. A particularly small Bual harvest.

The north side of the island produced some exceptional wines as less than usual rain fell during the growing season. At the same time growers have improved their treatment of the vines, for example only spraying when absolutely necessary. These two factors resulted in grapes ripening with exceptional levels of sweetness. The south side of the island saw more variable climatic conditions. In the Calheta region, renowned for its Bual production, the crop was reduced by as much as 70 to 80 per cent because of mist and light rain during flowering. In Camara de Lobos results were excellent for Tinta Negra Mole and Malmsey.

## 1993☆to☆☆☆

A difficult year as various adverse conditions struck when the vines were at their most vulnerable. Rain and hail fell during both flowering and "*pintar*" (when grapes begin to change colour).

The Camara de Lobos and Estreito regions were the worst affected, but some areas did manage to escape. Good wines were produced in the Campanario and Calheta regions. Overall, the better wines are the result of careful selection.

## 1992 ☆☆☆☆

A successful year for Madeira with particularly advantageous climatic conditions. Rainfall was below average and when it did occur, it was at times least harmful to the vines. These kind conditions allowed for minimal use of fungicides and pesticides.

Picking began on the southern side of the island in the Campanario on August 28 with the final wave beginning in the Jardim da Serra on October 6. A little rain fell during the harvest and the crop was slightly smaller than average.

## 1991 ☆☆☆

A good quality vintage, with the grapes being free of any disease. The resulting wines have plenty of fruit and promise well for their future development. Production in 1991 was much greater than in 1990. In particular, the Jardim da Serra area produced much more Sercial than usual, and production of Bual at Calheta is estimated to have more than doubled, thanks largely to the new government-sponsored plantings of the varietal to replace the former hybrid vines.

The months of June, July and August were notable for their fine weather and although some rain fell during the vintage, picking was barely affected and, as mentioned above, the grapes reached the winery in good condition.

## 1990 ☆☆☆☆☆

A generally excellent vintage, particularly for the noble varieties. The picking commenced on August 16 in the classic lower-lying districts of the south – Camara de Lobos and Campanario, particularly famous for their Bual and Malmsey. The Sercial and Verdelho harvest on the north side of Madeira started during the first week of September.

The weather was cool during picking with some rain, though this was accompanied by wind quickly drying the grapes which were generally in perfect condition with good sugar readings. Crop slightly smaller than 1989.

## 1989 ☆☆☆

June and July very cold with haze affecting the higher vineyards, all of which delayed development and reduced the crop potential – by as much as 50 per cent in the southerly Camara de Lobos, Estreito and Campanario districts. Heat returned at the end of July and continued throughout August.

Overall, however, the quality of grapes was good, and the size of the crop on the north of the island compensated for the shortfall in the south. Clearly there was some improvement in the growth and harvesting of the Sercial grapes: large bunches, and potentially high alcohol.

## 1988☆☆☆☆

One of the best vintages of the decade, all the major grape varieties were suitable for high quality blends, with true vintage potential. Near perfect climatic conditions, but June and July were cooler than usual, delaying development. But, the quality of the late harvest was high. The vineyards of the northern part of the island were particularly successful with quantity and quality; in the south the crop was somewhat reduced, especially from the higher vineyards affected by low cloud and mist.

A notable increase of *Vitis vinifera* on the island, thanks to the Regional Government's programme to switch from hybrid and ungrafted varieties to the classic madeira grape types.

## 1987☆☆☆☆

A satisfactory growing season. Rain, even snow on the higher ground during January and February. Beneficial spring rains and, despite strong winds in April and May. Satisfactory flowering.

The harvest was three weeks early, commencing the second week in August and continuing in the higher vineyards until the end of September. Towards the middle of September an easterly Sahara wind raised temperatures to 38°C (100°F) necessitating cooling of the must. A substantial crop of good quality.

## 1986☆☆

A poor start to the year: cloud and rain between January and March, also much snow on the high ground – delayed seasonal vineyard work. To compensate, the late budding and flowering missed damaging winds. Heavy rain fell in May and July.

Happily, in contrast to some previous years, the farmers had appropriate facilities to treat the vines. Rain again during the harvest necessitated speedy picking. The net result was an abundant crop of moderate richness.

## 1985

One of the worst vintages in living memory. The production was one of the lowest on record since oidium and phylloxera swept the island in the mid-19th century.

Winter was cool, but torrential rain throughout the island caused considerable damage to vineyards: terracing and soil were washed away. Spring was cool and abnormally wet; high humidity during leaf break and flowering resulting in viral diseases and mildews, affecting the development of early shoots. Flowering was late and, because of extremely humid conditions, uneven and often incomplete. June, July and August were hot but also relatively humid causing the spread of mildew and rot. The harvest picking was spasmodic, from the first week in September through to early October. Some farmers did not pick at all.

## 1984

Unfortunately, there were atrocious weather conditions this year, with a harvest to match. This was the result of extremely heavy rainfall from late February, and continuing through March.

This then caused landslides and much damage to the crops. The pruning was also interrupted by the rain and, sadly, by the need to replace soil and repair terracing.

The flowering was delayed 4 to 5 weeks and when it did begin (late April early May) there was a further period of high winds and torrential rain; also, in the north, severe hail damage. Damp, humid conditions persisted through to early July causing large areas of powdery mildew. July, August and September were hot though often cloudy. The late and uneven ripening delayed the start of picking until September 15 in the lower vineyards of the south and as late as September 28 in the north: this was one of the latest vintages on record. Indeed, in the higher vineyards planted with Sercial and Verdelho the harvest, such as it was, did not begin until the second week in October.

Overall, the production was 40 per cent less than normal and the grapes had a low sugar content. This all caused a severe problem in stock levels.

## 1983 ☆☆☆☆☆
This was an outstanding year. Of vintage quality wine and for top-class blends. A fairly cold and prolonged winter rested the dormant vines and discouraged premature growth, which can be a problem on the island.

Spring was cool and damp bringing problems of mildew , but flowering, though late, was generally satisfactory. July and August were both very hot, with scorching winds from the Sahara necessitating picking as early as August 10 in the lower southern vineyards of Camara de Lobos.

The Bual and Verdelho had exceptionally high sugar readings. However, the Sercial crop was reduced by mildew, wind damage and late ripening. The small crop of Terrantez was of the highest quality and is being nurtured by the Madeira Wine Company to produce an outstanding vintage of this rare wine.

## 1982 ☆☆
An exceptionally mild and dry winter did not provide an adequate vegetative rest period, and the low temperatures of mid-April and May resulted in uneven and late flowering. The higher than normal rainfall in the early summer hampered development, causing some mildew damage.

However, despite the cooler temperatures than normal, the weather during the vintage was dry and though it was late – some 12 days later than normal in the south, eight days late in the north – it progressed well. Crop 15 to 18 per cent down on previous vintages. Moderate quality.

## 1981 ☆☆☆
An average-sized harvest of good quality grapes. Winter was warm and dry, pleasant for tourists but not for vines. An equally pleasant, sunny and dry summer resulted in satisfactory, though later than usual, ripening. Grapes such as Sercial, grown on higher ground, did best.

## 1980☆☆☆☆

An unusually mild spring and warm summer, free of damaging winds. Picking began on August 25 in south coast vineyards and from September 8 in the north, yielding an above average crop of good quality grapes with higher than usual sugar content.

What was particularly noticeable, and welcome, was the larger crop of European grafted vines following the Government assisted conversion scheme – which was started in 1975 – from hybrids; wine from the latter used only for island consumption. However, apart from inflation, running at very high levels ever since the revolution of 1974, unfortunately, interest rates at 18.25 per cent since May 1978 made the necessary stock-holding a great burden for the major shippers.

## THE DECADE OF THE 1970s

Detailed weather statistics and quality ratings for this period either unavailable or unreliable.

## MATURE MADEIRA VINTAGES

**1968**☆☆☆☆ **1967**☆☆☆☆ **1964**☆☆☆ **1960**☆☆☆ **1957**☆☆☆☆ **1954**☆☆☆☆

## OLDER MADEIRA VINTAGES

**1952**☆☆☆ (particularly Verdelho and Malmsey), **1950**☆☆ **1944**☆☆☆ **1941**☆☆☆☆ (particularly Bual and Malmsey), **1940**☆☆☆☆ (especially Sercial), **1939**☆☆☆☆ **1936**☆☆☆☆ (Cossart's Sercial the best of the century), **1934**☆☆☆☆ (all grape varieties and districts excellent), **1933**☆☆☆ **1932**☆☆ **1931**☆

**1927**☆☆☆☆ **1920**☆☆☆☆ (Cossart's Malmsey☆☆☆☆☆), **1916**☆☆☆ (particularly Malmsey), **1915**☆☆☆ **1914**☆☆☆ (small crop, noted for its Bual), **1913**☆☆☆ **1910**☆☆☆☆☆ (the best all round vintage of the period), **1907**☆☆☆ **1906**☆☆ (small crop, Malmsey especially good), **1905**☆☆☆ (small but good), **1900**☆☆☆☆ (great vintage).

## PRE-1900

**1899**☆☆☆☆ **1898**☆☆☆☆ (the best since the phylloxera scourge), **1895**☆☆☆ **1893**☆☆☆☆ **1892**☆☆☆ (small crop), **1891**☆☆☆ **1890**☆☆ (small crop), **1883**☆☆☆☆ **1880**☆☆☆ **1879**☆☆☆☆ **1878**☆☆ **1877**☆☆☆ **1875**☆☆☆☆ (miniscule crop), **1883**☆☆☆☆ **1880**☆☆☆ **1879**☆☆☆☆ **1878**☆☆ **1877**☆☆☆ **1875**☆☆☆☆ (a tiny crop), **1874**☆☆ **1872**☆☆☆ (the year the phylloxera struck), **1870**☆☆☆☆ (the last of the good post-oidium vintages).

**1869**☆☆☆ (Bual excellent), **1867**☆☆☆ **1866**☆☆☆ and **1865**☆☆☆ (all small crops), **1864**☆☆☆ (small but particularly good for Bual and Malmsey), **1863**☆☆☆☆ (Malmsey excellent), **1862**☆☆☆☆☆ (the Terrantez still magnificent, one of the best-ever old madeiras), **1860**☆☆☆☆ **1856**☆☆☆.

Between 1851 and 1855 the vineyards, and trade, were devastated by oidium, a mildew destroying the leaves of the vines. **1850**☆☆☆☆ (the last of the pre-oidium vintages), **1846**☆☆☆☆☆ (particularly Terrantez, Bual and Verdelho, and still magnificent),

**1845**☆☆☆ (especially Bual). **1840**☆☆☆☆ (particularly Sercial and Verdelho), **1839**, **1838**, **1837**, **1836**, **1835**, **1834** and **1830** all ☆☆☆☆ years, **1827**☆☆☆☆☆ **1821**☆☆☆☆☆ **1811**☆☆☆ **1808**☆☆☆☆☆ (Cossart's Malmsey in particular still magnificent), **1802**☆☆☆☆☆ **1795**☆☆☆☆ **1792**☆☆☆☆

## POSTSCRIPT

If these pre-1900 years seem to the reader unrealistic, "cloud cuckoo land", bottles still exist; they appear from time to time at auction, either from private cellars in England and America, or from the cellars of the old Madeira families – they are one of life's glorious experiences.

# Appendix

The relationship between sun and rain through the growing season is, as we have seen in the text, crucial. The elements each have a direct bearing on the quality and quantity of wine from a given year. The following table summarises the average temperature, in degrees Celsius and Fahrenheit, the total rainfall in millimetres and the hours of sunshine through the growing season in Bordeaux from June to September over the past 35 years. The relationships make interesting reading. Note the low rainfall in a great year such as 1961 and the comparatively monsoonal conditions of the atrocious 1968. Also the remarkable combination of heat and sun in the two fairly recent excellent years 1989 and 1990. Although these figures are salutory, several elements are of course missing, for example the often devastating effects of spring frosts, of poor flowering in inclement weather – not to mention pests and diseases. The most important factors are, of course, mentioned in the main text.

## ANNUAL WEATHER STATISTICS: BORDEAUX

|  | Average Temperature | Total Rainfall | Hours of Sunshine |
|---|---|---|---|
| **1997** | 20.3˚C (68.5˚F) | 342mm | 781 hrs |
| **1996** | 24.0˚C (75.2˚F) | 305mm | 995 hrs |
| **1995** | 20.8˚C (69.4˚F) | 272mm | 935 hrs |
| **1994** | 20.5˚C (68.9˚F) | 582mm | 788 hrs |
| **1993** | 19.3˚C (66.8˚F) | 459mm | 836 hrs |
| **1992** | 18.6˚C (65.4˚F) | 387mm | 820 hrs |
| **1991** | 21.2˚C (70.2˚F) | 236mm | 950 hrs |
| **1990** | 20.9˚C (69.6˚F) | 165mm | 1,055 hrs |
| **1989** | 20.9˚C (69.5˚F) | 173mm | 1,055 hrs |
| **1988** | 19.5˚C (67.1˚F) | 204mm | 932 hrs |
| **1987** | 20.3˚C (68.5˚F) | 292mm | 813 hrs |
| **1986** | 19.6˚C (67.3˚F) | 212mm | 933 hrs |
| **1985** | 19.2˚C (66.6˚F) | 128mm | 991 hrs |
| **1984** | 19.1˚C (66.4˚F) | 252mm | 930 hrs |
| **1983** | 21.1˚C (70.0˚F) | 200mm | 881 hrs |
| **1982** | 20.3˚C (68.5˚F) | 235mm | 826 hrs |
| **1981** | 19.7˚C (67.5˚F) | 169mm | 818 hrs |
| **1980** | 18.8˚C (35.8˚F) | 223mm | 698 hrs |
| **1979** | 18.0˚C (64.4˚F) | 149mm | 852 hrs |
| **1978** | 18.8˚C (65.8˚F) | 178mm | 860 hrs |
| **1977** | 18.5˚C (65.3˚F) | 266mm | 860 hrs |
| **1976** | 20.8˚C (69.4˚F) | 222mm | 995 hrs |
| **1975** | 20.1˚C (68.2˚F) | 241mm | 920 hrs |
| **1974** | 19.1˚C (66.4˚F) | 211mm | 888 hrs |
| **1973** | 20.4˚C (68.7˚F) | 296mm | 872 hrs |
| **1972** | 17.6˚C (63.6˚F) | 179mm | 824 hrs |
| **1971** | 19.3˚C (66.9˚F) | 328mm | 943 hrs |
| **1970** | 19.6˚C (67.2˚F) | 149mm | 1,024 hrs |
| **1969** | 19.9˚C (67.8˚F) | 312mm | 835 hrs |
| **1968** | 18.9˚C (65.9˚F) | 324mm | 900 hrs |
| **1967** | 19.2˚C (66.6˚F) | 142mm | 963 hrs |
| **1966** | 18.6˚C (65.4˚F) | 234mm | 885 hrs |
| **1964** | 20.2˚C (68.3˚F) | 160mm | 1,020 hrs |
| **1962** | 19.2˚C (66.5˚F) | 125mm | 1,114 hrs |
| **1961** | 19.8˚C (67.7˚F) | 97mm | 908 hrs |
| **1960** | 18.7˚C (65.6˚F) | 354mm | 881 hrs |